Dreams and Spirituality

Dreams and Spirituality

*A Handbook for Ministry, Spiritual
Direction and Counselling*

Edited by

Kate Adams

Bart J. Koet and

Barbara Koning

CANTERBURY
PRESS
Norwich

© Kate Adams, Bart J. Koet and Barbara Koning 2015

Published in 2015 by Canterbury Press
Editorial office
3rd Floor, Invicta House,
108–114 Golden Lane,
London EC1Y 0TG, UK

www.canterburypress.co.uk

British Library Cataloguing in Publication data

A catalogue record for this book is available
from the British Library

978 1 84825 731 3

Typeset by Manila Typesetting Company
Printed and bound by
CPI Group (UK) Ltd

Contents

Acknowledgements   ix

About the Authors   xi

Introduction   xv

Part 1 Multi-Disciplinary Points of Departure   1

1   Dreams as Revelations: Food for Theological and
     Philosophical Thought
     Bart J. Koet   3
2   Dreams, Societies and Worldviews:
     A Cross-Cultural Perspective
     Charles D. Laughlin   16
3   The Role of Dreams in Psychological
     Maintenance and Growth
     Robert Hoss   37
4   The Dream as a Scientific, Aesthetic and
     Therapeutic Object
     Marc Hebbrecht   58

Interlude

Dream Narrative 1   Dreamlife of an Episcopal Priest: How
                         Dreams Were Helpful to Me as a Priest
                         and Pastor
                         Bob Haden   74
Dream Narrative 2   No Leaf Falls from a Tree Unnoticed:
                         Dreams and Stories of a Condemned
                         Murderer
                         Wouter Koek van Egmond   80

Part 2 Dreams and Religion: Empirical Data, Theory and Reflections 89

5 Varieties of Religious Dreaming: Some Explorations from the Point of View of Descriptive Psychology of Religion
Barbara Koning 91

6 The Wonder of Dreams: How Dreams Advance in Contemporary Miracle Stories
Anne-Marie Korte 102

7 Psychosystemic Engagement of Dreams
Larry Kent Graham and Shyamaa Creaven 116

8 Rabbinic Dream Work: An Introduction to the Dream Discussions in the Babylonian Talmud (Berachot 55a–57b)
Bart J. Koet 134

9 Muslim and Freudian Dream Interpretation in Egypt
Amira Mittermaier 147

Interlude

Dream Narrative 3   Renewed Through an Invitation to Dance my Life
Annette Dubois-van Hoorn 161

Dream Narrative 4   Guidance Through Dreams and Synchronicities at a Major Turning Point in Life
Barbara Koning 165

Part 3 Dreams and the Practice of Pastoral Care 171

10 Dreams in Everyday Pastoral Care
Wim Reedijk 173

11 Benefits of a Parish Dream Group
Geoff Nelson 182

12 Working with Dreams in Spiritual Direction: A Catholic Perspective
Gerard Condon 192

13 Out of the Mouths of Babes . . . : Hearing the Dreams of Children and Adolescents
Peter Green and Kate Adams 203

CONTENTS

14 'For He gives to his beloved even in his sleep' (Psalm 127.2):
    Pastoral Care and Dreams in Hospitals and Nursing Homes
    Hans Dornseiffen   210

15 Some Lessons from Prison Dreams: A Personal Account
    Bart J. Koet   217

16 A Dream Friendly Attitude in Ministry and Chaplaincy:
    Dreams in Pastoral Supervision
    Sjaak Körver   231

Interlude

Dream Narrative 5   Finding Deep Emotional Healing and
                       Reconciliation through a Dream
                       Russ Parker   243
Dream Narrative 6   Christ's Message to a Diplomat
                       Edy Korthals Altes   247

Acknowledgements of Sources   251

IASD Dreamwork Ethics Statement   252

Index of Biblical References   253

Index of Names and Subjects   255

Acknowledgements

The editors offer their appreciation to Riny Zwemmer for her careful translations of three chapters and to Margreet Oudenes for her meticulous attention to detail in copy-editing.

Finally, we thank Christine Smith and her team at Canterbury Press for their commitment to the book and for their advice and support throughout the publishing process.

About the Authors

Dr Kate Adams is Reader in Education at Bishop Grosseteste University in Lincoln, Lincolnshire. Her research focuses on children's spirituality, with a particular emphasis on their spiritual dreams. Kate is a former board member and Secretary of the International Association for the Study of Dreams.

Gerard Condon is a Catholic priest living in Cork, Ireland. He is an adviser for religious education and lectures in spirituality at St Patrick's College in Thurles, Co. Tipperary. During 1995–2002 he was the spiritual director at the Irish College, Rome. He has written *The Power of Dreams: A Christian Guide* (Columba 2008).

Shyamaa M. Creaven is a licensed professional counsellor in Denver, Colorado, and an adjunct professor at Naropa University teaching Gestalt Therapy Theory and Trauma Recovery. Currently a doctoral student at Iliff School of Theology and the University of Denver, Shyamaa is exploring the dialogue between spiritual life and psychological health.

Hans Dornseiffen read theology at the Catholic Theological University Amsterdam, and specialized as a dream worker. During 1976–2011 he worked as a pastoral counsellor in a hospital and a nursing home. In his role as a pastor he has used dream analysis to support his clients.

Annette Dubois-van Hoorn is a pastoral care worker with her own practice in Utrecht. She offers personal coaching and therapeutic artistic classes in painting, drawing and writing. These creative means help to find the way to one's inner self. She is also a minister for church celebrations in institutions and on camping sites. Her website is www.praktijksporen.nl.

Larry Kent Graham is Professor of Pastoral Theology and Care at Iliff School of Theology in Denver, Colorado. He wrote *Care of Persons, Care of Worlds* (Abingdon Press 1992) and *Discovering Images of God:*

Narratives of Care with Lesbians and Gays (Westminster John Knox 1997). His current work is on the impact of war on families.

Dr Peter Green is an Anglican priest and is currently Dean of Chapel at Bishop Grosseteste University in Lincoln, Lincolnshire. He served in parish ministry before becoming Chaplain and Head of Religious Studies at Abbots Bromley School in Staffordshire. His research interests include the phenomenological approach to religion and Lacanian literary theory.

Robert L. Haden Jr is an episcopal priest and a practising pastoral counsellor and spiritual director with a Jungian orientation. He is founder and director of The Haden Institute in North Carolina, website: www. hadeninstitute.com. He is author of *Unopened Letters from God: Using Biblical Dreams to Unlock Your Nightly Dreams* (Haden Institute.com 2010).

Dr Marc Hebbrecht is a psychiatrist, psychotherapist and psychoanalyst in Belgium. He is connected with PC ASSTER Sint-Truiden and with the psychoanalytical service of the UPC KU Leuven, campus Kortenberg. He is a training analyst with the Belgian Society for Psychoanalysis.

Robert J. Hoss, MS is a director and past president of IASD, director of the DreamScience Foundation for research grants and a faculty member of the Haden Institute, North Carolina. He is author of *Dream Language* (Innersource 2006) and *Dream to Freedom* (Energy Psychology Press 2013), and his work is published in 12 other books and three professional journals. His website is www.dreamscience.org.

Wouter Koek van Egmond is a visual artist. He read theology at the Catholic Theological University Amsterdam. From 1984 he was a minister in the penitentiary institutions of Amsterdam and Almere. Finding meaning on the edges of being human fascinates him, as well as space, form and perception. Since 2006/07 he has displayed his artwork in exhibitions.

Dr Bart J. Koet is Ordinary Professor of New Testament and Extra-ordinary Professor of Early Christian Literature at the University of Tilburg. For most of his life, Bart has combined pastoral practice with his scholarly work. He worked as a prison chaplain for 15 years. For a list of his publications, see www.tilburguniversity.edu/nl/webwijs/show/?uid=b.j.koet.

Dr Barbara Koning is a clinical psychologist of religion and spiritual director in The Netherlands, with expertise in academic inter-disciplinary practical-theological empirical research. She is running a Centre for Dreams and Well-Being. Her website is www.dreampilgrims.com. She is a member of the faculty of the Haden Institute in North Carolina.

Anne-Marie Korte is Professor of Religion, Gender, and Modernity at the Faculty of Humanities of Utrecht University, and Scientific Director of the Netherlands School for Advanced Studies in Theology and Religion. Her current research projects are *Figuring the sacred: A systematic exploration of contemporary miracle stories* and *Gendered blasphemy: Gender and sexuality in religious controversies.*

Edy Korthals Altes is an economist, diplomat and a former ambassador in Warsaw and Madrid, from The Netherlands. Since 1986 he has been active in Peace and Security, East–West relations, inter-religious cooperation, and Spiritual Awakening. He is former President of the World Conference Religions for Peace and is a Fellow of the World Academy of Art and Science.

Dr Sjaak W. G. Körver is a lecturer, researcher, pastoral supervisor and trainer in Clinical Pastoral Education at the University of Tilburg, The Netherlands. He has worked for 18 years as a hospital chaplain and in psychiatry. In 2013 he completed his PhD on spiritual coping strategies in lung cancer patients.

Charles D. Laughlin is emeritus Professor of Anthropology and Religion in the Department of Sociology and Anthropology at Carleton University in Ottawa. He has done ethnographic fieldwork among the So (Tepes) of Northeastern Uganda, Tibetan lamas in Nepal and India, Chinese Buddhists in Southeast Asia, and Navajo people of the American Southwest.

Amira Mittermaier is an Associate Professor in the Department for the Study of Religion and the Department of Near and Middle Eastern Civilizations at the University of Toronto. Her book *Dreams that Matter: Egyptian Landscapes of the Imagination* (University of California Press 2011) was won multiple awards.

Geoff Nelson is a retired Presbyterian pastor in Whittier, California, with over 35 years' experience working with his own dreams. He has a DMin degree on 'Dream Groups in the Church' and is a trained spiritual director.

Dr Russ Parker has been the Director of Acorn Christian Healing Foundation, UK, since 1995. He is the author of a number of books, including: *Healing Dreams* (SPCK 2013); *Healing Death's Wound* (Eagle 2002); *Free to Fail* (Triangle Books 1998); *Forgiveness is Healing* (SPCK 2011); and an anthology of prayer poems for public and private use, *Wild Spirit of the Living God* (Eagle 2007).

Dr Wim M. Reedijk works as a minister in the Protestant Church in The Netherlands, and is currently serving the community in Nieuwegein. He is co-editor of a Dutch ecumenical quarterly magazine on mysticism and spirituality. He writes on biblical topics, hermeneutics, pastoral care and guidance.

Introduction

Around the world people find guidance and inspiration in their dreams, and at times many need support in dealing with nightmares. However, many ministers and counsellors do not feel fully equipped to deal with this area of human consciousness. This situation occurs despite the fact that dreams have a long-established role in many world religions. We as editors introduce the potential of this book with a short narrative. It is drawn from the days Bart was working as a chaplain in a prison. At the time he worked closely with an imam who has agreed to share this incident.

> My colleagues knew that I studied dreams and that from time to time I talked to the prisoners about dreams. On one occasion, as we chatted over coffee, the imam related one of his dreams to me:
>
>> In my dream a big, black dog jumps on me; he is almost as tall as I am myself. It seems that he wants to knock me over, but I manage to stay standing.
>
> The dream had upset my colleague so he proceeded to ask me how I would interpret it. Such a request poses ethical issues because dream workers need to take great care when supporting people who seek to discover the meaning(s) of their dreams.[1] Thus I replied using the phrase: 'If it were my dream . . .' In doing so, I suggested that if it were my dream the dog would have represented my flock here in the prison: our inmates. For a moment both the imam and I paused, our thoughts drifting to the pain we felt as we reflected on the tragic circumstances of their lives, ridden with excess alcohol, drugs and various criminal behaviours. Then I moved on to suggest that if it were my dream, and according to some Islamic religious texts, the dog seems unclean and

---

1 The International Association for the Study of Dreams offers an ethical statement for dream workers (see p. 252 of this book). It is available in several languages on the website at www. asdreams.org/ethics.htm.

the strength of the uncleanliness tries to overpower me but I do not fall. That, I suggested, would be my interpretation of the dream and simultaneously a reflection of the strength of my friend. Afterwards it was clear that his unease about the dream had been taken away.

This story shows how dreams can serve as a bridge between different cultures and different religions, and can even deepen insights into the professional work of specialists in pastoral roles. But in order that pastoral counsellors fully comprehend the dreams of those in their care, they need to have an understanding of the hermeneutics – complementary and sometimes contrary to the culturally shared awareness of psychological-oriented theories. For example, while the Bible notes that dreams can come from much business (Eccles. 5.2 (or 5.3)), one finds dream narratives that are storied as divine communication. Similarly the belief that dreams can be a special revelation (cf. the so-called 'big dreams' as Carl G. Jung referred to them) is alive for many in the world today; in those from different faiths as well as those without a religious affiliation.

It is the purpose of this interdisciplinary edited handbook to contextualize the place of dreams in pastoral counselling by bringing together scholars from around the world in one volume. It combines a small number of previously published foundational texts (where appropriate, amended for this volume) together with invited, original chapters offering contemporary insights from varied areas of expertise. In so doing, it provides an original, broad, systematic, research-informed, theoretical and practical guide for ministers, spiritual directors and counsellors across a range of caring professions which enables them to understand the nature of dreams and the roles they may play in the lives of those in their pastoral care.

The design of the volume is intended partly as an enterprise of pastoral theology, which is considered an academic discipline in its own right. As such, this branch of science develops sound theoretical understandings of, and practical guidelines for, the ministry of care. Three main lines of epistemological thought are being distinguished in its overarching field of empirical practical theology: descriptive, strategic and normative. This book takes a descriptive approach in the following way. It is in three main parts, which are interspersed with six dream narratives. The narratives are offered by a variety of people, some of them pastors, who have encountered meaningful dreams either themselves or with their clients.

Part 1 offers multi-disciplinary points of departure with regard to dreams. The approaches include: scientific biblical theology; a cultural-anthropological analysis of the role of dreams in religions and societies around the globe; a neuroscientific understanding of how the brain restores by creating dreams; and a view on dreams related to the setting of clinical mental health care.

Part 2 reflects on ways of linking dreams and religion. Supplementary theoretical models are offered, one departing from a descriptive psychology of religion and the other from the standpoint of psychosystemic pastoral care. Cases of dream sharing as presented in a Dutch television programme are analysed and recognized as miracle stories. We also find a vista in historical rabbinic and contemporary Islamic dream traditions.

In Part 3, the focus is on a more practical and applied level. Attention turns to how to deal with dreams in a variety of specific pastoral contexts. Here we first explore the themes of dreams in the daily pastoral caretaking of a local church, in a dream group, and in spiritual direction. We hear of the dreams of children and adolescents arising in educational settings; an important topic given that the majority of texts on dreams relate to adults, yet children are also a key focus of pastoral care. We then read accounts about the hospital and prison: for pastoral clients in institutional settings also have dreams, as well as their pastors. We conclude with a chapter on the value of working with dreams when educating the pastor in pastoral supervision.

As such, it should be noted that the views offered are those of the individual authors. We the editors are fully aware that our perspective is primarily focused on western practice and we lament the fact that there is no space to include voices of the people of, for example, Africa[2] or other indigenous peoples. However, we offer this book so that it may enrich understanding of working with dreams in a range of contemporary western settings for the benefit of dreamers.

Kate Adams, Bart J. Koet and Barbara Koning

---

2 For an interesting perspective on Africa, see e.g. Jędrej, M. C. and Shaw, R. (1992), *Dreaming, Religion and Society in Africa*, Leiden: Brill.

Multi-Disciplinary Points of Departure

Dreams as Revelations

Food for Theological and Philosophical Thought

BART J. KOET

In a fascinating philosophical study the Frenchman Pierre Carrique (2002) tries to assess the value and significance of dreaming. His thesis is that at the primary level of each experience the difference between waking on the one hand and sleeping and dreaming on the other is at stake. But the phenomenon of the 'dream' is, in that context, the most alarming.

Even a person who is not very contemplative will occasionally be amazed by one of their dreams. The most astonishing fact is that during the dream, the dreamer is not surprised by the dream, for while dreaming the dream world seems realistic.

The ambiguity of dreaming is one of the reasons why it is very difficult to define it. Carrique explores the act of thinking about dreaming within different philosophical systems. First he discusses some of Descartes' works and those of his 'disciple' Sartre. Leibnitz, Kant, Hegel and Husserl follow. Then, in the second part of the book, Carrique turns to ancient Greek wisdom, to Plato and Aristotle, but also to older texts, like those of Heraclitus and Pindar, often with Heidegger as his guide.

In Greek wisdom it seems that the poet wins over the philosopher. It is the poet Pindar who, with the help of dreaming, defines human beings. First he asks:

'Creatures of a day! What is somebody?
What is he not?'
And then he seems to answer: 'Man is a dream of a shadow.'[1]

---

1 σκιᾶς ὄναρ ἄνθρωπος, Pythian Odes, VIII (Pindar: *c.* 522–443 BC). I cannot deal here with the fact that the translation of this text is quite difficult and that there are quite different possibilities. Compare, however: William Shakespeare, *The Tempest* (Act 4, scene 1, 148–58): 'We are such stuff as dreams are made on; and our little life is rounded with a sleep.'

According to Pindar, the dream helps to define and to determine a human being. According to Carrique, the dream as a border-crossing helps to make clear what becomes evident when consciousness diminishes. The twilight and the morning sun are necessary to understand the day.

Nowadays, one can find these puzzling cross-overs between reality and dreams and fantasies present in movies. It is precisely the difficulty to determine differences between dreams and facts that makes these movies so appealing.

The Matrix (1999) depicts a world in which reality as perceived by most humans is actually a simulated reality, created by sentient machines. In the movie there are constant cross-overs between the dreamlike world as made by the Matrix, the computer simulation of the world, and the 'real world'. It is no accident that the name of one of the protagonists is Morpheus (the Greek word for sleep and thus Morpheus is Mr Sleep) and that *Simulcra and Simulation*, a book by the philosopher Jean Baudrillard, is visible onscreen. That work was supposed to be read by the actors prior to filming and this also indicates that *The Matrix* deals with philosophical questions about the relationship between reality and signs. The theme of *Inception* (2010) is bringing real life to life in dreams (and in dreams within dreams) and thus it plays with the border-crossing between waking life and dreaming world.

However, dreams are not only an important philosophical, literary or cinematic topic. It is also important for theologians and pastors to think about dreams. It is the aim of this chapter to offer some theological, and above all, biblical points of departure. I will first sketch some theological aspects and, after drawing the broader lines of biblical views on dreams, I will discuss one biblical dream narrative more extensively.

An example of a theologian who as both a theologian and a philosopher thought about dreams is Augustine of Hippo (Koet 2012 and the literature mentioned on p. 110). In a very succinct but clear book about Augustine as a philosopher, Gareth B. Matthews discusses three philosophical dream problems according to Augustine (2005, pp. 65–75). Matthews distinguishes three different dream problems:

1 The first problem is the Epistemological Dream Problem: How do I know whether I am *now* dreaming or not?
2 Matthews calls the second the Metaphysical Dream Problem: How do I know whether all life is my dream?
3 He typifies the third as the Moral Dream Problem: Can I be immoral by doing something immoral in my dream?

Matthews refers to several of Plato's dialogues to show that Socrates had already dealt with these questions.

However, there are other theological issues. One of the most important is the fact that dreams can be seen as revealing the divine will, as argued by A. L. Oppenheim (1956, p. 184) in the introduction to his important book:

> For the ancient Near East it can be stated – with the oversimplification which is reserved only to preliminary remarks – that dream experiences were recorded on three clearly differentiated planes: first, dreams as revelations of the deity, which may or may not require interpretation; second, dreams which reflect, symptomatically, the state of mind, the spiritual and bodily 'health' of the dreamer, which are only mentioned but never recorded; and third, mantic dreams in which forthcoming events are prognosticated.

Oppenheim worked with Assyrian and Sumeric texts. In Greek and Jewish realms there was also a possible relationship between divine revelation and dreams. As argued by A. H. M. Kessels (1978, p. 154), in the Homeric poems all dreams are described as being sent by a God. And although quite a few other Greek authors referred to the divine origin of dreams, the philosopher Aristotle did not accept that dreams were from a divine source. Hence there was no single common idea about dreaming in ancient Greece.

When we look in the next section to the ideas on dreams in the Old Testament, we will also hear some different opinions. In the long history of the biblical books as an emerging canonical tradition, there were a variety of visions of dreams that were written down in the different stages of the development of the Old Testament (for dreams in the Old Testament, see Husser 1999; Lanckau 2006).

Views on dreams in the Bible

During the Requiem Mass for the assassinated president of the USA, Monsignor Philip M. Hannan, auxiliary Bishop of Washington, said that John F. Kennedy had quoted Joel 2.28: 'And it shall come to pass afterward, that I will pour out my Spirit on all flesh; your sons and your daughters shall prophesy, your old men shall dream dreams, and your young men shall see visions' (ESV) during his last dinner on 21

November 1963. He combined that reference with Proverbs 29.18: 'Where there is no vision, the people perish' (KJV). The Joel quotation and the way in which Kennedy combined two biblical texts, show two important aspects of biblical views on dreams: dreams and visions seem to be, to a certain extent, interchangeable and civilization needs them.

However, there is a lot of discussion about what a dream actually is. In English the word 'dream' can mean a fantasy or a daydream as well as something that happens during sleeping. It is quite difficult to give a concise definition of a dream. A well-known dream researcher told me at a congress of the International Association for the Study of Dreams that, as far as he was concerned, in dream research we have come no further than Aristotle (see his *De Somno* and *De Insomniis*).

There is no biblical definition of dreams and it is not possible to verify the authenticity of the dream stories that we read in the Scriptures. Did they really happen or are they a literary device? What is clear is that when dreams are mentioned in the Scriptures, often these narratives are indicative of a divine communication. As we have seen above, in classical times dreams were seen as a means of contact with the divine. This was the case in ancient Mesopotamia and ancient Greece, as well as ancient Rome and Israel. Instances of this are found in the narratives about the dreams and visions in Genesis, in which God manifests himself in different ways to Abimelech (Gen. 20.3), Jacob (Gen. 28.10–16; 31.11–13) and Joseph (for example, Gen. 37.40–41).

One of the most important texts about divine communication is Numbers 12.1–8. Aaron and Miriam, the brother and sister of Moses, had been lamenting: 'Has the Lord only spoken through Moses? Hasn't he also spoken through us?' Moses does not defend himself, but God does. According to Numbers, the Lord called Moses, Miriam and Aaron to the Tent of his presence. They obeyed, and the Lord came down in a pillar of cloud and called out:

> 'Hear my words:
> If there is a prophet among you,
>   I, the Lord make myself known to him in a vision
> I speak with him in a dream.
>   Not so with my servant Moses;
> he is entrusted with all my house.
>   With him I speak mouth to mouth,
> clearly and not in dark speech;
> and he beholds the form of the Lord.'
>
> (Num. 12.6–8, ESV)

This passage teaches us that God speaks in dreams and visions to the prophets, but to Moses he speaks mouth to mouth, face to face. Our concern here is the fact that God speaks to the prophets in dreams and visions.

In the Bible we often come across passages where God speaks through visions and dreams. From Numbers 12.6 we learn that dreams and visions may have the same function even though there can be some differences. Both serve as the vehicle of divine communication. That dreams and visions are interchangeable in a certain way is – as we saw above – also suggested in the parallel between visions and dreams in Joel 2.28–32, a text quoted in Acts 2.17–21 (for the parallelism and the divine origin of dreams, see also Job 7.14).

In the comparatively older books of the Old Testament dreams are freely interpreted as communication with the divine, and in the later books of the Scriptures other origins of the dreams are also proposed. The Ecclesiast says that dreams come from working too hard (see Eccles. 5.2 (or 5.3); compare also 5.6). And the learned Jew Ben Sira, who summarized the Hebrew Torah in proverbs for the Jews living in the diaspora – which ended up in the canon of the Septuagint thanks to the translation by his grandson – states that dreams are a delusion (Sir. 34.5). However, he adds one condition. Only when the dream has been sent by the Almighty can men attach value to it (34.6). Ben Sira was a representative of the Judaism that increasingly valued the Scriptures in the making and its interpreters, a group of men who in later times became known as the 'scribes'. In the Judaism of those times there were also more apocalyptic movements and they attached more importance to dreams and visions.

Consequently a dilemma arose: which dreams come from God and which ones do not? In the later books of the Old Testament, in the writings of the New Testament and in the Early Church only the dreams that are accompanied by reference to that other holy revelation, the Scriptures, are considered a credible divine revelation. This can be seen, for example, in the dreams in Matthew 1–2, where there are also references to the Scriptures (see Koet 2006; 2009).

Dreams in the New Testament

In the popular *Theological Dictionary of the New Testament* Albrecht Oepke writes under the term 'dream' that dreams in the New Testament are no longer so important, since Jesus, God, no longer speaks in a mysterious manner, but speaks openly (Oepke 1954, pp. 228–31). Dreams have not – according to him – been necessary since Jesus. This is one of the many examples in the dictionary of 'debunking' the Old Testament. Gerhard Kittel, the editor of this reference work, which is often used uncritically, was an active anti-Semite. Further, as Professor of Evangelical Theology and New Testament, and as one of the founding fathers of the *Reichsinstituts für Geschichte des Neuen Deutschlands* (in 1935, the Nazi Institute for the History of the New [sic] Germany), he published 'scientific' studies depicting Judaism as the historical enemy of Germany, Christianity and even European culture in general. It is thus not totally unexpected that in quite a few lemmas of that dictionary, authors suggest too wide an opposition between the 'dark' sides of the Old Testament or of Judaism on the one hand and the enlightened views of Jesus and the New Testament on the other. This seems to account also for the part that deals with dreams. After all, it may be so that in the Gospel little is said about dreams, but it does not mean that in the history of Christianity the part of dreams should be wiped out.

Only in Matthew 1–2 and in the story of Pilate's wife (Matt. 27.19) do we hear about dreams as a communication with the divine. In Matthew 1–2 we find five different dreams (see Gnuse 1990; Frenschkowksi 1998). The first dream is in 1.20–25, where Joseph is asked to take Mary for his wife. The second dream is a warning to the magi to leave the country (2.12). Then in a dream Joseph is told to go to Egypt (2.13–15). He is also informed about the death of Herod and that he can go back to Israel (2.19–20). A last dream warns Joseph not to go to Galilee (2.22).

Let me discuss one example. In 1.20–25 it is told how Joseph was in a very difficult situation. According to the Law (e.g. Deut. 24.1) he must leave his wife. In the dream there is a reference to a prophetic text. The law about sending an unfaithful wife away was overruled by two divine revelations. This dream is trustworthy, because the message that Mary will have a child conceived by the Holy Spirit is confirmed by a prophecy in the Scriptures. A dream and the Scriptures show Joseph a new way (see Koet 2006, pp. 44–5). Apparently, Jesus, like Moses, needs no dream to communicate with God. In Luke too we find a reference to dreams as a possible channel of communication with the Divine. Luke does not mention it in his Gospel, but in the Acts of the Apostles. Also, in the literature of the early church accounts of many dreams are told (for more details, see Koet 2006, pp. 11–24).

For a better understanding, let us focus on one of the dreams from Acts: the dream of Paul in Troy (Acts 16.9–10; see Koet 2006, pp. 147–71 and Koet 2008). This dream comes at a special moment. Paul is on the verge of making the crossing to Europe. At that moment he gets an 'epiphany-dream', a dream in which a person manifests himself, in this case a Macedonian man. This kind of dream is commonly known from Greek works, as found in Homer, for example. To readers in ancient times Troy (and the surrounding area) was a symbolic place. According to Homer it was here that the first confrontation between Hellas and the East had taken place. Time and again great leaders had come to this place to relive this confrontation. For one, Alexander the Great made a stop in the region of Troy on his way to punish the Persians. Troy was also of great significance to the Romans. Virgil, when he had almost finished the *Aeneid*, tried in vain to make a journey to Troy but it became the death of him. And then, more or less in the middle of the Acts, at a decisive moment, on that crucial spot of the Trojan plains, Luke marks the crossing to Europe with a dream story in Hellenistic attire. Crossings between Europe and Asia were frequently accompanied by dream stories. Thus Luke, expertly drawing on his roots in the biblical tradition, enrols his principal character, Paul, into Hellenistic history.

Solomon's dream (1 Kings 3): the perfect combination of a dream narrative and an ideological vision

Thus, in Scripture the meaning of dreams is interpreted differently. The thoughts are more subtle. Not just any meaning is given to a dream. Dreams occur, but a meaning is not given indiscriminately. Later on in the Scriptures a dream had to be accompanied by a cross-reference to other verses in the Scriptures to have credibility. In crucial moments stories of dreams are used to wake the reader. At that moment the reader knows: 'Be alert, wake up!' Earlier, Jacob had experienced this: 'Certainly, God was here and I didn't know it' (Gen. 28.16). Another example of a dream mentioned in a biblical narrative is the dream of King Solomon (1 Kings 3). This dream narrative teaches not only the king but the reader as well about how to be a good king. We will take a closer look at this story in order to get an impression of how stories in dreams are used to convey a vision (for some scholarly exegetical literature, see Carr 1991 and Seow 1984).

Kingdom in Scriptures

What makes a king a good king? Does a professional profile for kings exist? What is the code of honour for rulers of a country? In the Scriptures we are told that God does not like autocrats. Why would one person rule

9

over another person? Wouldn't God be sufficient as the only ruler over people, and certainly over the people of Israel? Of course people need judges, but God's sovereignty would be ultimately sufficient, for he is the King. However, blood is thicker than water. In Samuel 8 it is written how the Israelites want to appoint a king. When the sons of Samuel, the latest judge, are not up to their task, the elders of Israel ask Samuel to give them a king: 'Give us a king to be our judge.' Neither Samuel nor God likes this request. Nevertheless the Eternal One comforts, because the people did not reject the old judge, but him.

God advises Samuel to listen to them, but also warns them of the disadvantages of an autocrat. This ruler will require their sons as war material. He will take their farmlands, vineyards and olive gardens and give these to his servants (1 Sam. 8.11–18). In short, they won't have a better life if they have a king, but the Israelites don't listen and get their king.

Then it becomes obvious that life with a ruler isn't always favourable. The wonderful Saul gets trapped by his power. Even though David becomes the ideal king in the biblical tradition, his reign still has negative consequences. For example, he has an eye for Bathsheba, the wife of his friend and one of his best generals, Uriah. This is the beginning of a chain of fatal consequences, which leads to the death of this general and also the death of the 'illegitimate' child of David and Bathsheba (2 Sam. 12.15). Also the succession to the throne of David does not pass without problems. Finally Solomon comes to the throne after David. At the start of his reign we get a written lesson in how to be a king in answer to the question: What makes a king a good king?

A lesson in kingship (1 Kings 3)

What does it take to be a king? In 1 Kings 3 this question is examined within a dream narrative. One would think that the biblical author had already read Freud, for just at the outset of his kingship, King Solomon receives an extraordinary dream. At the time of Solomon's early kinghood there is no temple in Jerusalem. David had not been allowed to build the temple of the Lord because his hands had been tainted with too much blood. Solomon will be the king to build the temple, but in his early days sacrifices were still made on high mountain tops. So too does Solomon, as he offers sacrifice on the heights of Gibeon, after which he spends the night there. During the night the Lord manifests himself in a dream to the young king. God says: 'Ask! What will I give you?' (1 Kings 3.5). You are one of the world's youngest rulers and then comes this dream in which the Almighty presents the world on a plate to you. What a temptation!

At this point it is good to step outside the story for a minute and ask ourselves what we would choose if we were asked. Our answer may be private, but in 1 Kings 3 we hear Solomon's answer. God gave his servant David great favours, says Solomon, and David responded by following God's ways. These words sound pious and they probably are, but the situation may still be a little different from what we think. Surely, Solomon says, David was God's servant, but the Hebrew word used here, *oveed*, was also an honorary title. It comes from the verb 'to work' but in fact you are the one who works for God. Moses had that title and Joshua received it after his death. It is indeed very special to be allowed to be God's worker. And are Solomon's words true? Did David always follow God's ways? Solomon adds that one of God's favours given to David was that the son of David would sit on the throne. He himself is that son. He is the new servant. Good for him. Nevertheless, the young king is aware of his own limitations. To him God's people seem endlessly great. And so does his mission. In his answer the king shows some self-knowledge. He admits he was a young man when he succeeded his father.

In the Hebrew text as well as in the Greek translation the word used to describe Solomon shows that he is still very inexperienced. How can a young man like him lead a people? He is still as green as grass! Solomon asks something that may help him fulfil his royal task: Give your servant a listening heart (Hebrew: *lef sjomea*) to do justice to your people and to be able to discern good from evil. In the dream this answer pleases God so much that indeed he gives him a special gift: a wise and intelligent heart. Furthermore, because he has asked for something humble and not for all kinds of attributes such as a long life or the lives of his enemies, Solomon will also receive other royal benefits such as wealth and honour (but not the lives of his enemies).

Possibly, in the context of sleeping on the sacrificial height after making offerings, a sort of incubation may have taken place. Dream incubation is a ritual in which a person may, after fasting, present questions to the Deity hoping that these questions will be answered in the dream. In the Hellenistic era these rituals took place at the sanctuaries of Asclepios. The dream narrative is more important than the possible historical background in the construction of stories about the kingship of Solomon.

As 1 Kings 3.5–15 is placed at the beginning of Solomon's reign, it is clearly also meant as a kind of abstract of his kingship. Writers often place indications in a text in order to give the reader a clue about the themes of a story. In literary theory such a sign, a guide to the reader, is called a disclosure. At crucial points in the text the author tries to explain what the text is about by means of such disclosures. One way to do this is by presenting at the beginning of the story what the following story is about. Dream stories are a good vehicle by which to shape a disclosure.

In 1 Kings 3 we learn that King Solomon receives a very special dream at the outset of his kingship. A dream narrative gains extra attention and the reader knows that something extraordinary is about to happen. In biblical tradition, as well as in Greek and Roman culture, dreams could sometimes disclose a divine revelation. There are also many dream stories that announced that the person in the dream would have a very special life. Tradition has it that Olympias, mother of Alexander the Great, had a dream about her future child before his birth (see Plutarch, *De Alexandro* 2.3–5). On the eve of the wedding night she dreamt that a flash of lightning entered her and lit a fire inside her. Alexander would have used this dream to prove his divine descent.

In 1 Kings 3 the dream functions as a sort of prelude to the stories about Solomon. In the dream the setting of the aim of the kingship of this son of David is established. His kingship will be based on listening. Solomon is allowed to formulate his own vision of a ruler, after his sacrifices and in a communication with the Divine. According to Solomon, a real king is a king who listens. He has to be able to understand with heart and soul the people he will have to judge. In a visionary way the story presents the direction, the aim of his rule. This is the way in which Solomon wants to be king and judge: with a listening heart. Scripture gives a lesson in kingship in a narrative way.

The proof of the pudding is in the eating

King Solomon's profile of a king, in the first lines of 1 Kings 3, is immediately followed by an example from real life, in which Solomon proves to be the king who really listens with his heart. After the dream he travels to Jerusalem and offer sacrifices again. Subsequently, he serves a banquet to all his servants. Does the possibility to serve festive meals and eat together also belong to the tasks of the king? The rest of this chapter deals with Solomon as king and judge.

In the story of Solomon's dream the role of the king concentrates itself on the judicial function of a king at that time. In 1 Kings 3.16–18 the biblical author narrates how a listening heart helps the king to solve an almost impossible case.

In the days of the dream two women visit the king and present him with a difficult problem (1 Kings 3.16–28). They are both prostitutes and maybe for convenience of their shared profession they had been living together. They were both pregnant and both delivered a boy within the space of three days. One child dies, possibly because the mother had lain on him during her sleep. The women come into conflict. The first mother says that the other mother has exchanged her own dead child during the night with the living child of the former. The other mother denies this most emphatically. What is to be done, when DNA testing was not in existence? Solomon demonstrates that he has a heart that listens. He knows a mother only wants what is best for her child. He asks for a sword. His verdict is that the living child will be cut in two so that both women can have one half each. The rest of this famous story goes without saying. The mother of the dead baby agrees. After all, her child has died and she does not object to the death of the other child. The real mother does not want her child to die and she pleads with the king to let the child live and give it to the other woman. This way the women have shown their hand and Solomon can give the child back to the real mother.

Lessons in kingship: for whom?

In these fairytale-like stories we find ideas about the principles and the practice of kingship. True kingship is based on listening. Nowadays in our world there are only a handful of kings left. Today there is little audience for these lessons in biblical kingship. But appearances can be deceptive, for there are quite a lot of people who secretly dream of being a king or queen, even only for just one day.

In Indonesia this dream is ritualized in the wedding ceremony. At a certain moment in the service the couple disappear and then stride in again. In the meantime they have been dressed up and both wear a royal sarong. For one day they are a royal couple: prince and princess.

But to be prince and princess does not mean you can claim the other person for your own whims. At the wedding you give yourself away and you receive the other. To be there for the other means opening up your ears and listening with your heart. Married people, fathers and mothers, teachers, but also managers and executives can take lessons from the story of Solomon's dream of how a listening heart is the main thing for a king, a judge, and a teacher. Only those who try to listen with their heart can successfully judge other people's acts. Of course, this is easier said than done, but that is intrinsic to gaining wisdom. The stories about the kings of the Old Testament are narrative pedagogics. They teach us what is non-royal behaviour and what could be royal. The story of King Solomon's dream is a key story because it describes that the main attribute of an ideal king, an ideal parent, a teacher or a judge, is a listening heart, which will make a human being into a king or queen. This is true royalty.

Epilogue

I once met with an elderly theologian, and because we both wrote about dreams we became friends. His favourite topic was dreams in the Bible in relation to pastoral ministry. When he was very old, he had to be taken into hospital. At the time when he was in hospital I gave a lecture somewhere about rabbinic views on dreams. After my lecture a colleague theologian came to me and told me that he had made a mistake during a visit at the hospital to the old theologian just mentioned. Apparently, the old theologian was very ill and his life was in danger. During the visit the old man had mentioned to the colleague that he had had a dream, but the colleague theologian had failed to react to the dream of this old and sick man.

Religious ministers are often inclined to ignore the dreams of their flock. In the western world, since Freud published his ideas, the interpretation of dreams has been considered to belong to the psychological realm and maybe to the adherents of New Age movements. However, in biblical traditions dreams and visions are signposts. They stimulate people to look for new roads. As we saw above, Solomon had a dream at a crucial time in his life. Biblical stories of dreams are also used to wake the reader. At that moment the reader knows: 'Be alert, wake up and listen carefully to this dream.' This approach does not stop with the Bible for there have always been people who have experienced their dreams as divine revelations, such as Perpetua and Saint Francis and also, for example, Don Bosco.

I myself think that Luther, with his emphasis on faith and Scripture alone, was one of the first theologians to be totally against the interpretation of dreams as a form of revelation. A second blow came from the Enlightenment. Although Swedenborg was a protagonist of the Enlightenment, he claimed that many of his inventions were based on visions. This was offensive to Kant, who always stressed the rational and even wrote a book against dreams: *Träume eines Geistersehers, erläutert durch Träume der Metaphysik* (Königsberg 1766; see Johnson 2002).

Theologians and ministers are inclined to dismiss the dreams of their 'clients', that is, those who come to seek their advice. This is a pity, because

Scriptures (and later Christian traditions) show that dreams and visions have inspired human beings again and again. Thus, neglecting the dreams in the Scriptures or the dreams of people today is closing the door to possible revelations of wisdom. The creative tension between dreams as a revelation from God on the one hand and authorities such as Scripture and Tradition on the other in biblical and Christian traditions can be a mirror for contemporary struggles with authorities and traditions. Attention to dreams in the ancient wisdom traditions and to dreams in real life today creates new space for opening up to new wisdom.

References

Carr, D. M. (1991), *From D to Q: A Study of Early Jewish Interpretations of Solomon's Dream at Gibeon*, Atlanta GA: SBL Press.

Carrique, P. (2002), *Rêve, Vérité: Essai sur la philosophie du sommeil et de la veille*, Paris: Gallimard.

Frenschkowksi, M. (1998), 'Traum und Traumdeutung in Matthäusevangelium: Einige Beobachtungen', in G. Schöllgen, S. de Blaauw and W. Löhr, eds, *Jahrbuch für Antike und Christentum* 41, Münster (Westf.): Aschendorff, pp. 5–47.

Gnuse, R. K. (1990), 'Dream Genre in the Matthean Infancy Narratives', in *Novum Testamentum* 32, pp. 97–120.

Husser, J. M. (1999), *Dreams and Dream Narratives in the Biblical World*, Sheffield: Sheffield Academic Press.

Johnson, G. R., ed. (2002), *Kant on Swedenborg: Dreams of Spirit-Seer and Other Writings*, West Chester PA: Swedenborg Foundation.

Kessels, A. H. M. (1978), *Studies on the Dream in Greek Literature*, Utrecht: Hes Publishers.

Koet, B. J. (2006), *Dreams and Scripture in Luke-Acts: Collected Essays*, Leuven: Peeters.

Koet, B. J. (2008), 'It started with a Dream: Paul's Dream (Acts 16.9–10) and Aeneas as a Biblical Example of Dreams as Intercultural Legitimation Strategy', in *Dreaming: Journal of the Association for the Study of Dreams* 18 (2008), pp. 267–79.

Koet, B. J. (2009), 'Divine Dream Dilemmas: Biblical Visions and Dreams', in K. Bulkeley, K. Adams and P. M. Davis, eds, *Dreaming in Christianity and Islam: Culture, Conflict and Creativity*, New Brunswick NJ: Rutgers University, pp. 17–31.

Koet, B. J. (2012), 'Jerome's and Augustine's Conversion to Scripture through the Portal of Dreams' (Eph. 22 and Conf. 3 and 8), in B. J. Koet, ed., *Dreams as Divine Communication in Christianity: From Hermas to Aquinas*, Leuven: Peeters, pp. 93–124.

Lanckau, J. (2006), *Der Herr der Träume: Eine Studie zur Funktion des Traumes in der Josefsgeschichte der Hebräischen Bibel*, Zürich: Theologischer Verlag.

Matthews, G. B. (2005), *Augustine*, Oxford: Wiley-Blackwell.

Oepke, A. (1954), 'Traum und Traumdeutung im Alten Testament', in G. Kittel and G. Friedrich, eds, *Theologisches Wörterbuch zum NT* 5, pp. 220–38, especially 228–31 (German original).

Oppenheim, A. L. (1956), *The Interpretation of Dreams in the Ancient Near East, With the Translation of an Assyrian Dream Book*, Philadelphia: Transactions of the American Philosophical Society, Vol. 46, Part 3, pp. 184–373.

Seow, C. L. (1984), 'The Syro-Palestinian Context of Solomon's Dream', in *Harvard Theological Review* 77, pp. 141–52.

2

Dreams, Societies and Worldviews
A Cross-Cultural Perspective

CHARLES D. LAUGHLIN

Why should she give her bounty to the dead?
What is divinity if it can come
Only in silent shadows and in dreams?
Shall she not find in comforts of the sun,
In pungent fruit and bright green wings, or else
In any balm or beauty of the earth,
Things to be cherished like the thought of heaven?
                    Wallace Stevens, 'Sunday Morning'

The most common alternative state of consciousness among human beings is dreaming. All normal humans sleep, and during sleep they dream. Yet as common as is this alternative state, it is still a phenomenon of mystery and confusion to many westerners, and of fascination to scientists wishing to understand how the mind works, both in terms of the neuropsychology of embodied consciousness and within the context of culture (see Laughlin 2011 for a more complete list of references). Dreaming is a function of neurophysiological processes that are universal not only to human beings but to all animals with cortical brains. Infants in the womb, and as newborns, spend much of their time dreaming, most of it in rapid eye movement (REM) sleep (Feinberg 1969), and people continue to dream until they die. Sleep and dreaming are obviously critical to the healthy development and adaptation of humans and animals of any age. Yet what people dream about, the physical conditions in which they sleep and dream, whether they pay any attention to dream content in their waking lives, how they interpret and integrate dream material into their self-identities, how groups put dreaming to social uses – all of these factors vary enormously among individuals, and especially across cultures. Small wonder then that dreaming has been of interest to anthropology since the inception of the discipline.

In this chapter I will discuss dreaming from the standpoint of being a neurologically trained anthropologist (neuroanthropologist). My commitment, as always, is to science. In Susan Parmon's (1991, p. xii) words, 'the framework of science, with its assumptions of testability and commitment to phenomenon as object rather than subject is, as science should be, useful, practical and down-to-earth'. I will show how the cross-cultural variation in meaning is integral to a full scientific understanding of the role played by dreaming in people's lives (see Laughlin 2011; Laughlin, McManus and d'Aquili 1990, pp. 12–18).

Pre-assumptions about the dreaming brain

Experience unfolds in each and every one of us as a stream of consciousness that forms recurrent patterns of content called 'states' (Tart 1975). States of consciousness are componential (that is, they are the product of many neurophysiological processes that combine in a distinct and recurring organization of content and relations, making each state introspectively identifiable. This is even true for the simplest manifestation of consciousness, what Antonio Damasio has called 'core consciousness' that 'provides the organism with a sense of self about one moment – now – and about one place – here' (see Damasio 1999, p. 16 for a more detailed account). Even core consciousness is comprised of content mediated by discrete neurophysiological structures. More complex states are relatively stable and are cognizable by the individual, and within a culture, as distinct from other states, e.g. 'awake', 'hyper', 'drunk', 'high', 'dreaming', 'dozy', 'blue', and so forth. Many of the same components will be involved in different states. For instance, those functions requisite to core consciousness are always there to some degree. Moreover, there is a certain area of the cortex known as the fusiform and lingual gyri, which processes the colour sense. If this area is destroyed, colour disappears from perception in waking life, from dreams and even from memory (Edelman and Tononi 2000, p. 53; Damasio 1999, p. 268). In other words, the same area of the brain produces colour for all states of consciousness. On the other hand, certain components of states will differ. For instance, there is a particular neurochemical that is present during waking states that is absent during dreaming. In sleep states, sensory input and motor output are massively inhibited, while they are relatively active in waking states. Adding additional components to core consciousness changes the experience within the dream.

There are two further states that bear mention for ethnographic reasons, those being the *hypnagogic* imagery that may arise during sleep onset and the *hypnopompic* imagery that can arise during sleep offset. The hypnagogic and hypnopompic states have very short durations (something like five seconds or less) in typical western subjects. As we fall asleep we may experience a blending of both external stimuli and internal imagery as the body relaxes and slips into Stage 2 sleep. The same occurs as we leave sleep and enter the waking state. We westerners tend to ignore such imagery for all the reasons I have mentioned above, and hence tend not to remember them later on, but they do become memorable, salient and interpretable among dreamers in some non-western societies, most notably those that use various ritualized forms of *dream incubation* as oracles. (Dream incubation is the method by which dream rituals evoke and direct dreaming towards the solution of a problem, as seen for example in the practice of *dharnā* among Bengali Hindu pilgrims (see Morinis 1982), and in meditative practices involving dreaming such as those used in Tibetan dream yoga.

The anthropology of dreaming

Human experience seems to be distributed across a range of states, from those concerned primarily with adaptation to extramental reality to those oriented towards internal relations within the being. The most common alternation here is between what we call 'waking' and 'dreaming' states.

Monophasic cultures

In modern, materialistic technocratic societies like our own Euro-American-Australasian societies, as well as modern industrial Chinese, Japanese and other Asian societies, children are typically taught not to attend to their dreams and to focus on adaptational interactions with the external physical world. The common cultural message is that dreams are not real ('It's only a dream, dear'), they just happen and should be ignored. Schools typically do not address one's dream life, and information obtained in dream life bears little or no relevance to the waking world, except perhaps during the course of psychotherapy. These technocratic societies exhibit what we call *monophasic cultures* (Laughlin 2011; Laughlin, McManus and d'Aquili 1990, p. 293), which tend to skew the development of consciousness away from alternative states of consciousness and towards perceptual and cognitive processes oriented to the external world. Monophasic orientation towards dreaming leaves its mark on the research and accounts of western anthropologists for whom dreams often have to be demythologized in order for them to become meaningful – that is, the dream must make sense to rational thought in the waking state to make any sense at all (Tedlock 1992, p. 4; Bourguignon 2003, p. 137). So extreme is the disattention to alternative states in technocratic societies that complementary spiritual movements have arisen over time to assuage the sense of spiritual poverty felt by many – movements that include those focused on dreaming (Hillman 1988).

Polyphasic cultures

The state of affairs among technocratic societies stands in sharp contrast to both our own pre-industrial history and the pre-industrial histories of other modern, industrial societies such as Japan, China and Brazil, during which dreaming and dream interpretation were highly valued. People in the medieval and early modern period often saw dreams as communications from God – or from the Devil. For the ancients, dreams were perhaps more like visitations. Dreams might predict the future or carry messages. Aside from western European societies, there are in excess of 4,000 cultures on the planet today, and roughly 90% of them seek out and value experiences had in alternative states of consciousness, and especially in dreams (Bourguignon 1973; Bourguignon and Evascu 1977).

We say that these are polyphasic cultures, meaning that they value experiences had in the dream life, as well as those had in trance states, meditation states, drug- and ritual-driven visions, etc. These experiences are often conceived by the people as different aspects of reality, not unreality – indeed, the people rarely if ever make a distinction between experienced and extramental reality the way science does today. Their sense of identity incorporates memories of experiences had in dreams and other alternative states, as well as in waking life. Indeed, the people may not have a word in their native tongue that exactly connotes 'dream' in our everyday English sense. What we call a 'dream' may be considered by others to be the polyphasic ego of a person experiencing another domain of reality (e.g. Herr 1981, p. 334 on fuzzy boundaries among Fijians between what we call dream, hallucination and vision; Merrill 1992 on this issue among the Ramámiru of Mexico). Dream experiences, just as waking experiences, inform the society's general system of knowledge about the self and the world – that is, their *cosmology*, as well as the development of a person's identity. One can thus understand why ethnographer Jean-Guy Goulet's Guajiro (a South American people) hosts would not allow him to live with them unless he 'knew how to dream' (1994, p. 22). One may also understand why the anthropology of dreaming has for generations focused upon polyphasic cultures, perhaps because they are so at odds with our own everyday ethnocentric and monophasic expectations.

Ethnographic studies of dreaming cultures have shown how social expectations, symbolic attributions and environmental conditions may impact dreaming and the interpretation of dreams. For instance, it was said by traditional Eastern Cree hunters of Labrador that, 'If a man could no longer remember his dreams upon awakening, he could no longer hunt' (Flannery and Chambers 1985, p. 4). Cree hunters, beginning in their teens, sought to have special spirit visitors appear to them in their dreams and establish a relationship with them. These visitors would then mediate between the hunter and the animals being hunted. So attention to dreaming was very important to the Cree, and they considered the loss of dream recall as aberrant. Likewise, in Fiji where people live on many small islands and where a great deal of tension exists between the sexes and repression of divisive feelings is necessary to keep local harmony, the incidence of negative dreaming and nightmares is notable (Herr 1981). Not surprising, Fijians show a great, but negative interest in dreams, and will greet each other in the mornings with the question: Did you [not] dream last night? – meaning, did you sleep well without being disturbed by any nasty dreams (ibid., p. 333). Sex in Fiji is fraught with all sorts of taboos, especially for women, and so what in another society might be a pleasurable erotic dream becomes a fearful one.

Sociocultural uses of dreaming

As we have seen, dream experiences are of great interest to many peoples all over the planet. Moreover, they put dreaming to use. Just as a hunter or gatherer might elaborate with considerable drama the story of their daily adventures in the bush, so too may people in some societies relish hearing about the adventures had during what we call 'dreams'. The information derived from these dream accounts may have an important role to play in a people's self and social identity, decisions made in everyday life, planning future actions, and accruing spiritual understanding. Take, for example, the routine sharing of dreams among the Mehinaku people of the Xingu river headwaters in Brazil (Gregor 1981). People sleep in hammocks close together in a long house. During the night, they wake up to add fuel to the communal fire and reflect upon their dreams. In the morning they recall a number of dreams from the night and share them with others immediately upon waking. Dreams are the adventures had by one's 'eye soul' during sleep when it detaches from the body and wanders around. Another classic example are the Aborigines of the western desert lands of Australia (Tonkinson 2003, p. 92). Each individual has a dream spirit that can leave their body at night and wander places and see and do things (e.g. seek out and request the aid of rainmaking spirits). This is a very common theme cross-culturally, for people often understand their dreams as the wandering of their spiritual selves during sleep.

Holocultural studies

Although dreaming is a species universal, not all societies emphasize the importance of dreaming, or do so in exactly the same way. There have been some holocultural studies done correlating the content and use of dreaming with certain sociocultural factors. Holocultural research involves statistical analysis of correlations between different cultural traits using a large sample of human societies taken from all over the planet. They usually consider only those societies for which there exist sufficient ethnographic materials. The best study to date is Roy d'Andrade's (1961) statistical study of anxiety and attempts to seek and control supernatural powers by way of dreaming (hereafter called 'control dreams'). D'Andrade reasoned that subsistence patterns range from those societies that emphasize adherence to social norms, sanctions and procedures (agricultural and animal husbandry) to those that emphasize individualism, isolation and self-reliance (hunting and fishing). Peoples of the latter kind tend to place individuals in anxiety-producing situations more often than those of the former kind – hence the emphasis upon dreaming as a means of seeking and controlling supernatural powers via dreaming. D'Andrade also reasoned that the farther away a male has to move from his parents, the more likely he would tend to feel 'on his own' and anxious, and thus seek control dreams. In a similar way he showed a significant correlation between post-nuptial residence (where people live after marrying) patterns and control dreams among males.

Erika Bourguignon (1972) carried d'Andrade's work further by reasoning that 'hallucinogenic trance' states are closely allied with control dreams; so closely in fact that it is hard to tell where trance leaves off and dreaming begins. She combined her holocultural research on trance states with d'Andrade's work, and examined the correlation between trance and control dreaming using a sample of societies that overlapped with d'Andrade's. She was able to confirm that the use of control dreams does indeed correlate with the use of trance states. This would seem to add support to the notion that peoples that face uncertainty, individualism and conditions that demand self-reliance do take measures to gain control over their situation by way of trance states, prayer and dreaming.

In another interesting use of holocultural methods, Kenneth Colby (1963) examined content differences in the reported dreams of men and women cross-culturally. He analysed 549 dreams reported by 366 men and 183 women from 75 traditional societies and looked for sex differences in the occurrence of 19 'qualities' or themes. Themes that were particularly distinct were men dreaming of 'wife' (his or someone else's) and women dreaming of 'husband' (hers or someone else's). Men also tended to dream of weapons, coitus, death and animals more often than women, and women dream of mother, clothes and female figures more often than men. These findings were consistent with the findings of an earlier and similar study of western college students.

Finally, in a remarkable cross-cultural study of Jungian archetypal themes, analyst Vincenza Tiberia (1981, p. 73) notes that Jung drew a distinction between personal and collective dreams, which Kruger later called 'everyday' and 'archetypal' dreams. This is precisely the distinction made by many traditional cultures to distinguish their normal dreaming from very special dreams that have socially significant portent, especially those in which there is communication with gods, spirits or ancestors. Tiberia used the data from roughly 300 societies available in the Human Relations Area Files to collect some 62 archetypal dreams from 43 different cultures spread over seven world areas. In analysing these dreams she isolated the cultural saliency of six archetypes: 'the Archetypal Feminine' (anima, Great Mother), 'the Self', 'the Marriage', 'the Ancestor Archetype', and 'Losing Teeth'. The first three archetypes were as described by Jung himself, while the last two were discovered in analysing the cross-cultural data.

Oneirocritics

As Irving Hallowell (1976) has shown, in many human societies dreaming and dream sharing are thoroughly social acts. There are many uses to which dreaming is put by many societies, and when specific uses are of social importance, be it for the purposes of relieving anxiety, healing, prediction of future events, finding of lost objects, seeking of initiatory visions, prescription of appropriate ritual acts, a form of prayer, etc., those uses are typically institutionalized. The dream-as-dreamt becomes a dream-as-text in the telling, and as such invites attention, reflection, discussion and interpretation by others, as well as ritual activity that may operate as a mediator between the individual's dream experience *cum* text and the society's mythopoeic worldview.[1] Dream interpretation is typically standardized and the meanings attributed to dreams are usually couched in terms that confirm, instantiate, and are consonant with the prevailing worldview. As Murray Wax (2004) mentions, in many small-scale hunting and gathering societies, dream sharing is an everyday, immediate social practice. We have seen with the example of the Mehinaku dream sharing above that dreaming and dream telling are commonplace. Among the nineteenth-century Zulus of southern Africa, dreaming was a very practical affair in which communications from ancestors might necessitate ritual actions to keep them happy (Chidester 2008). In this case dreams not only invited social engagement, but social action as well.

To add to these examples, Waud Kracke (1992, p. 32) notes for the Parintintin, a small, previously hunter-gatherer group in Brazilian Amazonia:

> Dreams like myths . . . are to be told. Waking at daybreak, or in the middle of the night at 2–3 a.m., one may often hear someone narrating a dream to a few others as they warm themselves by the fire. During the day over work, a person may interrupt gossip about current events to entertain work companions with a dream.

Dreams complete their usefulness in their telling, in their sharing. Among such small groups, everybody seems to be an oneirocritic – a dream interpreter – and the content of the dream becomes as it were public property as individual interpretation approaches group consensus. Among the Andaman Islanders of the Bay of Bengal in the Indian Ocean (Pandya 2004), hunter gatherers would share their dreams around the fire at night and in the morning just after waking, and the group consensus as to the meaning of a person's dream will have an influence upon the activities of that person during the day.

Where there is this routine sharing of dreams, the meaning of dream objects and events is fairly standardized. For the Mehinaku, dreaming of a wide clear path may forecast the dreamer will go bald later in life,

---

1 I am specifically avoiding the issue of how the dream as directly experienced, and the dream as remembered and expressed socially may relate.

dreaming of white men or their artefacts may portend illness, and dreaming of eating fruit assures an active sex life. The nineteenth-century Zulu understood the Jungian 'law of opposites' in which the real meaning of a motif was its antithesis, e.g. to dream of marriage means death, to dream of death means marriage, and so forth (Chidester 2008, p. 31). Of course, not all societies share dreams quite so freely. Among the Mekeo people of Papua New Guinea, dreams 'are regarded as dangerous knowledge, to be handled with the greatest discretion . . .' (Stephen 1995, p. 139). When Mekeo share dreams, it is usually with family members and other intimates, and messages derived from dreams almost always pertain to one or more of a short list of portends considered crucial to people (ibid., p. 120). Mekeo shamans heal people by travelling in their dreams to power places in search of their patients' lost souls (ibid., p. 198). The shaman appears to be an adept at dreaming, more so than laypeople, and able to dream lucidly and organize their dream experience around a specific intention. It is intentional dreaming like this among shamanic cultures that may be considered a kind of prayer or meditation.

Other peoples may recognize an institutionalized role of oneirocritics. These are specialists in the art of interpretation to whom one may turn for help in understanding portentous dreams. Images in such dreams are associated with symbols in the people's cosmology which becomes seamlessly realized in direct experience. The dream events enliven and make immediately accessible the stories that are at the core of the cosmology. In his classic study of dreaming and dream theory of the Iroquois, Anthony F. C. Wallace (1958) describes a people among whom dreaming is of prime importance to everyday decision-making. In a dream theory very similar to Freudian psychoanalysis, the Iroquois believed that the soul has certain desires that may be unconscious to the waking person. If these deep-seated desires are not in some way met, bad things may happen, especially sickness. The soul is thought to reveal the desires in dreams. But the person may not be able to interpret the dream in the correct way in order to elicit the desire. Thus people consult oneirocritics, who are adept at analysing the real desires underlying the dream story. In other words, the Iroquois posited a clear distinction between what Freudians later on would call the 'manifest' and 'latent' content of dreams, and recognized that a specialist might have to be called in to explicate the latent meaning of the dream. Once the 'latent' soul desire is laid bare, every effort was made to satisfy the soul's desire so that sickness was healed or avoided.

Benjamin Kilborne (1981, p. 296) makes the interesting point that in Morocco, where dream symbols are standardized and there are dream books available to anyone who wishes to consult them, few people interpret their own dreams, but rather rely upon the professional oneirocritic (often the Koranic schoolmaster) to help them reach the proper understanding of special dreams. In the process of interpretation, the interaction between dreamer and oneirocritic is important, and as Kilborne says, the dream-as-reported becomes a text upon which both the dreamer and the oneirocritic project meaning. Of course, the meaning reached during a session is always consistent with a Koranic belief system. Barbara Tedlock (1981) also notes the importance of the dream interpreter among the Quiché Maya. Many people become initiated as oneirocritics and they function as healers and diviners as well. Tedlock states that the interpreter will apply a number of general rules in attributing meaning to symbols while at the same time taking into consideration the dreamer's everyday situation.

As Roy d'Andrade (1961, p. 313) points out, the relationship between culture and dreaming is anything but a simple one – the dream may exhibit content from the outer world, but the internal dynamics within the individual's psyche determine the structure of the dream – the 'grammar' of dreaming, if you will. Institutionalized oneirocritics will operate to conserve social understanding of the world, and return individual experience to the mosaic of the society's worldview. It helps to understand that there is probably no such thing as a dream that admits of one and only one possible interpretation. Traditional oneirocritics will generally choose an interpretation most consonant with the cosmology. Yet in a very subtle way, the enactment of myth in dreaming operates to *revitalize* (Wallace 1966) the cosmology by instantiating the myth within the present, thus resulting at times in an ever so subtle transformation of the cosmology. This interaction between dreams and the cosmology make dream reality pragmatic; that is, bringing the timeless cosmology alive, renewed and useful to people in their contemporary lives.

A marvellous example of the dynamic relationship that may obtain in a polyphasic society between an individual's dream experiences and the society's worldview is the remarkable description Laura R. Graham (2003) offers of the Xavante people of Brazil. An elder may have a dream (obviously lucid considering the extent of focus, clarity of detail and working memory involved) which he then retells around a camp-fire to other elders. The dream may involve a meeting with the gods of mythological lore in which new ritual instructions and new songs are revealed. The elder retells the dream and sings the songs to teach the other elders. This leads later on to a ritual enactment of the dream by costumed dancers and singers. The ritual drama is conceived locally to be both a re-enactment of the history of mythopoeic drama and the introduction of new and creative material that becomes part of the ritual tradition of the people. As Graham notes, 'A myth has a life that is born through its tellings. And each new telling has the potential to vary, even minutely, details of the previous tellings' (2003, p. 8).

Dreaming as a window into the invisible

For monophasic peoples, dreams are synonymous with *un*-real, but for most peoples on the planet, dreaming is at least as real as waking experience, and often considered *more* real. Why? Because dreams are often understood to make normally invisible forces visible – the same function that myths perform (Laughlin 2011). As Roger Lohmann writes, 'Sleep is a doorway, and dreams are roads and destinations. In dreams, people visit other places, change the shape of reality, and gain insight into causes and connections secreted beneath the cosmos of waking life' (2003, p. 1). Both the world religions, and those of smaller-scale societies, recognize certain motifs as spiritually salient in their dreams – those that feature death, gods and ancestors, totemic animals like snakes and bears, sexuality, healing and diagnosis, prophecy, demons and nightmares, soul-flight, and so forth. Spirits, ghosts, long-dead ancestors, gods, heroes, etc., whose presence one may only sense, but not observe in the waking life, may take on form when they appear as characters in a dream (d'Andrade 1961, p. 298). Dream characters may communicate in one way or another with the dreamer. As a consequence, people may understand dreaming as a means of communicating (we might say 'praying to') with the normally invisible forces that influence their daily lives, and perhaps obtaining valuable information.

Among many African peoples, the belief is quite common that the ancestors pass on to a higher plane of existence and that they may mediate between divine (normally hidden) forces and the living (Parrinder 1962, p. 61). They may communicate via dreams of a distinctive character, and may warn the living of impending events, and even suggest the cause of the events. Among the North American Indians of the Great Plains, the quest for spiritual vision dreams was as common as it was important. Dreams had (and have today) a role that was central to native religious systems among most if not all Plains cultures (Irwin 1994). In the context of their cosmologies, dreaming is a state in which people experience both the 'known' and the 'mysterious' (ibid., p. 21). Dreams instantiate the mythic worldview and at the same time empower the dreamer with direct knowledge of the mysteries.

Among Haitian people the dead are known to walk at night in the form of such horrors as zombies and werewolves. The dead come alive in the dreams of children in their nightmares (Bourguignon 1954, p. 263). Moreover, the gods and the dead may visit the dreamer in order to offer messages. Talking in one's sleep is understood to be a message from the dead or the gods, often in a language that only the gods and the priests can understand. If disturbing dreams and nightmares are confusing to the dreamer, they may consult a *vodun* priest who is considered to be an oneirocritic. As is typical in traditional societies, the dream will be interpreted within the *vodun* worldview. The message may be read as a demand from the gods for certain ritual procedures to be carried out.

Dreaming is for some peoples a direct source of learning, knowledge and power. As Robin Ridington (1988) makes clear, 'hunting dreams' among the Subarctic Dunne-za enable the hunter to establish a relationship with the animals he hunts and with the normally invisible spirits that influence his success or failure. Moreover, one may be directly instructed and guided towards paths of knowing while dreaming. Denise Nuttall (2007, p. 345) reports that during her lengthy apprenticeship with the great Indian tabla player Usted Zakir Hussain, she repeatedly had what she called 'tabla dreams' in which Zakirji would visit and instruct her. The same experience was reported by Katherine Ewing (1994, p. 574), who was visited by her teacher in dreams while researching Sufi practices in Pakistan. The Ese Eja of Peruvian Amazonia seek the names of their children from dreams (Peluso 2004). In their dreams, people interact with animals and receive the 'true name' of their child. This process brings direct experience in dreaming, naming and notions of personhood into accord with the spiritual aspects of Esa Eja cosmology.

The classic example of the integration of dreaming and cosmology is that found among the Australian Aborigines (Tonkinson 1978, pp. 15–17, 93; 2003; Poirier 2003). The Aborigines believe that in mythical times, called The Dreaming or Dreamtime, hero spirits created the world people later inhabited. People understand that the Dreamtime happened a long time ago, and yet is still present today. Individual dreaming is an expression of the Dreamtime, the link between contemporary dreaming and the Dreaming being seamless. All the power accrued by shamans derives from the Dreamtime and is accessed by way of dreaming, and is in a sense timeless. Interpretations of dreams are always in terms of Dreamtime characters, landscape features, power sources and adventures. Every person has a dream spirit that can travel anywhere it wishes in this Dreamtime domain. Every landmark has its place in the mythic stories of the Dreamtime and these features are recognized during individual dreaming. As Robert Tonkinson writes, 'Their human forefathers who first peopled their territory must have sensed a need to ground metaphysical conceptions in the stones, sand, and streambeds of the physical world, to unite spirit and substance and in this way render much more immediate and meaningful the essential unity of the two realms' (1978, p. 15). People seek and receive instructions and knowledge in dreams, and conceive of such information as having been bestowed upon them by mythopoeic forces. New rituals may be derived from inspiration in individual dreams, and then as time passes and the rituals spread from group to group, such rituals may be viewed as having derived collectively from the Dreaming (2003, p. 94). Nancy Munn, in reporting on a Walbiri Aborigine's dreaming, noted that 'the dreamer felt himself to be both a kind of observer of the events of the dream and at the same time an actor in the dream, identified with the ancestors' (1973, p. 114).

Dreaming and healing

Dreams may be utilized in diagnosing disease – what might be called medical oneirocritics. Among the Navajo people of the American Southwest, among whom I spent some years on and off researching their spiritual and cosmological system, if one should dream about spirit beings such as the *Yei* ('Holy People'), this may portend future danger and perhaps disease. William Morgan (1932) describes a shaman who had a recurring dream that the gods, including *Yei*, were trying to drag him away to a mountain. The shaman 'was familiar with gods, dreams, and sickness, and believed that they were causally related. He was convinced that his dream was a warning, and that unless something were done, he would be sick' (ibid., p. 391). The shaman checked out his diagnosis with other specialists and they agreed with him. This interpretation of the dream was consistent with Navajo cosmology. The universe is inhabited by normally invisible forces, collectively known as the 'Holy Wind' (see McNeley 1981), forces that are extremely potent and are potentially dangerous if not in balance. Much of Navajo healing is about restoring balance and 'beauty', or *hozho*. The shaman's recurring dream was for him an indicator that forces in his body and life were spiralling out of balance, and this required an effective response in order to avoid the calamitous outcome sure to follow.[2] Linking certain dreams with future negative

---

2 Lest the reader think that diagnosis of disease by attending to dream content and associations is rather fanciful, modern medicine recognizes the same diagnostic utility in certain cases; e.g. a dream disorder termed REM sleep behaviour disorder has been shown to be a predictor of neurological degenerative diseases later in life (see Britton and Chaudhuri 2009).

outcomes is fairly widespread among traditional societies. Another example is the Sambia people of Papua New Guinea (Herdt 1992), who share certain dreams because they appear to foretell events. They do not report just any dream, but rather those that are emotionally and portentously 'heavy'. 'Dreams are interpreted primarily because Sambia believe they reveal bad omens about future events such as warfare, hunting, birth, death, gardening, sickness, and travels' (ibid., pp. 64–5). Shamans use their own dreams to bolster the appearance that they have predicted important events correctly. In a curious variation on this theme, among the Ramámuri (aka Tarahumara) people of Northern Mexico, to have a good night's sleep means that one's soul has remained asleep and safely in one's body, and thus one does not dream at all (Merrill 1992). But if someone should wish you harm, then your soul awakens and leaves its refuge and you dream of doing battle: '. . . dreaming precludes peaceful sleep because malevolent beings – evil people, coyotes, and personified illnesses were specifically mentioned – attack or otherwise attempt to harm the dreamers or their souls' (ibid., p. 195).

Dreaming and witchcraft

The wanderings of the dream body may be interpreted positively or negatively, depending upon the society. In many African societies, a witch may take on a dream body to do mischief while the waking body remains where it lays. Prince (1961) mentions that among the Yoruba of Nigeria, a witch may morph her dream body into a bird and travel to a target's home and attack them while they sleep. The victim may in turn experience nightmares related to this activity. Dreaming and witchcraft are also associated in Papua New Guinea. The Kuma people manifest a great deal of tension in their social lives. A lot of their anxiety finds its way into their dreams, which they term 'sweet witchcraft while you sleep' (Reay 1962, p. 460), meaning that what at first blush may look attractive may well be evil in disguise. The 'sugar-coating' falls away and the underlying conflict and anxiety become manifest to the dreamer, and they are unable to resolve the situation. Among the people of Gawa Island, dreaming is seen as 'seeing . . . during sleep; seeing is the prototypical form of knowing . . . Dreams in particular are regarded as crucial means of giving visibility to the invisible witch and witch activities' (Munn 1990, p. 6). Dreams of a sick person may be interpreted by a healer as indicating that the source of the illness is witchcraft, and perhaps as revealing the identity of the witch.

Oneiromancy

Many societies tap into dreaming for the purpose of divining the future – for seeking information about events that have yet to happen, or that have not finished happening, through prophecy and portends. For many peoples, ancestors, spirits and gods may intervene in the course of human affairs by communicating what may or may not happen in the foreseeable future. Like so many peoples dependent upon hunting, the Eastern Cree of Labrador (Flannery and Chambers 1985) considered knowing just where game was to be found to be crucial. Oneiromancy (dream divination) was therefore well developed for the Cree, with dream visitors mediating between hunters and the animals they hunted. There were many types of dreams; some could be talked about and some could not. Positive portend dreams were reported far from the morning's fire, while negative portend dreams were spoken of as close to the fire as possible. Likewise, Navajo (Morgan 1932) interpret dreams as an indication that disease is present, or may come, and the diagnosis might well lead to a healing ceremony. Dreams are warnings, and bad dreams (nightmares) are warnings of bad things to come.

Among the Guajiro of Columbia the ancestors are believed to live on an island where they have plenty to eat and there is no conflict, unlike conditions among the living (Watson and Watson-Franke 1977). Dreaming is considered to be just another phase of life. The dream world is real and dreamt events are as real as waking events, often 'depicting and foretelling actual events that will occur in the future, warning of upcoming developments, and commenting on the dreamer's true physical and spiritual status' (ibid., p. 394). The same may be said for the Aguaruna of the South American Andes, among whom all states of consciousness are different views on reality (Brown 1992). Dreams are as integral to Aguaruna everyday decision-making as is waking experience. But it is by way of dreams that they may anticipate the future, able at times to see the end of a process that, in waking life, is far less certain. Dreaming, as with so many peoples, is a prerequisite to successful hunting, and dreaming of a dead warrior is necessary for one who wishes to be successful in battle (ibid., p. 163).

Shamanic dreams

Dreaming has been integral to most of the spiritual traditions among the world's societies. 'Shaman' is the label that anthropologists use for traditional mystics, spiritual practitioners and healers, and as such shamans represent humanity's ancient encounter with and interpretations of alternative waking and dreaming states. Dreaming is often integral to the calling and empowerment of shamans, and presumably has been since time immemorial. Among the Dunne-za, a Subarctic hunting people, the initiation of each man is by way of a vision quest (Ridington 1971). The vision is sought through a series of dream experiences in which the would-be hunter encounters mythical animals described in myth who initiate him and binds mythic time with the present. His relationship with the archetypal 'boss' of each animal species he hunts depends upon these early encounters. His success as a hunter is determined by the knowledge and power bestowed by the respective animal 'boss'. Shamanic initiation is an extension of this series of dream encounters, but more explicitly through death, initiation by a community of shamans in heaven and then rebirth on the earthly plane. Through these dream visions the shamanic initiant establishes a relationship with the 'boss' of humans, and obtains his 'god songs', which give them the power to guide the 'shadows' of men along the path to heaven. Among the Paviotso, a Plateau Shoshonean tribe in Nevada, USA, shamans may be of either sex, and commonly obtain their calling and receive their powers through dreaming (Park 1934, p. 99):

> A man dreams that a deer, eagle, or bear comes after him. The animal tells him that he is to be a doctor. The first time a man dreams this way he does not believe it. Then he dreams that way some more and he gets the things the spirit [ancestor] told him to get . . . Then he learns to be a doctor. He learns his songs when the spirit comes and sings to him.

Transpersonal dreaming

Dreaming among some traditional peoples may confound our western consensus understanding of what is normal and what is real, as is the case in what we may call transpersonal dreaming. As I have taken pains to emphasize, from the cross-cultural perspective what constitutes 'normal' and 'real' varies enormously. Despite the common psychoanalytic reduction of transpersonal dreaming to 'transference', unresolved unconscious conflict and other Freudian notions, actual transpersonal dreaming (see Laughlin 2011), especially dreaming containing 'paranormal' elements such as co-dreaming, precognition, out-of-body experiences, etc., is amply illustrated in the ethnographic literature (see Young and Goulet 1994;

Goulet and Young 1994; Goulet and Miller 2007). Transpersonal dreams are those that stretch one's experiences of self beyond the normal limits of the ego (Walsh and Vaughan 1980).

One of the most fascinating types of transpersonal dreaming is the phenomenon of 'co-dreaming' ('shared dreaming', 'mutual dreaming'); that is, when two or more people share the same dream content at the same time. Anthropologist David Young (1994) reports that he had visions of human figures entering his bedroom as he awoke from dreaming. When he described these visions to his Cree healer friend, the healer recognized one Amerindian figure as one of his spirit helpers. There are many such anecdotes to be found in the ethnographic literature and elsewhere (see Krippner and Faith 2001). One of the most remarkable are the dream experiences reported by anthropologist Marianne George (1995) while she was in the field among the Barok of New Guinea. She had developed a close relationship with an important female leader who was her sponsor. To make a long story short, George had dreams of her host telling her to do things. In the morning the host's sons, who also shared the dreams, dropped by to make sure she understood the old woman's instructions during the night, and repeated to her verbatim what the old woman had told her in the dreams. They told George that it made no difference how far away they were, when their mother wished to communicate with them, they would dream about it. This happened again a number of times after the old woman had died. Again, the old woman's sons would verify the dream visitation and message, in one case directing George to the precise location of an ancient long-house hearth she had been seeking for carbon dating purposes.

Conclusions

We have seen that the uses to which societies put dreaming vary a great deal. They range from simply ignoring dreams as pointless hallucinations to societies that pay close attention to and value dreams. It seems very likely that all polyphasic cultures attend to dreaming as being another domain of reality. The ways they use dreams are various, and most find multiple uses for such experiences. Dream sharing is very common among polyphasic peoples. Dreams are sometimes the first thing they speak about in the morning, and everybody is interested in the information imparted by the dream report. In some societies everybody participates in dream interpretation, while in other societies there are recognized dream interpreters. The most common uses put to dreams in polyphasic cultures are those that deal with those 'matters of ultimate concern' (Tillich 1963) that are the principal drivers of religious thought: birth, death, sickness, invisible causation, catastrophes and the uncertainty of future events. Pastoral and theological readers should be cautioned to be wary of misunderstanding the use of dreaming in religious and spiritual practice among polyphasic peoples, for many of the uses to which dreaming are put appear to be types of prayer or meditation. Societies very commonly seek information about future events, or seek to intercede in future events, for the purposes of increasing success in hunting and other endeavours, in divining the causes of and avoiding illness, to remove the uncertainty of the outcome of plans, and to fulfil wishes.

One of the obvious problems that ethnographers have in doing dreaming-related fieldwork is taking their informant's claims about co-dreaming and other 'paranormal' phenomena at face value. As Poirier (2003, p. 109) notes, 'it is unthinkable, on the basis of western objectivity, that dreams might well be addressed to another person, or that while dreaming, one's spirit might penetrate someone else's dream'. We simply do not know what to make of such reports from our informants – unless, of course, like Marianne George, we were to experience such dreams ourselves. Edith Turner (1992) has taken anthropologists to task for this enduring kind of ethnocentrism, and has suggested we step back from our western biases further than ever and try to believe our hosts when they speak of the reality of spirits, or conversations with spirits in dreaming. This issue has long been bound up with the taboo against ethnographers 'going native' – embracing the world as described by our hosts. This taboo has unfortunately been applied at times as proscriptions against incorporating extraordinary experiences had by fieldworkers in ethnographic reports.

What readers in theological and pastoral studies might take away from this study is that prayer and other states of consciousness are heavily impacted by institutional strictures and custom. The terrible mistake that many old-school Christian missionaries made was being overly concrete in their interpretation of alien customs. They would, for example, fail to recognize variations in the practice of prayer and meditation carried out by their host nations. North American native peoples were thoroughly spiritual in their belief systems, yet at the same time did not recognize a henotheistic interpretation of their experiences had in dreams and other alternative states. Because European missionaries were normally not conversant with their dream lives, they failed to understand that certain special dreams were prayerful conversations with the divine (with the Holy Wind, as the Navajo would say). The cross-cultural perspective I have sketched here should instil a humble sense of caution about non-European belief systems and spiritual practices, especially among polyphasic peoples who may actually have a better grasp on the sublime dimensions of reality than do their visitors.

References

Bourguignon, E. (1954), 'Dreams and Dream Interpretation in Haiti', in *American Anthropologist* 56(2 – Part 1), pp. 262–8.

Bourguignon, E. (1972), 'Dreams and Altered States of Consciousness in Anthropological Research', in F. L. K. Hsu, ed., *Psychological Anthropology*, 2nd edn, Cambridge MA: Schenkman, pp. 403–34.

Bourguignon, E. (2003), 'Dreams That Speak: Experience and Interpretation', in J. M. Mageo, ed., *Dreaming and the Self: New Perspectives on Subjectivity, Identity, and Emotion*, Albany NY: State University of New York Press, pp. 133–53.

Bourguignon, E. and Evascu, T. L. (1977), 'Altered States of Consciousness within a General Evolutionary Perspective: A Holocultural Analysis', in *Behavior Science Research* 12(3), pp. 197–216.

Britton, T. C. and Chaudhuri, K. R. (2009), 'REM Sleep Behavior Disorder and the Risk of Developing Parkinson Disease or Dementia', in *Neurology* 72(15), pp. 1294–5.

Brown, M. (1992), 'Ropes of Sand: Order and Imagery in Aguaruna Dreams', in B. Tedlock, ed., *Dreaming: Anthropological and Psychological Interpretations*, Cambridge: Cambridge University Press, pp. 154–70.

Chidester, D. (2008), 'Dreaming in the Contact Zone: Zulu Dreams, Visions, and Religion in Nineteenth-Century South Africa', in *Journal of the American Academy of Religion* 76(1), pp. 27–53.

Colby, K. M. (1963), 'Sex Differences in Dreams of Primitive Tribes', *American Anthropologist* 65, pp. 1116–22.

Damasio, A. (1999), *The Feeling of What Happens: Body and Emotion in the Making of Consciousness*, New York: Harcourt.

D'Andrade, R. G. (1961), 'Anthropological Studies of Dreams', in F. L. K. Hsu, ed., *Psychological Anthropology*, 1st edn, Homewood IL: Dorsey, pp. 296–332.

Edelman, G. M. and Tononi, G. (2000), *A Universe of Consciousness: How Matter Becomes Imagination*, New York: Basic Books.

Ewing, K. P. (1994), 'Dreams from a Saint: Anthropological Atheism and the Temptation to Believe', *American Anthropologist* 96(3), pp. 571–83.

Feinberg, I. (1969), 'Effects of Age on Human Sleep Patterns', in A. Kales, ed., *Sleep: Physiology and Pathology*, Philadelphia: Lippincott, pp. 39–52.

Flannery, R. and Chambers, M. E. (1985), 'Each Man Has His Own Friends: The Role of Dream Visitors in Traditional East Cree Belief and Practice', in *Arctic Anthropology* 22(1), pp. 1–22.

George, M. (1995), 'Dreams, Reality, and the Desire and Intent of Dreamers as Experienced by a Fieldworker', in *Anthropology of Consciousness* 6(3), pp. 17–33.

Goulet, J.-G. (1994), 'Dreams and Visions in Other Lifeworlds', in D. E. Young and J.-G. Goulet, eds, *Being Changed by Cross-Cultural Encounters*, Peterborough, Ontario: Broadview Press, pp. 16–38.

Goulet, J.-G. and Young, D. (1994), 'Theoretical and Methodological Issues', in D. E. Young and J.-G. Goulet, eds, *Being Changed by Cross-Cultural Encounters*, Peterborough, Ontario: Broadview Press, pp. 298–335.

Goulet, J.-G. and Miller, B. (2007), *Extraordinary Anthropology: Transformations in the Field*, Lincoln NE: University of Nebraska Press.

Graham, L. R. (2003), *Performing Dreams*, 2nd edn, Tucson AZ: Fenestra.

Gregor, T. (1981), 'Far, Far Away My Shadow Wandered . . . : The Dream Symbolism and Dream Theories of the Mehinaku Indians of Brazil', in *American Ethnologist* 8(4), pp. 709–20.

Hallowell, A. I. (1976), 'The Role of Dreams in Ojibwa Culture', in A. I. Hallowell, *Contributions to Anthropology*, Chicago: University of Chicago Press, pp. 449–71.

Herdt, G. (1992), 'Selfhood and Discourse in Sambia Dream Sharing', in B. Tedlock, ed., *Dreaming: Anthropological and Psychological Interpretations*, Cambridge: Cambridge University Press, pp. 55–85.

Herr, B. (1981), 'The Expressive Character of Fijian Dream and Nightmare Experiences', in *Ethos* 9(2), pp. 331–52.

Hillman, D. J. (1988), 'Dream Work and Field Work: Linking Cultural Anthropology and the Current Dream Work Movement', in M. Ullman and C. Limmer, eds, *The Variety of Dream Experience*, New York: Continuum, pp. 117–41.

Irwin, L. (1994), *The Dream Seekers: Native American Visionary Traditions of the Great Plains*, Norman OK: University of Oklahoma Press.

Kilborne, B. (1981), 'Pattern, Structure, and Style in Anthropological Studies of Dreams', in *Ethos* 9(2), pp. 165–85.

Kracke, W. H. (1992), 'Myths in Dreams, Thought in Images: An Amazonian Contribution to the Psychoanalytic Theory of Primary Process', in B. Tedlock, ed., *Dreaming: Anthropological and Psychological Interpretations*, Cambridge: Cambridge University Press, pp. 31–54.

Krippner, S. and Faith, L. (2001), 'Exotic Dreams: A Cross-Cultural Study', *Dreaming* 11(2), pp. 73–82.

Laughlin, C. D. (2011), *Communing with the Gods: Consciousness, Culture and the Dreaming Brain*, Brisbane: Daily Grail.

Laughlin, C. D., McManus, J. and d'Aquili, E. G. (1990), *Brain, Symbol and Experience: Toward a Neurophenomenology of Consciousness*, New York: Columbia University Press.

Lohmann, R. I. (2003), 'Introduction: Dream Travels and Anthropology', in R. I. Lohmann, ed., *Dream Travelers: Sleep Experiences and Culture in the Western Pacific*, New York: Palgrave, pp. 1–17.

McNeley, J. K. (1981), *Holy Wind in Navajo Philosophy*, Tucson AR: University of Arizona Press.

Merrill, W. (1992), 'The Ramámuri Stereotype of Dreams', in B. Tedlock, ed., *Dreaming: Anthropological and Psychological Interpretations*, Cambridge: Cambridge University Press, pp. 194–219.

Morgan, W. (1932), 'Navajo Dreams', in *American Anthropologist* 34(3), pp. 390–405.

Morinis, E. A. (1982), 'Levels of Culture in Hinduism: A Case Study of Dream Incubation at a Bengali Pilgrimage Centre', in *Contributions to Indian Sociology* (NS) 16(2), pp. 255–70.

Munn, N. D. (1973), *Walbiri Iconography: Graphic Representation and Cultural Symbolism in a Central Australian Society*, Ithaca: Cornell University Press.

Munn, N. D. (1990), 'Constructing Regional Worlds in Experience: Kula Exchange, Witchcraft and Gawan Local Events', in *Man* (NS) 25(1), pp. 1–17.

Nuttall, D. (2007), 'A Pathway to Knowledge: Embodiment, Dreaming, and Experience as a Basis for Understanding the Other', in J.-G. A. Goulet and B. G. Miller, eds, *Extraordinary Anthropology*, Lincoln NE: University of Nebraska Press, pp. 323–351.

Pandya, V. (2004), 'Forest Spells and Spider Webs: Ritualized Dream Interpretation Among Andaman Islanders', in C. Stewart, ed., *Anthropological Approaches to Dreaming*, special issue of *Dreaming* 14(2–3), pp. 136–50.

Park, W. Z. (1934), 'Paviotso Shamanism', in *American Anthropologist* 36(1), pp. 98–113.

Parman, S. (1991), *Dream and Culture: An Anthropological Study of the Western Intellectual Tradition*, Westport CT: Praeger.

Parrinder, G. (1962), *African Traditional Religion*, New York: Harper and Row.

Peluso, D. M. (2004), 'That Which I Dream is True: Dream Narratives in an Amazonian Community', in C. Stewart, ed., *Anthropological Approaches to Dreaming*, special issue of *Dreaming* 14(2–3), pp. 107–19.

Poirier, S. (2003), 'This is Good Country: We Are Good Dreamers', in R. I. Lohmann ed., *Dream Travelers: Sleep Experiences and Culture in the Western Pacific*, New York: Palgrave, pp. 107–25.

Prince, R. (1961), 'The Yoruba Image of the Witch', in *Journal of Mental Science* 107, pp. 795–805.

Reay, M. (1962), 'The Sweet Witchcraft of Kuma Dream Experience', *Mankind: Official Journal of the Anthropological Societies of Australia* 5(11), pp. 459–63.

Ridington, R. (1971), 'Beaver Dreaming and Singing', *Anthropologica* 13(1/2), pp. 115–28.

Ridington, R. (1988), 'Knowledge, Power, and the Individual in Subarctic Hunting Societies', in *American Anthropologist* 90(1), pp. 98–110.

Stephen, M. (1995), *A'aisa's Gifts*, Berkeley CA: University of California Press.

Tart, C. (1975), *States of Consciousness*, New York: Dutton.

Tedlock, B. (1981), 'Quiché Maya Dream Interpretation', *Ethos* 9(4), pp. 313–30.

Tedlock, B. (1992), 'Dreaming and Dream Research', in B. Tedlock, ed., *Dreaming: Anthropological and Psychological Interpretations*, Cambridge: Cambridge University Press, pp. 1–30.

Tiberia, V. A. (1981), *Jungian Archetypal Themes in Cross-cultural Dream Symbolism*, unpublished doctoral dissertation, School of Human Behavior, United States International University, Ann Arbor MI: University Microfilms International.

Tillich, P. (1963), *Systematic Theology*, Chicago: University of Chicago Press.

Tonkinson, R. (1978), *The Mardudjara: Living the Dream in Australia's Desert*, New York: Holt, Rinehart and Winston.

Tonkinson, R. (2003), 'Ambrymese Dreams and the Mardu Dreaming', in R. I. Lohmann, ed., *Dream Travelers: Sleep Experiences and Culture in the Western Pacific*, New York: Palgrave, pp. 87–105.

Turner, E. (1992), *Experiencing Ritual: A New Interpretation of African Healing*, Philadelphia: University of Pennsylvania Press.

Wallace, A. F. C. (1958), 'Dreams and Wishes of the Soul: A Type of Psychoanalytic Theory among the Seventeenth Century Iroquois', in *American Anthropologist* 60(2 – Part 1), pp. 234–48.

Wallace, A. F. C. (1966), *Religion: An Anthropological View*, New York: Random House.

Walsh, R. N. and Vaughan, F. (1980), *Beyond Ego: Transpersonal Dimensions in Psychology*, Los Angeles CA: J. P. Tarcher.

Watson, L. C. and Watson-Franke, M.-B. (1977), 'Spirits, Dreams, and the Resolution of Conflict Among Urban Guajiro Women', *Ethos* 5(4), pp. 388–408.

Wax, M. L. (2004), 'Dream Sharing as Social Practice', in C. Stewart, ed., *Anthropological Approaches to Dreaming*, special issue of *Dreaming* 14(2–3), pp. 83–93.

Young, D. E. (1994), 'Visitors in the Night: A Creative Energy Model of Spontaneous Visions', in D. E. Young and J.-G. Goulet, eds, *Being Changed by Cross-Cultural Encounters*, Peterborough, Ontario: Broadview Press, pp. 166–94.

Young, D. E. and Goulet, J.-G., eds (1994), *Being Changed by Cross-Cultural Encounters*, Peterborough, Ontario: Broadview Press.

3

The Role of Dreams in Psychological Maintenance and Growth

ROBERT HOSS

Introduction

The role that dreams play in the maintenance and restoration of psychological health has often been considered limited to the use of the dream in conjunction with some form of therapeutic or self-help exercise. There, however, appears to be a natural learning, internal maintenance or healing process taking place during the dream sleep, whether we recall or use material from the dream or not. Understanding that natural process taking place and working with it can be of great value to the therapist, dream worker and/or the dreamer themselves.

Understanding what is happening as we dream is complicated by the bizarre nature of dreams. This is attributed to the unique combination of active and inactive centres in REM sleep when our more vivid dreams occur, and to the natural figurative 'language' of those centres (such as the associative cortex) where the imagery is produced. If we closely examine dream narratives we can also observe actions in the dream plot which appear to reflect known processing functions of the brain centres that are active during REM. The implication is that the dream is not meaningless, but our observing the normal processing activity of internal information, in the absence of external sensory information and rational thought. Determining the specific function of the dream has been controversial, however, due in part because there are only a few studies that have captured and grossly correlated neural activity with dream content. Even then there remains an uncertainty of whether the dream itself plays a role or is simply a projection of the processing taking place. This distinction does not need to get in the way of discussing the beneficial processes that take place during REM state dreaming, however.

This chapter discusses what is taking place while we dream and how to observe it in the dream, the objective being to better understand how to work with dreams in the natural way that our dreaming mind works with them. This knowledge has been described in a number of papers, and incorporated in a complete dream working protocol and worksheet, that can be downloaded from www.dreamscience.org.

Our dreaming brain

In order to most effectively apply dreams to the healing profession it is best to understand what dreaming truly is and what psychological signifi-cance it holds for us. The understanding of dreams began centuries ago as a matter of religious and cultural beliefs, then as the psychology of dream-ing evolved (influenced by Freud, Jung and others) the understanding of dreams became a matter of theoretical and psychological debate as well as personal insight.

With the discovery of the REM sleep cycle in 1953, more accurate scientific dream research began. Sleep stages were defined, based on brain wave signatures, from waking to deep sleep. This included a lighter stage of sleep called REM (for rapid eye movement) which occurred approx-imately every 90 minutes, each occurrence lengthening in duration over a night's sleep. The deeper stages are called non-REM or NREM. Upon waking subjects in the laboratory during REM sleep, dreams are reported from 80% to 100% of the time; as opposed to the NREM stage where dream reports are in the order of 20%. While some studies have found the dream narratives to be similar, most others report REM dreams to be more vivid and emotionally charged, while NREM dreams are more thought-like replays or rehearsals of daily events. Human studies began revealing that REM sleep appears to be needed for memory consolidation and psy-chological restoral. For decades, however, much of the scientific commu-nity debated whether dreaming had a function or if it was just the brain trying to make sense out of the random firing of neurons. Neuroscience and psychology appeared far apart until the late 1990s when neuro-imaging technology began to support some of what psychologists had observed and theorized. The technology of this 'new psychiatric couch' has helped both neuroscientists and psychologists to converge their theories towards a better understanding of the dreaming process.

In addition to imaging technology, direct neural microprobe studies with mice, by Matthew Wilson at the RIKEN-MIT Neuroscience Research Center, have captured real-time evidence of learning taking place in both

NREM and REM sleep and that the process activates the visual cortex – thus dreaming – even in animals! NREM learning appears to be more of a replay of the task in proper time and sequence; whereas REM appears to bring in memories of similar tasks, perhaps associating them with pieces of the recent experience, in compressed time and out of sequence.

Figure 1 is a composite of information from neuroimaging surveys by Harvard Medical School researcher Alan Hobson and others (2003), derived from PET scan studies performed by researchers Pierre Maquet, Allen Braun and Eric Nofzinger (Hoss and Hoss 2013). Hobson states that the combined activity of these brain centres appears to account for not only the unusual characteristics of dreams, but also some of the functions that psychologists and theorists have attributed to dreaming. The centres that are active as we dream are known to perform much of their information processing unconsciously, below our level of aware-ness, or before their output reaches or triggers consciousness. Harvard researcher Robert Stickgold noted that dreams appear to be constructed within networks of associated memories that we don't normally access directly. In contrast, the rational thinking and self-reflective parts of the brain which create our sense of waking consciousness are deactivated, along with episodic memory and primary sensory and motor functions. As researcher Allen Braun puts it, dreaming is a 'state of generalized brain activity with the specific exclusion of executive systems'.

Waking state neurological studies, on the centres that appear highly activated in REM, suggest that a significant information processing cap-ability may exist in the dream state. High activity in the limbic system or 'emotional brain' has led researchers to believe that dreams selectively process emotional memories, perhaps unresolved emotionally important issues triggered by a waking event. Active cognitive centres in the frontal regions suggest that dreams may perform a psychological and emotional restoral, problem resolution and emotionally driven learning function. High activity in the visual or sensory association regions (the visual association cortex in particular) supports the idea that dream imagery is a picture representation of connections being made between associated emotions, memories and conceptualizations within. These topics will be discussed in more detail below.

Carl Gustav Jung, founder of analytical psychology, considered dreams to be 'the most readily accessible expression of the unconscious', and to reveal 'the unconscious aspect of a conscious event' whereby the unconscious mean-ing (the deeper emotional impact of the event) is expressed (Jung 1971, p. 29; 1964, p. 5). If true, the therapeutic value of dreams becomes apparent as a means of revealing the deeper inner issues a person is struggling with, issues that might be difficult to reveal using cognitive dialogue-based approaches. The concept of dreams revealing the unconscious aspect of a conscious event can be illustrated in the following example.

The dreamer was enjoying a spiritual retreat and embracing new spiritual concepts. These new concepts, however, were in conflict with the long-established beliefs of his Latin American Catholic upbringing. That night he dreamed, 'I was in an airplane that landed in a spiral motion on the rim of a large circle in a Latin American village. In the centre of the circle was a priest dressed in black with a gun, protecting the village from my intrusion.' Here the dream pictures the unconscious aspect or internal conflict created by the event, but the conscious event itself (the retreat) was not explicitly presented in the dream. The inner conflict between the new belief (the arriving airplane) and the threat to the old belief (the Latin American village) was appropriately pictured as the priest with the gun protecting that village from the intrusion.

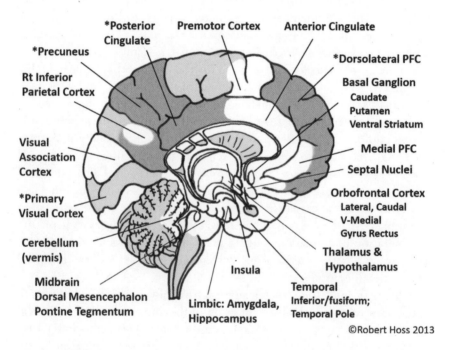

Figure 1: The dreaming brain.

The language of dreams

Although therapies do exist which utilize dreams as a form of expression, without an understanding of the nature of their content, it is of benefit to the therapist and the dreamer to understand the 'language' of dreams. Jung observed the language of dreams to be the language of the unconscious, that of 'symbols' or an 'emotionally charged pictorial language'. Ernest Hartmann, Professor of Psychiatry at Tufts University, makes a similar observation. He states that the dreaming brain makes new connections that are presented as picture-metaphor, which picture emotional similarities and reveal new perspectives (Hartmann 2011). The picture-metaphors connect seemingly unrelated information, or describe a first entity as resembling a second entity in some way; perhaps combining linked associations into a single image (which Freud called 'condensation'). The following example illustrates this concept:

> The dreamer was bothered by the dreams she was having about the relationship with her husband. She stated that he was the source of the problems in their marriage. She had a series of recurring dreams where she was arguing with him then turning and running away. In the last dream, however, she turned around and looked at his face . . . It was her father's face! Here the dream had connected the unresolved issues with her father to her attitudes about her husband and their relationship. The connection was simply yet clearly presented as a picture-metaphor of the projection of her father onto her husband.

The figurative nature of our dreams is likely due to the images, and other dream experiences, being created in parts of the brain that associate sensory information with 'meaning'. For dream imagery, this appears to occur in the visual association cortex, which creates visual associations with the information being processed from within. This might involve visual representations of our inner feelings, memories and beliefs as well as representations of connections being made and other mental processes taking place in the brain. The organization of all this visual information into the dream space is believed to involve the right inferior parietal cortex, which helps organize our perception of a visual space in the waking state (Hobson et al. 2003). Although dreams are predominantly visual, other areas of the brain such as the temporal lobe along with parts of the cerebellum and certain premotor and sensory areas can also become activated, supplying the dream with other internally generated fictive sensory associations (moving, hearing and tactile sensations, and to a lesser degree taste and smell).

Understanding that dream images and actions are representations of what is being processed within helps us understand how to work with a dream – by exploring the dreamer's own associations with the imagery, rather than pondering its literal form. With the possible exception of some instinctive archetypal patterns (to be discussed below), it is important to understand that dream imagery is formed from the dreamer's own experiences and memories, not something that can be found in a symbol dictionary nor 'interpretations' projected on the dream by another. It is also important to keep in mind that the rational literal mind is inactive in REM; it is the associative cortex creating the imagery, so what might appear as a 'message' is association or metaphor; it is rarely literal. The following case (Hoss and Hoss 2013, p. 14) illustrates these principles:

'I was in a clinic and a nurse was checking me over. She felt some lumps in my groin area and exclaimed, "She is riddled with cancer." I asked the nurse if she could do something to keep me from going through all the pain. A subsequent medical exam resulted in no cancer.' When the dreamer came to my workshop she was upset and confused as to why her dream was telling her she had cancer! When we looked past the literal 'message' and worked with her associations it became obvious. It was discovered that the dreamer saw her relationships in terms of astrological signs. Working with her associations with 'groin area' and 'Cancer' led to the discovery that she had a boyfriend who was astrologically a Cancer. In waking life she wanted to break up with him but was uncertain (the 'riddle') as to how to go about it without going through a lot of pain. When we replaced the literal words in her dream narrative with these associations, it revealed that her 'riddle' was how to go about getting rid of the 'Cancer' (her boyfriend) without going through all the pain! While it is good to check the situation out when dreams reveal medical conditions or warnings, it is always best to remember that dreams speak in metaphor, and to look at the dream from the standpoint of our personal associations to gain a balanced understanding.

Although the source of most of our dream imagery is personal association, Jung observed dream imagery originating from a deeper level of the psyche common to all humans, which he called the collective unconscious. He termed this imagery 'archetypes'. Archetypes appear as patterns and characters of a mythical nature which he found to be present across time and cultures, in the dreams and myths of all humankind. They are representations of primal, instinctive mental forces that drive the evolution of our personality, integrating conscious and unconscious processes, and driving a transcendence from one state to another, in a process he called 'individuation' – becoming an individual. Understanding all Jung's observations and working with this imagery is beyond the scope of this chapter; however, it is worthy of greater study to gain a deeper understanding of dreaming (Jung 1971). For example, one of the most often occurring patterns is that of reintegrating our fragmented conscious and unconscious mind so that they work together in harmony. This connecting process appears in dreams as the merging of opposites (dark/light, the cross, male/female, sex, marriage, balanced geometric or mandala imagery, etc.). Also the cycle of death and rebirth appears to symbolize a cycle in our mental growth which first requires a 'death of the ego' so that the new self can be discovered and emerge. This imagery includes themes of death, loss, darkness, descending followed by a journey of trials, guidance and discovery, and eventual emergence or rebirth images such as a child, spring, and beautiful sunlit nature settings. The unknown, often dark or shadowy, wise and guiding characters in our dreams he attributed to the guiding forces of the unconscious. These images are conceptually reflections of the common instinctive neurological processes taking place in the frontal areas of the brain during REM that drive the dream plot towards resolution.

The exception to dream imagery as picture-metaphor is in extreme PTSD-related dreams. Stanley Krippner, Professor of Psychology at Saybrook University in San Francisco, states that PTSD nightmares are not characterized by metaphor or symbol but are lifelike replays of the event and therefore are not treated by interpretation of the narrative or imagery. An active visualization technique, aimed at modifying the nightmare, called Imagery Rehearsal Treatment (developed by Barry Krakow), is often used to treat PTSD nightmare cases. Recovery can be seen as the nightmares begin to incorporate images of mastering the situation and references from the present and from the pre-trauma past, and become more symbolic and include more illogical dreamlike imagery and metaphors.

Emotion stimulates dream action and imagery

As indicated above, high activity in the limbic system or 'emotional brain' has led researchers to believe that dreams selectively process emotionally important memories via interplay between the cortex and the limbic system and that emotion does not simply arise from the dream, but rather drives the dream plot. Centres such as the basal ganglia and medial prefrontal cortex, which are known to be involved in emotional regulation, are highly active in REM. Researcher Els van der Helm at UC Berkeley discovered a dampening activity taking place in REM whereby emotional memories are reactivated in the amygdala to hippocampal network, as the amygdala is calmed by stress-reducing hormones in the forebrain. Psychiatrist and sleep physician Milton Kramer also observed a mood regulation process taking place during REM. This may be why we often experience going to sleep pondering a problem that has us emotionally disturbed, only to wake in the morning less concerned.

Emotion may even guide a learning process. Ernest Hartmann (2011) contends that dreams weave new material into established memory and that emotion helps organize that memory based on what is important to us. Later I will discuss the observation of and emotionally guided learning process taking place as dreams appear to emotionally reinforce (produce a rewarding ending) when a dream plot or scenario is successful.

Aside from the role emotion plays in influencing the dream plot, it may also create the dream imagery itself. Hartmann (2011) states that the dream image is a picture of emotion or the 'feeling state' of the dreamer, 'contextualizing' those feelings in relation to the dreamer's inner and outer life. This can be illustrated in a dream of a man who went to bed extremely angry about a work situation. That night in his dream he was introduced to a character named 'Willy Pistoff' – a somewhat humorous image which clearly pictured his 'feeling-state'.

Exploring the emotions within the dream images

Fritz Perls, best known for his work in developing Gestalt Therapy, saw dream images as 'alienated fragments' of the dreamer's personality, containing emotional material that is in conflict with the dreamer's desired view of her or himself (Perls 1969, pp. 71–72). He developed a role-play technique whereby he asked clients to 'become' and experience the images in their dreams, and express the emotions they contained (Perls 1969, p. 74). An example (Hoss and Hoss 2013, p. 16) is the dream of a man with a strong 'male ego' who disliked working for a new female boss.

The dreamer felt he was an expert worker but when his female boss was around he would nervously fail which would end with her disapproval.

He dreamed, 'I am standing in a sweet potato patch across from my boss who is on the other side of a barbed wire fence.' When asked to 'become' the sweet potato he stated, 'I am a sweet potato, butter me up and I'll be good.' This was an expression of an emotional need which he was reluctant to admit to himself and certainly reluctant to admit to his boss – an emotional barrier which was undermining his performance.

Recognizing that dream images picture our feelings, and having access to a therapeutic approach for revealing those hidden feelings in the dream images, is a great benefit when working with clients or with your own dreams. Reactivating the unconscious by 'giving the dream a voice' rather than engaging the dreamer in a cognitive exchange re-engages the part of the brain that was active and 'awake' in the dream as opposed to the rational brain that was inactive or 'asleep' at the time. It becomes the quickest and most effective way at revealing underlying conflicts and emotional barriers.

A simple script is suggested here for leading a client or dreamer through this Gestalt role-play. It takes about ten minutes and is designed to reveal role issues, inner conflicts and motivating factors that have left the dreamer emotionally stuck. The dreamer re-enters the dream and picks some element in the dream that draws their attention. The dreamer then imagines themselves as that dream element, 'becomes it' as best they can, in order to 'give it a voice'. The dreamer is then asked to stay in the role of that dream element and answer six questions (usually asked by the practitioner) as they imagine the dream element would answer them:

1 What are you?
2 What is your purpose or function?
3 What do you like most about being this dream element?
4 What do you dislike about being this dream element?
5 What do you fear the most?
6 What do you desire the most?

The dreamer is then brought out of the role-play. When the answers are read back, however, the dreamer is asked to switch perspectives and listen to the answers, not as the dream element stating them, but as if they themselves are making those statements about a recent situation or feeling in their own lives. Any connections that the dreamer makes between the statements and their waking life feelings are noted. The dreamer then discusses the connections with their waking life situation.

The questions were designed to reveal three layers of emotional content that might be contained within the dream element. The 'what are you?' and 'what is your purpose or function?' questions were designed to reveal the dreamer's role perception. The 'what do you like?' and 'what do you dislike?' question pair was designed to uncover underlying emotional conflicts. Finally, the 'what do you fear?' and 'what do you desire?' question pair was designed to explore the motivating factors that leave the dreamer stuck in the conflict. This is illustrated in the following case example (Hoss and Hoss 2013, pp. 77–81):

'Karen' was about to end a beautiful relationship, not due to any rational reason, but driven by a growing anxiety that she did not understand. It occurred when she thought about helping her boyfriend through a medical procedure. Fortunately, Karen had a dream that she shared in our workshop: 'I am in the home I shared with my ex-husband, looking out over trees that contained black things. My mother is there and we are trying to decide whether they are birds or bats. The dream was upsetting.'

We asked Karen to re-enter the dream and look for something in the dream scene that draws her attention. She was drawn to 'a lone bird's nest' in the tree. We took her into the bird's nest and, once there, asked the bird's nest to speak – guiding her with the six scripted statements. Role-playing the bird's nest, she stated, 'I am a lone bird's nest, my purpose is to be warm, and enveloping, and to provide a safe landing spot', and 'my desire is to be there and strong when needed'. This was an apt description of how Karen saw her role in helping her boyfriend through the procedure. When we asked the bird's nest what it disliked and feared, she stated, 'I dislike getting crapped on and fear getting blown out of the tree!' It became apparent that this is not just a 'bird's nest' speaking, but Karen's own unconscious expression of a conflict she was stuck in – and the fear that created it.

We then asked Karen to recall a specific incident where she felt that way. She stated, 'The moment I decided to divorce my "ex". I had gone all out to help him and he showed up two hours late and began yelling at me for not having done enough.' The source of the anxiety was revealed, she was terrified that if she once again helped someone she loved, she would once again get 'crapped on'.

Note that all of the conflicted emotions that were the source of the anxiety were contained within the picture-metaphor of this one dream element – the lone bird's nest. Once revealed the source of the anxiety could be dealt with – which we pursued in the remainder of the workshop. Her joy returned and at that moment her boyfriend entered the room and she went up and embraced him, later telling him she would stay in the relationship.

Colour combines with imagery to reflect emotion

A surprising fact about dreaming is that most dreams originate in colour. Sleep laboratory research by Professor Dr Michael Schredl, involving waking the subjects during their REM cycle and asking them about the colour of the images in their dreams, resulted in from 80% to 100% of subjects recalling some colour. Recall of colour seems to diminish as does other dream content, but perhaps more rapidly.

Research by this author (Hoss 2010) suggests that dream colour is associated with emotion and combines (or 'condenses' as Freud termed it) with dream imagery to provide an emotional intensity to that image. Research in the field of colour psychology has demonstrated that the human brain and autonomic nervous system respond unconsciously (below our threshold of awareness) to colour (Hoss 2010). The research found that colour evokes a relatively common set of neural responses, different for different colours, which in turn has a relationship to emotion. For example, red excites the brain and nervous system into action, while blue has a calming effect. The research by Hoss concludes that the same emotion to colour associations continue into the dream state. This makes sense because the limbic and autonomic nervous systems should naturally retain the same associations in either state. The compilation of waking state data on emotional response led to my development of the 'Color Questionnaire' as a supplemental aid in researching and working with colour to emotional associations in dreams. It is a tabulation of common subliminal emotional responses to colour intended as an aid in triggering the dreamer's own emotional associations. It can be downloaded from www.dreamscience.org.

Do dreams have the capability for problem resolutions and learning?

As discussed previously, there are many active centres in the frontal regions of the brain, adjacent to the limbic region that are involved in varying degrees of cognition. These centres together appear to perform functions such as psychological and emotional self-maintenance, creative problem-solving, and adaptive learning. The benefit to the therapist or dream worker in understanding these processes is in recognizing them in the dream plot so as to understand how the dreamer's own mind was attempting to resolve the issue the dream is dealing with. Following the natural healing approach taking place within the dreamer's own mind may be the healthiest and more expedient approach to therapy.

The problem resolution capability of the dreaming brain

Scripps College professor Gayle Greene states that, far from being idle fancies, dreams are enablers of 'the most sophisticated human cognitive functions'. The benefit in knowing this is in recognizing the activities in the dream and using the cues in helping the dreamer to work through a conflict and move forward in a manner that the dreamer's own unconscious has suggested. Waking state studies suggest that the dreaming brain may have the capacity to support problem resolution and adaptive learning. This hypothesis is based on a compilation of results from a number of waking state neuroimaging studies on those centres found to be active during REM sleep (25 studies cited in Hoss and Hoss 2013). The following functional capabilities were observed when these centres were studied individually or when networking with other centres also active in REM:

1 Detecting a problem.
2 Planning a resolution scenario.
3 Providing cues to guide or mediate the outcome.
4 Testing and monitoring the scenario.
5 Learning by emotionally reinforcing a successful scenario.

Although there are no neuroimaging studies that have traced the activity in these regions to coincide with the ongoing content of a dream, it is promising that these activities can be observed in dreams. The following example (Hoss and Hoss 2013, p. 147) will be used, along with a further discussion of the study results, to illustrate the hypothesis:

The dreamer was offered a teaching position in a field that he was once an expert in but no longer working in. His conscious attitude was, 'It has been too long, I can no longer resurrect those talents they are gone forever.' He had decided to turn down the offer but then had the following dream: 'I was wandering through a desert and saw an old rusty car. I looked inside and found a man who was not moving. I was going to give him up for dead, but my unknown companion said he was just asleep and urged me to wake the man. I argued that it was useless but after much discussion reluctantly gave in and shook the man. When I did, both the man and the car came to life and the car transformed into a newer car.'

1 Detecting a problem

The basal ganglion, anterior cingulate, and parts of the orbitofrontal cortex (all active in REM) have been found to play important roles in the detection of errors and conflicting perceptions, inspecting events that deviate from expectation, and the monitoring of conflict and anomalies. The anterior cingulate acts as part of a general performance monitoring system that detects conditions under which errors in reasoning have occurred or might occur. Such problem detection might be observed in dreams as an introductory scene, a picture-metaphor that is representative of the situation or conflict. This is observed in the example as the 'old rusty car' and the 'man who was not moving' that the dreamer 'gave up for dead' – an apt metaphor that pictures the dreamer's waking attitude about his 'old rusty' talents.

2 Planning a dream scenario

The anterior cingulate has been found to act when there is a violation in expectancy, initiating and mediating action aimed at choosing between conflicting perceptions. It networks with the basal ganglia (thought by some to be the brain locus for reward-based planning and learning) particularly when it involves novel, unexpected situations. Similar activity might be observed in dreams as a character or event that initiates a plan or 'what if' scenario aimed at reversing the direction or attitude of the dream ego. In the above example this mediating action can be seen as the unknown shadowy companion who initiates the plan to 'wake the man' ('what if he is just asleep?') and continues to negotiate with the dream ego to bring about a reversal.

3 Providing cues to guide or mediate the outcome

Although the dream appears to self-organize, the anterior cingulate may play a mediating role in developing the dream plot towards an eventual goal. It has been found in waking studies to mediate resolution by providing cues to other areas of the brain; to monitor performance and outcome; and to select an appropriate response based on placing a reward value on anticipated outcomes. The insula, basal ganglia and medial prefrontal cortex, also active in REM, may network to provide input that also influences the dream plot. The insula is found to be involved in our sense of self, subjective feelings, sudden insight, and guiding perceptual decision-making. The basal ganglia has been shown to select which response to make or inhibit as well as motivate us to seek eventual rather than immediate reward. The apparent sense of authority and guiding wisdom in our dreams may be a result of the medial prefrontal cortex, which is known to monitor learning and provide a confidence judgement or 'sense of knowing'. These cues might be observed in dreams as a moment of surprise or insight, something that is unexpected, or a guiding event, words or a character who points out, suggests, negotiates, or commands some new way of proceeding. In the example this guiding action is apparent as the shadowy companion urges the dream ego to wake the man. The surprise and subsequent insight is also apparent as the man and car come back to life.

4 Testing and monitoring the scenario

The anterior cingulate has been shown in waking state studies to work together with the medial prefrontal cortex to plan and test an activity; to generate performance expectations; to monitor and observe the outcome; and to adapt behaviour depending on whether the outcome met expectation. The medial prefrontal cortex is involved in simulating, rehearsing and processing self-referential, goal and reward-directed behaviours and together with the basal ganglia is involved in dampening and extinction of emotional response. The activity in these two centres during the REM state may be why we commonly observe dreams to organize into segments with abrupt scene changes; each segment appearing to test a new scenario that incorporates additional associations. Since dreams attempt to correct our behaviour by compensating for our misconceptions, dream scenarios are often observed to bring about a reversal or acceptance by the dream ego; a moment when the dream ego reverses its course of thinking or actions, or accepts the cues it has been given to follow in the dream. In the example the dream tested the planned scenario by bringing about a reversal in the thinking of the dream ego which tested the solution when he shook the man.

5 Learning by emotionally reinforcing a successful scenario

Dreams appear to emotionally reinforce successful scenarios. If this is the case, it may be in part due to action of the anterior cingulate which has been found to select an appropriate scenario out of various options, monitor the outcome, and place a reward value on that outcome. Together with the basal ganglia, the anterior cingulate has been found to be involved in focused, reward-based decision-making and learning, and adapting to changing conditions. The caudal and ventral medial orbitofrontal cortex is also involved in expectation, regulation of behaviour planning, and influencing ongoing behaviour, based on reward and punishment. With all these centres active during REM it is therefore not surprising that the dream would self-reward a dream scenario that meets expectation. Emotional reinforcement may also be a means of learning, 'organizing memory based on what is emotionally important', as Ernest Hartmann (2011) put it. Emotional reinforcement is suspected to be taking place in dreams with positive or promising endings. In the dream example above, the emotional reinforcement was apparent as the car and the man both came to life once the dream ego followed the cues it was given. There was an apparent learning taking place as well. Although the dreamer did not initially work on the dream, his behaviour was changed – he subsequently accepted the assignment and did exceptionally well.

What problems might dreams be resolving?

From the above discussion it appears that our dreaming mind has the capability for problem resolution, but what problems is the dreaming mind dealing with? This question has been debated by researchers and psychotherapists ever since Freud first suggested that dreams might have a meaningful function. The theories are many but for simplicity's sake might be summarized in these three areas:

1 *Restoring psychological balance.* A process of dealing with unresolved emotionally important issues, bringing the mind back to 'reality' and/or maintaining a sense of 'self' despite adverse waking experience.
2 *Adaptive learning.* Through weaving new material into established memory and testing and/or practising problem resolution scenarios, in order to arrive at a new inner model that better prepares us for waking life.

3 *Psychological growth.* An often long-term, cyclic process of compensating for misconceptions or dysfunctional beliefs in order to transcend
   old attitudes and evolve a more mature personality.

I will discuss each of these below and illustrate each concept with a dream
example. The problem resolution activities described in the previous section will also be noted in [brackets] in each dream example, as well as a
way to tie all these theoretical concepts together.

1 Restoring psychological balance

Jung (1964, pp. 12, 273) stated that the general function of dreaming
was to restore our psychological balance and bring the mind back to
reality. This might include the resolution of long-term internal conflict
or emotionally important unfinished business of the day. Jung stated that
dreams restore psychological balance through a process of 'compensation'. Dreams do this by presenting and compensating our conscious
misconceptions or distortions in order 'to bring the conscious mind back
to reality' or 'warn of the dangers of our present course' (Jung 1964,
p. 34). Researcher Patrick McNamara at Boston University School of
Medicine found that dreaming may involve a process of learning from
unexpected or negative outcomes by simulating alternative ways of handling these outcomes. In other words the dream creates and tests a number of 'what if' scenarios, or what McNamara called 'counterfactuals', in
order to find one that achieves the desired outcome. In one study of 50
dream reports he found that 97% contained corrective attempts by gener-
ating 'counterfactuals', which they considered to be the dream's attempt
to integrate new content into memory. Harry Fiss, PhD, University of
Connecticut School of Medicine, stated that one aim of this process might
be to maintain a healthy sense of 'self' despite adverse waking experiences.
French neurobiologist Michel Jouvet indicated that dreams achieve this by
reprogramming cortical networks to maintain psychological individuality.

   This process was illustrated in the example of the 'old rusty car' above,
where the dream attempted to compensate for the dreamer's misconception, and planned and guided the dreamer through a 'what if he is just
sleeping' scenario. The dream rewarded the outcome when the dreamer
followed the scenario – thus maintaining a more complete sense of 'self'.
Sometimes the emotional reinforcement comes as a warning, however, as
can be seen in the following example (Hoss 2005, p. 116):

This teen had deep fundamental religious beliefs. She frequently tried to suppress a side of herself she considered evil by going through a prayer ritual whenever she had what she considered 'evil thoughts'. After one such episode she dreamed: 'An evil person had come alive again and I feared that an "entity" was at work. I went through a ritual of exorcism to eliminate the evil person [picture-metaphor of her behaviour] but the more I tried the darker the sky became [compensating surprise – got worse not better]. Suddenly a voice said, "Stop – you are only making it worse" [guiding cue].' Here we see the dream 'compensating' for her misconception and warning against continuing this unhealthy practice of considering a side of herself as evil and trying to suppress it.

2 *Adaptive learning*

Dr Monte Ullman, founder of the Maimonides Medical Center in New York, believed that dreams serve some adaptive function. Antti Revonsuo, Professor of Neuroscience at the University of Turku in Finland, extended this thinking to include the evolution of a survival function through a process of threat rehearsal. Both Ernest Hartmann and researcher Robert Stickgold observe that dreams are where we make new connections, bringing material together in fresh, often startling ways. This permits us to draw on stores of knowledge from the past, present and imagined future, in order to find new patterns and combinations that break through old beliefs and behaviours and adapt to stress over time. Researcher Richard Coutts proposes that dreams improve our ability to meet waking needs by testing scenarios; those that appear to adapt are retained, while those that appear maladaptive are discarded. Alfred Adler, founder of the school of individual psychology, also suggested a similar process, which diverges from rational logic towards an inner logic that either reinforces or inhibits the contemplated action. The following are two examples of dreams that appear to be testing solutions in order to adapt to waking life situations (Hoss and Hoss 2013, pp. 150–1).

This is the dream of a young man who had acquired a defensive response of getting angry whenever he was teased, which only invited more teasing. 'I had a dream about a mean dog which was being beat on by three men [picture-metaphor of his situation]. Suddenly the dog rolled over and played dead [testing a what-if scenario, a reversal]. The men now thought it was cute and left it alone. A street lamp lit overhead at that moment [reinforcement of the new connection being made].' The dreamer learned to 'play along'.

The second example is a case where the dream appears to test a series of scenarios during a night's sleep, bringing in new associations each time, in an attempt to resolve a long-standing conflict.

In life this dreamer had gone through multiple traumatic experiences whenever she attempted to assert herself – symbolically expressing her 'masculine' side. She was given the message in her youth that assertive females are considered 'sinister' and the primary male figures in her life (father and alcoholic ex-husband) provided poor masculine role models and would 'squash' her attempts to assert herself. She was now at a point in life where she needed to become assertive – which triggered an internal conflict. She had the following dream which contained five sequences, each bringing in different associations; but as a series they appear to move towards the singular goal of integrating masculine and feminine:

1 Two sinister-looking men pulled another man out of a car that had been blocking traffic and killed him.
2 One man 'squashed' a beautiful dragonfly on the back of another man.
3 I am in a hotel room bed. I rolled over and a man was in my bed. I am upset that the hotel had booked the man in the same room with me.
4 I went to the office to change rooms, but had to crawl through a dark hole. A man and a woman pulled me 'up from the darkness' into a lit room.
5 I went back to the hotel room and finding a drunken couple lying on the bed, I was disgusted and left.

In sequences 1 and 2 we see two associations related to her conflict being detected and presented as picture-metaphor. Sequence 3 tests a scenario aimed at masculine integration – which is unsuccessful. In segment 4 a scenario is tested in which the dreamer experiences the rewards of masculine and feminine integration – pulling her out of the hole she is in. This appears successful and is emotionally reinforced, but when another attempt at integration is made in segment 5 (male and female together on the hotel bed again), the association with alcoholism enters the picture and appears to defeat it.

3 Psychological growth

Dreams also may help bring about a longer-term psychological growth and maturation. Jung claimed that dreams reveal a regulating tendency or 'transcendent' function, which brings about new awareness and gradually the emergence of a wider and more mature personality (Jung 1964, p. 161). He wrote that the dream achieves this through recognizing the motives of the ego and 'compensating' for these deficiencies by creatively integrating unconscious and conscious material (revealing new connections and viewpoints) in order to arrive at a new attitude, whereby the unconscious and the conscious self are more integrally connected and move together. Others agree that dreams help develop the ego (Jones 1962) and integrate our fragmented personality (Perls 1969). Clinical psychologist David Feinstein observed how dreams mediate conscious and unconscious perceptions in order to achieve the self-maintenance and transcendent functions that Jung describes. He indicated that dreams either find a way to accommodate the material within our existing internal model (the 'old myth'), strengthen a growing and opposing 'counter myth' or creatively develop a new inner model (a 'new myth') that better accommodates internal and external reality. Such is the case of a corporate executive whose company was restructuring and eliminating various divisions (Hoss and Hoss 2013, p. 154):

> The executive was told his department may be eliminated. He was trying to find a way out of his circumstance but was holding out for the possibility that a like position would open internally, out of fear that if he looked elsewhere he would never find a good job at his age and would also lose his retirement package. He had the following dream: 'I am a passenger in a boat on a dark underground river trying to find a way out and a "position" in the windows where I can see daylight [problem detected and presented as a picture-metaphor]. A tour guide appears behind me and points out an opening in the front of the boat [compensating scenario planned] that I had not seen before [surprise] and says, "You can walk out that door" [guiding cue]. I didn't understand and was reluctant, but finally at his constant urging I walked out the door [reversal and scenario tested] and found myself out in front. At that point the boat emerged from the cave and into a bright, beautiful, colourful sunlit setting of calm water [emotional reinforcement].' An apparent learning took place. Without even understanding the dream, the dreamer's viewpoint had been reversed. He subsequently accepted

what turned out to be a fabulous job outside, one that he had previously turned down, and literally 'walked out the door'.

Conclusions

Dreams appear to provide a wealth of information that can be invaluable to the therapist or the dreamer themselves in helping to understand and resolve inner issues that leave a person stuck in conflict; issues that might be difficult to reveal using cognitive dialogue-based approaches. Dreams reveal the unconscious emotional aspect of a conscious event, and the dream images themselves contain those underlying emotions and conflicts. By 'giving those dream images a voice' (rather than relying on rational dialogue) a therapist can provide a rapid and reliable means for revealing those underlying emotions and conflicts. Furthermore, if we are able to observe problem resolution and learning activities pictured in the dream, we can gain an understanding for how our unconscious mind is attempting to self-heal, which might provide helpful clues as to a more natural approach to dealing with the dreamer's situation that is revealed by the dream.

A dream-working protocol and worksheet, which combines all these approaches, can be found on and downloaded from www.dreamscience. org. The process begins with recording the dream narrative and the emotional situations taking place in the dreamer's life at the time. A first level of connecting the dream to waking life is performed by exploring the picture-metaphors in the dream narrative. The next level of exploration focuses on the underlying emotions, which uses the six question scripted Gestalt role-play, 'giving the dream a voice'. At that point the underlying emotions or emotional conflicts the dreamer is dealing with are typically revealed and related to their waking life situation. The dream is then explored to determine if it contains any obvious actions aimed at resolving the issue (the occurrence of surprise, a guiding event, a reversal). In particular, if the dream ends positively we look for the action that brought it about and relate that to actions the dreamer might take in waking life to help with what they are struggling with. If the dream is inconclusive or ends negatively then a spontaneous imaging technique is applied (similar in nature to Imagery Rehearsal Treatment) to complete the dream with a new imagined ending. This is then explored as a possible analogy to a waking life solution.

References

Hartmann, E. (2011), *The Nature and Functions of Dreaming*, New York NY: Oxford University Press.

Hobson, J. A., Pace-Schott, E. F. and Stickbold, R. (2003), 'Dreaming and the Brain: Toward a Cognitive Neuroscience of Conscious States', in E. F. Pace-Schott, M. Solms, M. Blagrove and S. Harnad, eds, *Sleep and Dreaming*, New York NY: Cambridge University Press, pp. 1–50.

Hoss, R. (2005), *Dream Language: Self-Understanding Through Imagery and Color*, Ashland OR: Innersource.

Hoss, R. (2010), 'Content Analysis on the Potential Significance of Colour in Dreams: A Preliminary Investigation', in *International Journal of Dream Research* 3(1), pp. 80–90.

Hoss, R. and Hoss, L. (2013), *Dream To Freedom: A Handbook for Integrating Dreams and Energy Psychology*, Santa Rosa CA: Energy Psychology Press.

Jones, R. M. (1962), *Ego Synthesis in Dreams*, Cambridge MA: Schenkman.

Jung, C. G. (1964), *Man and His Symbols*, New York NY: Dell.

Jung, C. (1971), *The Portable Jung*, edited and with an introduction by J. Campbell, New York NY: Viking Press.

Perls, F. (1969), *Gestalt Therapy Verbatim*, Moab UT: Real People Press.

4

The Dream as a Scientific, Aesthetic and Therapeutic Object

MARC HEBBRECHT

Introduction

From my own background as a psychotherapeutically trained psychiatrist working in a psychiatric hospital and associated with psychoanalytic education, I have gained much experience in working with dreams in clinical practice with patients. In this chapter, attention is given to the status of the dream as an object of study that is situated in the borderline area of numerous disciplines.

Science attempts to answer several questions relative to dreaming: Does the dream correspond with a reality that can be studied scientifically? Is the dream meaningful and interpretable? And what does contemporary psychoanalysis have to say about dreams? Are there risks involved, and if so, when must we be careful about a discussion of dreams? Here I will explore and give answers to these questions. Substantiated insights will be proffered, that the reader may consider in reaching their own answer to the question of whether it is meaningful to deal with dreams in the framework of counselling.

Phenomenological approach

Regardless of how respectable both traditions are, before we let science and psychoanalysis have their say, we will become familiar with a broader viewpoint. The dream can also be viewed as an aesthetic and poetic phenomenon that brings truths to light and cannot be exclusively understood by science and psychoanalysis. Early in the twenty-first century, Sharpe (1937) compared the dream to poetry. According to her, the dream uses literary procedures and expresses itself like poetry. Dreams, like language and other symbolic forms, are attempts to communicate to someone else the way the world is experienced. It is the task of the poet to communicate these experiences in a very personal manner. The poetic form of expression prefers to speak in images rather than to list factual occurrences. The poetic form avoids generalizing and prefers the particular; it does not like verbosity and avoids conjunctions and pronouns as much as possible. This also occurs in dreams. In the same way that a poem is a condensation of numerous images and feelings, extracted from former emotional experiences, a dream can be viewed as a condensation of latent thoughts, memories, affects, sensory observations, etc. A poem must evoke an effect, touch the reader; it may not leave them unmoved. The contemporary psychoanalyst will also ask themselves what effect the dream has on them. Some dreams do not affect us at all, whereas others arouse horror.

In what follows, we explore how science and psychoanalysis add something to our insight into the dream experience, yet without thereby reducing the dream to one small aspect of its reality.

Definition and characteristics

In the scientific literature various definitions of the dream can be found. The definition of Hobson et al. (2000) is as follows:

> Dreaming is 'mental activity occurring in sleep characterized by vivid sensorimotor imagery that is experienced as waking reality despite such distinctive cognitive features as impossibility or improbability of time, place, person and actions; emotions, especially fear, elation, and anger predominate over sadness, shame and guilt and sometimes reach sufficient strength to cause awakening; memory for even very vivid dreams is evanescent and tends to fade quickly upon awakening unless special steps are taken to retain it'.

Science sheds light on various characteristics. Dreams are an activity of the mind during sleep in which vivid series of depictions are formed, usually in fanciful variation, and the person thinks that they are experiencing all of this. In a few seconds, the dream creates a presentation that is experienced as real. According to Hartmann (2011, pp. 34–5), the great majority of our dreams are very common and are not bizarre. Only now and then do we have a bizarre or strange dream. Bizarreness can be a characteristic of dreams but is not limited to dreams. Dreams often have a powerful reality content: especially in dreams when we have the feeling that we are actually involved in it, a characteristic that our thoughts and day dreams lack. Analytical studies of the content of dreams indicate that we particularly dream about what is occupying us the most emotion-ally. Our dreams are not words, but are usually images or videos based on emotionally loaded associations. Dreams are metaphors in movement (Ullman 2006). The dream is guided by emotions; emotions select the images and bring several images together to create a new image. The dream image can be likened to a photo of an emotional condition.

Thoughts and impressions from waking life are replaced in dreaming by a hallucination (we see, for example, mountains, valleys, plains, cities . . .). Dream images are fleeting and changeable. From the hallucinatory images, the dream forms a situation, it represents something as real, it dramatizes an idea. Visual images form the main ingredient of the dream, although other sensory experiences are also possible. In the dream, physical activ-ities can occur that are in principle impossible: flying, for example. There is often disorientation in various areas: the person feels unsure about the space in which they find themselves, they do not know for sure when the dream occurred in their personal history, or there is confusion with regard to the gender, the age and the identity of the people in the dream. There is a spatial consciousness in the dream as in the waking condition; percep-tions and images are placed in an external space. The dream seems to occur in the present time. Dreams are especially affective occurrences: emotions are usually present, such as fear and anxiety. In the dream, a change of the reflective consciousness occurs: self-monitoring, purposeful and logical thinking and the will-function are decreased, which causes an inability to analyse situations, to test assumptions and to make decisions (Benca et al. 2005). Furthermore, while dreaming one is less able to form new memories.

Another characteristic of the dream is expressed in the choice of the material reproduced: the insignificant and inconspicuous are remembered, whereas the most important things are forgotten. Most dreams are quickly forgotten. Sometimes the dream memory is very vivid shortly after waking, but fades during the course of the day, or we know that we have dreamed but not what we have dreamed. It also happens that a dream is forgotten upon waking, but is remembered at a later time during the day. Other dreams remain persistently as vivid memories for a very long time.

Also, although the sleeping brain is disconnected from the real world because the main sensory functions are turned off (there is a turning away from the outside world), it is able to create a virtual world that looks like the real world and is also experienced as real. Dreams seem at first sight to be bizarre and irrational, but when one keeps track of them systematically and thinks about them, they are found to provide important insights and truths, and they are more connected to experienced reality than one might first suspect.

Does the dream exist? Can the dream be studied?

This brings us to the question of whether the dream really exists. Does the dream refer to an experience that really occurs during sleep, or does it relate to an occurrence that runs parallel with waking up? Or is the dream purely a story that is constructed after waking up? Kramer (2007, pp. 17–31), in his overview of empirical dream research, devotes an entire chapter to answering these questions. In a series of research projects he compared the degree to which the report of a dream differs from the report of a nightmare and from the report of a confabulated nightmare. When a participant is asked to write a fictional story of a nightmare, such stories differ significantly from reported dreams and nightmares. Fabricated or confabulated nightmares are more aggressive, more intense, less friendly, more colourful, relate to adversity, and are characterized by more movement and indoor scenes. A confabulated nightmare is reported with significantly fewer words than nightmares or dreams. There are also neurobiological arguments for the existence of dreams. For young adults, about 20% of the night consists of rapid eye movement (REM) sleep. After the discovery of REM sleep in 1953, it was assumed that dreaming only occurred in this phase (the dream being viewed as a epiphenomenon of REM sleep). This now appears not to be the case! One dreams mainly during REM sleep, but in the non-rapid eye movement (NREM) phases there is also mental activity. At present scientists assume that remembering dreams during NREM sleep occurs in 40% of cases and during REM sleep in 80% (Nielsen 2000). Thus dreaming is not an experience that is exclusively connected to REM sleep. Throughout the whole night there is psychological activity. A person can remember dreams more accurately when they are awoken from REM sleep. Dreams can even occur in the waking state (Foulkes 1993), a fact that is confirmed by contemporary psychoanalysis.

Thus empirical research indicates that the dream is a real phenomenon, not a confabulation or something that is purely imagined. The dream is real and really exists. The dream is even measurable. The dream is an organized phenomenon, not a phenomenon that occurs 'arbitrarily'; it is a meaningful experience characterized by regularity and variability.

The question of whether the dream can be studied by the positive sciences requires a methodological discussion. Methodologically considered, the dream is an exceptionally complex subject.

First, the dream is a multiple conscious experience, with perceptual, emotional and motoric dimensions. When one subjects the dream to scientific research, it is in fact reduced to a memory that is then converted into a story. This story is created after the dream experience in the waking state and is then reported to a researcher. The dream investigated in this way is, in other words, a retrospective event.

Second, how the meaning of the dream is viewed by both the researcher and the dreamer influences the dream content.

Third, research in a sleep laboratory is not equivalent to sleeping in natural surroundings: one is sleeping in a space that one does not know, a technician is present who is watching, electrodes are attached to the skin; the sleep of one night in a strange environment is less deep and is interrupted more often than in the regular sleeping environment. Furthermore, the experimental environment is included in the dream as an external element.

Fourth, the methodological mistake is often made of equating physiological activity in one zone of the brain with psychological activity (REM activity on the EEG is not the same as dreaming!). This confronts us with the complexity of the body-mind problem that leads to both neuroscientific and philosophical controversies (Kramer 2002).

Finally, episodic memory for recent occurrences during sleeping-waking changeovers and during sleep decreases, an item of information that does not make dream research any easier (Hobson et al. 2000).

In brief: the total range of possible dream experiences, as well as the phenomenal richness thereof, cannot be investigated exclusively by means of research in sleep laboratories.

Is the dream meaningful and interpretable?

Taking the current state of affairs in science into consideration, we can state that interdisciplinary research that includes epistemological, phenomenological, empirical, psychobiological, psychopathological and psychoanalytical approaches, confirms that a dream is usually meaningful. Its meaning is not always discernible, however. The meaning of some dreams cannot be discovered; these dreams evade interpretation and sometimes serve as an evasive manoeuvre. Freud, in *The Interpretation of Dreams*, also spoke about 'the navel of the dream': the place where the dream becomes unfathomable.

An essay about dreams is unthinkable without referring to psychoanalysis and its founder, Sigmund Freud. In *The Interpretation of Dreams* (1900), a book that is a succession of examples of the operation of the subconscious, he gives a model of the psychological apparatus and explains his theory of how the psyche works. Primarily, Freud views the dream as a fully fledged psychological act, a carrier of meaning. This makes the dream interpretable. The dream is an organized psychological activity, to be distinguished from the waking life, and obeying its own set of rules. Freud thereby not only goes against the popular interpretation of dreams (the deciphering of dreams with the help of symbolic codes to predict the future) but also against the scientists who claim that dreams are only unorganized productions, brought forth by internal stimuli. According to Freud, the dream is a psychological creation of the dreamer himself and not a message that is sent by a god or a demon. He defines the dream as psychological activity during sleep. The dream is experienced mainly visually and is played on a different stage from representations in the waking system. Yet, not every dream can be interpreted.

The question remains whether the freshly dreamed dream is meaningful in and of itself. The meaning of a dream usually comes to light most clearly in dialogue with another person. Meaning comes to light via an interpreter who introduces an external system of meaning assignment and consistently applies it to the dream. Viewed in this way, a comprehensive and complete meaning of a dream does not exist. There is not one true interpretation of a dream – several interpretations are possible that can all be true.

There remains a mysterious core in the dream that is best left alone; one can explore it as a phenomenon but preferably without becoming obsessed with its interpretation. This core might well be understood later after new dream sequences present themselves. But it might not. We may not forget that the dream itself is a kind of inner eye, a window to the inner world, which is quite free from all inroads: a volatile and intimate creation with aesthetic characteristics.

A practical rule of thumb in this regard is that the manifest dream, in other words, the dream as the dreamer remembers and tells it, deserves just as much attention as the associative thoughts that are connected with it.

Associative contexts in practice

Even though a dream appears bizarre at first, on investigation it will often add insights about experienced reality in a particularly clear way, more than one might suspect initially.

Continuity usually exists between the dream and the occurrences of the preceding day. Not all daily preoccupations are expressed in the manifest dream, but emotionally loaded interpersonal themes are. The dream can also contain intersubjective aspects, as is discussed below. The dream, as a mental activity, is not just the creation of the person himself but it can be thrust upon him from the outside. This is sometimes evident in group therapy. When someone tells a dream during group therapy, resonances occur from other members of the group. Dreams of group members often show similarities or are complementary. Sometimes a group member can introduce a dream that another group member cannot dream or put into words, as though one member of the group 'dreams' for the other member of the group.

The obsolete concept that the dream can be explained on the basis of external, supernatural concepts must be put into perspective but may not be completely pushed aside. We also recognize the dream as a communication: via a dream a patient can, for example, express their opinion about the quality of the relationship with the therapist. Or we can view the dream as a visitation, like the ethnopsychiatrist Nathan (2011) claims, which is clarified in the following section. Finally, a dream can play a role in socialization. Social dreaming is a method described by Lawrence (2003) in which dreams are used to develop a good relationship within the group. The exchange of dreams could bring clarity about a threatening crisis and increase the feeling of solidarity among the members. In addition it can lead to innovating ideas that meet the specific needs of an organization.

Beyond that, a dream can be an indication that a psychological problem has not been completely assimilated and solved, but needs additional processing. To this end a dream can be communicated to someone else. Also, a dream could indicate that one has discerned a physical, psychological, relational or social condition without yet being clearly conscious of it.

Is there still room for the traditional interpretation of dreams?

Increasingly it is becoming evident that psychoanalysis does not possess the exclusive right to interpret dreams. In this regard I refer, for example, to the recent contribution of Nathan (2011), who researches what ethnopsychiatry and cultural anthropology contribute to the interpretation of dreams. According to Nathan, the dream is located at the borderline between the nonsensical, the capricious and the sacred. He sees the dream primarily as a movement: a cinematic happening full of action, interaction, staging and succession and also as a paradoxical event that has its origin in the most intimate core of ourselves but which as a phenomenon appears strange to our own selves. We observe the dream as a phenomenon that descends on us as from another world.

The dream contains a message of which we know neither the sender nor the addressee. The dream is a dialogue with a partner who is of a radically different nature from the dreamer himself. The interpretation is the required complement of the dream, like the other side of a coin. A dream is a request for interpretation, the dream is searching for an interpreter. Also, a dream cannot be viewed separate from the interpreter. The function of the interpreter is not to make explicit, explain or translate – but to facilitate – so the movement of the dream can be extended to the external world (*'un interprète des rêves est donc un accoucheur de lendemains'*) (Nathan 2011, p. 124). In the view of Nathan, a dream is directed towards the future; every interpretation sketches and creates the future. In its vision, the dream still fulfils a prophetic function, an insight that lies in the extension of the supernatural approach of the dream that until the beginning of the nineteenth century was the dominant view. It must be stressed, following Koet (2009) who writes of the *divine dream dilemma*, that also in ancient times, several different viewpoints about dreams existed at the same time and these were not restricted to supernatural explanations.

Nathan ventures to make a classification of dreams. First he distinguishes eruptions (*'effervescences'* or outpourings of an excess, to be compared with evacuative dreams), then carriers (messages, visions) and finally signals. Thus a nightmare can be understood as a signal, directed to the dreamer and to his immediate environment, which warns about a potential danger for one's own survival, career or family situation. The dream can also be viewed as a public place in ourselves where a person can meet other fanciful beings. In addition, the dream gives a glimpse of the hidden strategies of others.

Nathan's primary criticism of psychoanalysis is that it participates in '*le culte du quiconque*' (the cult of 'just anybody'), which is typical of postmodern society. By this he means that what is most individual is in danger of being wiped out. From this view he cannot accept that typical dreams exist. According to him, psychoanalysis has contributed to the destruction of the sacred dimension of the dream. Nathan considers the function of the dream to be the regeneration of the singular identity of the person. Unlike Freud, he states that the dream is creative. After a deconstruction of sensory impressions, the dream process selects a number of significant elements and reassembles them according to a specific logic into a new construction that is finally converted into moving images. The dream is not a photographic reproduction of something in the past but the prefiguration of something in the future. The dream is the indefatigable creator of possible worlds and scenarios.

The interpretation of dreams, according to Nathan, ought to be based more on what traditional dream interpreters did long before Freud. First the interpreter must acquire information about the world and the culture in which the dreamer finds himself; the interpreter must become familiar with the dominant myths and legends from that world, and must also know the typical plays on words that are commonly used in the language of the dreamer. The dream is viewed as a projection into tomorrow: a veiled idea that will possibly become reality the following day. He asks the dreamer to tell all the details of the dream: the décor, the personages, the animals, the strange beings. Nathan gives the dream a name. He views the dream not as a form of impulse expression but as an abstract thought that wants to be observed and communicated. The interpreter will mainly make use of his intuition and notice the fantasies that come to his mind. Dreams reveal a deep truth about the person himself. Therefore one should not tell a dream to someone one does not know. Listening to a dream requires respect, which cannot be expected of just anyone. Some dreams are better left uninterpreted: dreams in the process of formation, dreams that are an exact copy of a situation in reality, wish dreams, or representations of the psychological condition of the dreamer. Dreams can bring a secret to light. Before a dream is interpreted the interpreter must weigh the consequences of his interpretation: first and foremost he may not cause harm; he may never use the dream as a weapon. Not all dreams relate to the dreamer himself; there are also dreams that are for the general good (for example, dreams of leaders).

The dream in contemporary psychoanalysis

Whereas in the past the emphasis was placed on interpreting, decoding and translating dreams, more attention is now given to the ability to dream, and this capability is welcomed as progress in psychological development (Fonagy et al. 2012).

Our ability to dream develops slowly during the childhood years. Dreaming as an attainment only comes into being in late childhood (Hartmann 2011, pp. 23–30). The ability to create completely formed dreams develops in parallel with the development of visuospatial capabilities and the narrative ability (the ability to tell stories). Dreaming relates not to passive perception but to active imagination and the telling of a story. Dreaming is a creative recombination of memories and knowledge.

With the help of his own reverie and intuition, the task of the contemporary psychoanalytical psychotherapist is to help the patient dream the undreamable and finish dreaming his interrupted dreams. Thus dream interpretation is not the interpretation of a latent content but a construction of meaning in a context. More than previously, an interactional view is applied in the interpretation technique. This does not contradict the concept that the dream is a primitive means of expression and communication – although the dream is now mainly seen as a transformation activity and an interpersonal statement, and is used less as an intrapersonal decoding of psychological hieroglyphics. This expands the Freudian concept of the dream in an impressive way. The dream is more than just an attempt to fulfil subconscious wishes.

The dream is also not just a thought like any other. The dream deserves a special status because it makes it possible to gain access to deeper, hidden meanings and in itself is a special context for the discovery and experiencing of new meanings. Some dreams arouse curiosity and cause one to want to know more, to desire knowledge.

The meaning contained in the manifest dream differs from the meaning that emerges through the investigation of free associations with the various dream elements. When listening to dreams, the emphasis often lies on the ability to intuitively understand metaphors. Here is an example of this. After she had to endure a cutting remark, a patient told me the following dream:

> The house that she has just bought has collapsed. Thieves broke in and emptied one side of the house. Only icons of Mary that she inherited from her parents have been taken.

Her further associations make clear that her job is a source of frustration. When she comes home after having been swamped by a wave of criticism, she feels empty and robbed. She no longer has the energy to spend time with her child. Mary-icons represent the close bond between mother and child. More can be said about this dream, but I am illustrating how an offence has influenced her self-image and is expressed metaphorically in the dream as a collapsed and plundered house.

Often the dream portrays a simple truth about how occurrences in daily life are experienced subjectively. In other cases the dream provides access to the inner dilemmas of the person. Dreams are dramatic portrayals of situations and relations between internal objects as they exist in the inner world. Figures in the dream can be understood as personified features of the personality of the dreamer.

In the dream a problem is stated that invites further unravelling and processing. When a problem is too painful because it is connected with a trauma, it will announce itself over and over through the dream. When there are repetitive dreams we ought to give consideration to an unprocessed trauma. On the other hand, the dream is the expression of a capacity of the person, namely the ability to symbolize – a talent that not everyone possesses. Dreams are indications of continuing psychological integration (or a sign that the integration has not yet succeeded and remains limited to an evacuation) (Lauret 2011).

Contemporary psychoanalysis concludes that a complete concept of the dream is not possible. We can accept dreams, appreciate and admire them, and discover various meanings in them. Especially, big dreams can be appreciated as works of art. The distinction between 'small' and 'big' dreams comes from Jung. Many people carry a dream with them that is very meaningful and emotional for them personally. Often such a big dream is the first dream that one tells others, according to Jung (1993). Big dreams make use of mythical themes that characterize the life of the hero.

The dream as an intersubjective phenomenon

With his intersubjective approach to the dream, Bion brought about a paradigmatic revolution in psychoanalysis that is only now coming to fruition. Dreams of patients have a vivid relationship with dreams of therapists, and conversely. The dream process continues day and night, and now and then eruptions are visible on the surface. In addition, we should not forget that a dream is already an interpretation of an emotional experience. Patients tell dreams to share psychological content with the therapist, which they themselves cannot dream, in order to be able to continue the dream process. A dream must therefore always be viewed as a 'work in progress' (Schneider 2010, p. 532).

From the intersubjective point of view, the function of dreams is the clarification of what is happening in therapy: dreams can provide commentary on the indication, the process, the subconscious intrapsychic and interpersonal dynamics of both patient and therapist, the transference and countertransference and the therapeutic relationship. Thus a dream can show a direction, indicate a border, contain an evaluation, make a risk situation visible, reveal blind spots or mistakes of the therapist, illuminate a countertransference problem or show a way out from an impending impasse. Some dreams open a new and refreshing perspective on the material and make the formulation of creative hypotheses possible. Thoughts that have not yet formed are often visualized in images through a dream. A dream is told to someone else to learn more about one's self, to clarify the enigmatic in a dialogue with the other person. A dream that arises during the course of treatment is currently understood as a creation that comes into being in the relational and emotional field. Then it is not the creation of one psyche but the cinematographic version of what is occurring at a deeper level in the patient/practitioner relationship. The dream can be viewed as a kind of dramatic scene that generates meaning and that serves as a starting point for new stories (Hebbrecht 2013).

Contraindications

There are circumstances in which a practitioner must be cautious in dealing with dreams that are reported. This is the case, for example, for recurring nightmares about one stereotypical theme or recurring dreams in which death occurs. Recurring nightmares are not banal. When the brain functions poorly, such as during confused states and some psychotic conditions, the dream fulfils, as it were, a release function by which the psyche empties itself of an excess of stimuli. Every psychiatrist knows that increasing nightmares can be a signal of a psychotic collapse, of a schizophrenic episode or of a manic phase. Dreams of psychotic patients make both regressive disintegration and deterioration visible, and the attempt at reorganization and restitution by means of delusion formation. Psychotic dreams (also the dreams of borderline patients) are very concrete, make violence and sexual sadism visible, and are characterized by sudden aggressive explosions and monstrous figures.

Nightmares are sometimes the consequence of a disturbance of neural networks in the brain, as a result of toxic (use of drugs), medicinal, organic and metabolic causes. Consider nightmares, for example, in the framework of the delirium of people who are very ill physically, or suffering as a consequence of withdrawal syndromes after protracted misuse of alcohol and tranquillizers. Especially with nightmares in adults, consideration must be given to medical and pharmacological causes. With children, nightmares do not necessarily have a pathological meaning. Recurring nightmares can also indicate that an earlier trauma is not being processed psychologically. A post-traumatic nightmare, for example, is an exact replication of the traumatic occurrence and is accompanied by physiological reactions that indicate a post-traumatic reliving of experiences. Such nightmares can recur for decades in unmodified form. They can be viewed as attempts to process the trauma. This sometimes succeeds, but usually the problem is only postponed, does not get solved and is continually repeated in the dream. In all these situations, a referral to a specialized physician is necessary.

Another problem can occur when the dream condition intrudes into waking life and the border between dreaming and real life becomes blurred. This is the case with dissociative disorders. With a depersonalization disorder, the person is bothered by persistent or recurring experiences in which he is disconnected from his feelings and observes, as it were, his own mental processes or his own body. He may suffer, for example, from the feeling that everything is happening in a dream. Also with trance, twilight states and auto hypnotic conditions, one can be awake but feel as though one is acting in a dream. The patient then withdraws from the real world or can become so involved in a book or in a film that they lose their own identity. The patient then does not see or hear what is happening in their immediate surroundings (Hebbrecht 2010, pp. 147–61).

In some cases it is difficult to make the distinction between a dream and an epileptic phenomenon. Patients with complex partial epilepsy can have attacks of dreamlike experiences both at night and during the day, that suddenly occur and just as suddenly end; these are sometimes (not always) followed by tonic-clonic grand-mal attacks, with tongue biting and incontinence. In such cases a neurological evaluation is necessary. Epileptic attacks are stereotypical phenomena, however; real dreams are more sophisticated, richer and more original. When nightmares coincide with bed-wetting, for example, the possibility of epilepsy must be considered.

Finally, caution is advised when counsellors have recurring dreams about patients they are counselling. These are called countertransference dreams. Such dreams indicate that emotional experiences of the patient that are difficult to digest psychologically are being deposited in the counsellor, who then has difficulty processing them. It can indicate a lapse in professionalism. Certainly if a therapist dreams repeatedly about a particular patient, advice should be obtained from an experienced colleague.

Working with dreams in the framework of pastoral counselling

By making use of dreams in the framework of counselling, clients can gain more insight into themselves: they can become more open to metaphorical meanings, they learn to make connections between various aspects of self-perception and to be amazed by personal psychological phenomena. Thus they develop curiosity about themselves and the feeling emerges that they are discovering something that they did not know before.

Sharing a dream with someone is an indication of confidence in the listener. A dream is, after all, a private matter that one does not easily share with others. When someone tells a dream in the framework of a counselling relationship, this is a moment of intimacy that requires a tactful attitude on the part of the listener. Each dream is a very personal thought that the dreamer can better understand by communicating to someone else. It is especially risky when the listener behaves like an all-knowing seer who can clarify a mystery that the dreamer knows nothing about.

On the one hand, there are dreams that have a fascinating power and remain as life-long memories; they can have a radical influence on a life and give it form. Consider the dream as a calling, for example, where the dream forms the foundation of a life choice. On the other hand, not all dreams are meaningful; there are dreams that do not divulge their meaning, while other dreams are exceptionally clear to the listener but the dreamer does not want to accept the meaning. Or, in a different vein, dreams can lead one away from a project, having a resistance function. Being occupied with dreams is then a way of not being occupied with the core assignment ('he is a dreamer').

Someone who listens to a dream ought to ask himself what effect the dream evokes: confusion, wonder, anxiety, excitement . . . or does it not evoke anything?

There are several ways to find the meaning of a dream depending on the theory and the personality of the therapist. The dream can serve as a starting point for the construction of meaning that comes into being through the co-operative thinking of the patient and the counsellor. Thus, one may not impose explanations. People who listen to dreams must place themselves in the role of an interested interviewer who encourages the patient to develop his story.

Based on psychoanalytical theory, a dream can be approached from various perspectives. Is the dream an attempt to fulfil a subconscious wish? Does it have to do with the processing of a trauma that has been only partially successful? Is the dream an expression of a compensation, with the dream serving as a warning that more attention must be given to something or someone being neglected? What question is being directed to the dreamer via the dream? What simple truth about the dreamer and their life situation does the dream contain? Is the dream a spontaneous self-portrait, a reflection of the inner condition at the moment? Is it an indication of the actual emotional state, the self-structure, the inner dilemmas, of mutual relations between internal objects? Is the dream a film of the inner world? (Blechner 2001). Does the dream reflect what the partner, children, close colleagues, other group members . . . do not want to know or cannot feel? Is it my own dream or is it someone else who is dreaming in me? Is the dream to be understood as a cinematic message that is sent to the dreamer from an outside supernatural reality that requires consideration? Is the fact of being able to dream and to tell the dream to someone else a creative moment that was not possible before? Thus, several explanations are possible for one dream; the dream is, after all, the poetic expression of many meanings by which each listener can discover new content depending on the system of meaning that is applied to it. Understanding dreams relates more to the construction of several meanings and less to the deciphering of one meaning.

Dreams are a special source of inspiration for literary, poetic and artistic activity. For the artist, the dream often forms the beginning of a discovery, something new and original. It is therefore unethical to remove the stimulus from the dream by wanting to explain and clarify it completely. A dream can be followed by a creative action.

Conclusion

The dream is a phenomenon that is situated on the borderline between the brain and the mind, between the inner and the outer world, between present and future, between the natural and the supernatural. In addition, the dream is an aesthetic phenomenon. Someone who wants to work with dreams must be willing to acquire in-depth knowledge in various fields of science. The actual neuroscientific theories cannot, however, explain the narrative aspects, the meaning, the content and the function of the dream. In some circumstances it is important to refer the patient to a specialized psychiatrist, especially when there are recurring nightmares and dream experiences that encroach on the waking condition. If a therapist dreams repeatedly about someone they are counselling, it is advisable to obtain counsel for themselves from a more experienced colleague.

References

Benca, R. M., Cirelli, C., Rattenborg, N. C. et al. (2005), 'Basic Science of Sleep', in B. J. Sadock, H. I. Kaplan and V. A. Sadock, *Kaplan and Sadock's Comprehensive Textbook of Psychiatry*, 8th edn, Philadelphia: Williams and Wilkins, pp. 280–94.

Blechner, M. (2001), *The Dream Frontier*, Hillsdale: Routledge.

Fonagy, P., Kächele, H., Leuzinger-Bohleber, M. and Taylor, D., eds (2012), *The Significance of Dreams: Bridging Clinical and Extraclinical Research in Psychoanalysis*, London: Karnac.

Foulkes, D. (1993), 'Data Constraints on Theorizing about Dream Function', in A. Moffitt, M. Kramer and R. Hoffmann, eds, *The Functions of Dreaming*, Albany: State University of New York Press, pp. 11–20.

Freud, S. (1900), 'De Droomduiding', in Freud, S. (2006), *Werken 2*, Amsterdam: Boom.

Hartmann, E. (2011), *The Nature and Functions of Dreaming*, New York: Oxford University Press.

Hebbrecht, M. (2010), *De Droom: Verkenning van een grensgebied*, Utrecht: De Tijdstroom.

Hebbrecht, M. (2011), 'Een Nieuw Paradigma: Droomduiding in het spoor van Bion', in *Psychoanalytische Perspectieven* 29, pp. 61–77.

Hebbrecht, M. (2013), 'Intersubjectieve Aspecten van Dromen', in *Tijdschrift voor Psychoanalyse* 19, pp. 3–15.

Hobson, J. A., Pace-Schott, E. F. and Stickgold, R. (2000), 'Dreaming and the Brain: Towards a Cognitive Neuroscience of Conscious States', in *Behavioral and Brain Sciences* 23, pp. 793–1121.

Jung, C. G. (1993), *Dromen*, The Kleine Jung-bibliotheek, Rotterdam: Lemniscaat.

Koet, B. J. (2009), 'Divine Dream Dilemmas: Biblical Visions and Dreams', in K. Bulkeley, K. Adams and P. M. Davis, eds, *Dreaming in Christianity and Islam: Culture, Conflict and Creativity*, New Brunswick, NJ/London: Rutgers University, pp. 17–31.

Kramer, M. (2002), 'The Biology of Dream Formation. A Review and Critique', in *Journal of the American Academy of Psychoanalysis* 30, pp. 657–71.

Kramer, M. (2007), *The Dream Experience: A Systematic Exploration*, New York: Routledge Taylor and Francis Group.

Lauret, M. (2011), *Lectures du rêve*, Paris: PUF.

Lawrence, W. G. (2003), *Experiences in Social Dreaming*, London: Karnac.

Nathan, T. (2011), *La Nouvelle Interprétation des Rêves*, Paris: Odile Jacob.

Nielsen, T. A. (2000), 'Mentation in REM and Non-REM Sleep: A Review and Possible Reconciliation of Two Models', in *Behavioral and Brain Sciences* 23, pp. 851–6.

Schneider, J. A. (2010), 'From Freud's Dream-work to Bion's Work of Dreaming: The Changing Conception of Dreaming in Psychoanalytic Theory', in *International Journal of Psychoanalysis* 91, pp. 521–40.

Sharpe, E. F. (1937), *Dream Analysis*, New York: Brunner/Mazel.

Ullman, M. (2006), *Appreciating Dreams: A Group Approach*, New York: Cosimo.

Dream Narrative 1

Dreamlife of an Episcopal Priest
How Dreams Were Helpful to Me
as a Priest and Pastor

BOB HADEN

Introduction

I do not remember any dreams from my childhood, from my adolescence or college years; no dreams as a teacher and basketball coach; no dreams around the marriage ceremony; no dreams when I felt my call to the priesthood or when I was ordained. But since I was forty, I have remembered several thousand dreams and recorded many of them. What made the big difference? At age forty I began to take dreams seriously and, therefore, they took me seriously.

Taking dreams seriously sprung from a four-day silent retreat searching for a renewed spirituality after a 'dark night of the soul' experience. Karen Armstrong (2001) says that religion from the beginning was composed of both logos and mythos (reason and mystery). Then, during the scientific era and the enlightenment we dropped mythos. I was in deep need of recovering mythos. Many of us in the spiritual world today are trying to recover mythos. Dreams play a big role in that – as do other sources of inspiration like the medieval mystics, desert mothers and fathers, Celtic spirituality and modern-day Pentecostals.

The ancient Chinese wisdom that 'when the student is ready, the teacher will appear' really is true. Dovetailing with the retreat experience, a teacher appeared: the Swiss psychoanalyst Carl Gustav Jung. One of the things that hooked me in the beginning of this adventure was Carl Jung saying he had a deep and abiding fear. His fear was that the Church was losing the experience of the Divine. And if the Church lost the experience of the Divine, it would go down the drain. And if the Church went down the drain, western civilization would go down the drain. When I read that I knew I had a renewed purpose and a partner in the journey.

So following the retreat, meditation and honouring the dream as 'God's forgotten language' became a part of my renewed spirituality. I would like to share some of that journey with you. These past 30 years I have learned that dreams come from a divine source offering us healing and wholeness. All this wisdom is coming from an autonomous source that is beyond me, but speaks in me. This Mystical Presence speaks in a metaphorical voice: the language of dreams.

Vestry dreams

As I began remembering my dreams on a regular basis, many of them continued to be about the vestry. There were vestry dreams about things as simple and straightforward as 'you are stepping on my toes' and more collective unconscious dreams like 'a snake in a cave'.

You are stepping on my toes

A vestry-woman came up to me at church and said, 'I dreamed last night that you and I were dancing and you were stepping on my toes.' Well, that certainly gave me a clue and caused me to be alert to how I was 'stepping on her toes' in vestry meetings. Actually, I was stepping on her 'standpoint', because dream symbols like legs, feet and toes often signify to what we stand on, so our standpoint in life. I was stepping on her standpoint in life. I began to ponder that. And, because of the dream, she was able to tell a critical thing that I needed to hear to facilitate our communication, friendship, and working together on the vestry. The 'grace' of the dream is that I did not get defensive when she communicated that message through a dream story. If she had pointed her finger and given me the straight message I would have become defensive. Dreams are much like Jesus' parables in that respect. We get involved in the story of the parable and hear the message non-defensively.

Snake in a cave

I never would have realized that the following 'snake in a circle in a cave' dream was also about the vestry. Who would have ever guessed that? But when I took that dream to my dream analyst, she immediately said, 'Is there a snake on your vestry?' Being naive and blind at the time, I said,

'No, there's no snake on my vestry.' I learned two weeks later there very definitely was a 'snake' on my vestry. I asked my analyst, 'Why did you ask that question?' She said, 'Because in ancient times the council of the tribe met in a circle in a cave and your council is the vestry.'

Several weeks later, the 'snake on the vestry' became very apparent. He was a big manipulator. He did all kinds of sneaky things behind the scenes. I got so mad at him. In fact I got *overly* mad at him. Well, luckily I had learned that if I get that mad at someone, there is something similar going on in me. So I asked myself, 'How do I manipulate?' I began by saying, 'I would never manipulate. It is a high quality with me.' Finally, after asking myself five times, I said, 'Oh, I am very sophisticated in the way I manipulate.' The moment I said this, my anger towards the vestry person dissolved. Although I did not share this with the vestry person, he lessened his manipulation. Jung says that when we do not own our shadow it is automatically projected onto people in society and those with traits like our shadow will receive it and be worse. Jesus says it very succinctly: 'First take the log out of your own eye and then you will see clearly how to take the speck out of your neighbour's eye.' The 'snake of a vestry person' was also my Shadow. I could be 'sneaky' also. Robert Johnson (1991) says that one of the highest moral acts we can do is to make friends with our own shadow. The reason I did not recognize the vestry person's shadow was that I was not acquainted with my own shadow. Can you imagine what a gift it would be for family members to do their own shadow work? What a different world we would have if not only families but vestries and parishes and businesses and nations would do their shadow work and become more conscious. One of the ways to become conscious of our shadows is by observing our nightly dreams.

Spiritual dream

Two monks just looking at each other

One night I had a simple dream of two monks sitting at a table just looking at each other. There was nothing going on. A few hours after I woke up from that dream, it suddenly hit me. There was 'nothing going on' in my spiritual life. The thing I love about dreams is that you hear stark truth about yourself in a way that you accept it and usually start to do something about it. This dream was telling me that I was off my path of growth towards wholeness, towards what God is calling me to be.

Pastoral care dreams

The black wisdom woman

I have found dreams a very helpful guide in church pastoral situations. One day I got word that a nineteen-year-old girl in our parish had died of cancer. I went immediately to see the family. That night I had a dream of a black woman standing behind me as I was sitting at my desk in my office. That's it. That's the picture God was drawing for me. It took a while, but all of a sudden it hit me. The dream symbol of the black woman represented 'soul' to me. I had not had a soul time with that family. So, I went back out to the house and sat on the floor in the girl's room and cried with her mother. Then the mother told me what her daughter had said to her, shortly before she died: 'Mom, I haven't had sex with a boy and now I am getting ready to die. Can you tell me what it is like?' If I had not listened to that dream I would have missed this opportunity for a more meaningful pastoral experience. God speaks through dreams.

Quadruple bypass

A parishioner came into my office and said, 'You know that John is having the quadruple bypass operation tomorrow. What you don't know is that I dreamed last night that he died. Does that mean that he is going to die?' Before working with dreams I would not know what to tell her and would have been scared to death. I said, 'Polly, I don't know, but I have been in the hospital room with you and you have not been taking this seriously and it is a very serious operation. My guess is that the dream is trying to tell you to take this seriously.' That was many years ago and her husband did not die. Most dreams in which 'literal' and concrete imagery of death occurs normally signify about something that needs to die in us. Dreams predicting actual physical death do occur, however, but that is conveyed in a much more symbolic language like going to make some kind of journey.

Guidance dreams

In the calling process

When I was in the calling process for a large south-eastern parish I had a dream of the church, which I had never seen. It had a wrought-iron fence around it and inside the fence was a clergy friend of mine all dressed up in his clerical garb. He was the one who was called and became the Rector of the church. It was not meant for me.

A second bishop's election

A couple years later I was a finalist in a bishop's election in another southern diocese. A week before the election I had a dream of a station wagon with four flat tyres. In the dream I was saying, 'Let's get these tyres pumped up,' but they wouldn't pump up. I was being foretold again that I would not be elected. There was something comforting about receiving this message from a dream. It had the essence of 'This is not what you are meant to be. Your path is elsewhere.'

Baby crib for the church

Having had previous dreams that had said 'no', when the 'yes' dream came I believed it all the more. I was in Washington DC for four days with a vocational consultant. The consultant asked me to come in after the weekend with the plan for the rest of my life. That night I had a dream of a doctor and his wife giving me $4,000 for a baby crib for the church. In the dream I was saying I could get a baby crib for cheaper than $4,000. Upon awaking I had confidence that this would be a new birth for the church and that there was the proper container for this baby. This dream is what gave me the courage to take the risk and set the plan in motion to establish The Haden Institute.

Two airplanes and six people

Guidance continued, even after I started The Haden Institute. One dream saved the Institute and me. If I had not listened to this dream, the Institute would not be and I would have had another wreck, ended up in the hospital and be financially broke.

The dream was of two small airplanes and six people. The idea in the dream was to go three and three. Robert, my oldest son who is very intuitive and fun, was the pilot of one of the planes. So, all six decided to go with him. Robert decided to take off on the beach rather than the runway. A voice said, 'Someone tried that yesterday and crashed.'

When, upon awakening, I heard the word 'crash' I knew I had better listen to this dream because it was a warning dream that I was about to crash. Upon reflection I realized that I, a high intuitive, was about to launch six new projects. And if I did that I would crash. There was a clue in the dream. Divide the projects three and three. So, I put three projects on the back burner and the Institute began to sail.

Conclusion

The discovery of silence, meditation, dreams, and Jung have re-awakened mythos and the experience of the Divine for me. Dreams have provided guidance all along the way, but it was only after I took dreams seriously that they took me seriously and could become a guide for me. All of this wisdom is coming from an autonomous Source that is beyond me, but speaks within me. In this light dreams deserve to be rediscovered and honoured again in the Church – as 'God's forgotten language'.

References

Armstrong, K. (2001), *The Battle for God: A History of Fundamentalism*, New York: Ballantine Books.

Johnson, R. A. (1991), *Owning your Own Shadow: Understanding the Dark Side of the Psyche*. New York: HarperCollins.

Dream Narrative 2

No Leaf Falls from a Tree Unnoticed[1]
Dreams and Stories of a Condemned Murderer

WOUTER KOEK VAN EGMOND

Translated by H. A. M. Zwemmer

Let me tell you Richard's story. I have learned a lot from Richard. He was a detainee in the prison where I worked as a pastor, and when we met in this capacity we entered into a conversation and we kept each other company for some time; a time in which Richard was confronted with the most extreme limits of (his) life, and during which he, like no one else, made an appeal for my solidarity.

Maybe one could say that the awareness of contingency, the restrictions of human existence, is decided by at least two fundamental experiences. First of all comes the experience of death: the definite loss of people around us, especially people who are dear to us. This forces us to deal with the inescapable fact of our own mortality. Consciously or unconsciously, all that we undertake, everything we are, is being limited and decided by this. But there is more that limits and decides our comings and goings, our freedom, our complete human existence. It is also our responsibility towards ourselves and each other, and our culpability which serve as the other side to it. Religious people add to this our responsibility and

---

1 Line from a poem, fragmentarily preserved, written by Richard, the principal character in this chapter:

I don't think good or evil exists
I think human beings are looking for something
But they do not know what
. . .
But oh God, good and evil do exist!
No leaf falls from a tree unnoticed.
. . .
And our names are written
On the sidewalks of Amsterdam
In the gutter.

culpability towards God. No matter how, our freedom stops when the other/Other asks us for an answer.

This is why I call the Bible the *holy* Scriptures, for all I read in it ultimately takes place on the boundaries of human existence. Being human, in all its glory and all its tragedy; that is what it is about, and this has given these stories mythical proportions. By this I mean that these stories belong not just to a historical but more so to a literary reality, the reality of the creative mind, the truth of the 'imagination'. The biblical story becomes truth the moment we see that it is *our story*: timeless, as it were, raised above the contingency of history. It confirms us in our contingency, because the story raises our consciousness. The biblical story calls for an answer and thus lifts us up out of our contingency.

Probably the same could be said of our dreams. Dreams are outside the contingency of history for they take no part in our actual daily reality. They belong to the domain of our inner world. But the moment we take our dreams seriously, seeing that they are truly expressing something real about ourselves, they hold up a mirror to our faces, and make us conscious of ourselves. Dreams show us the 'inner side' of our story, and this makes them true, just like the great myths of humankind. In our dreams we express ourselves, and we call for an answer.

Richard's story

I would like to tell you Richard's story. Of course I have changed his name, and the name of the victim is also fictitious. But the story is true. Richard has encountered the ultimate boundaries of being human: the boundary of death and the boundary of guilt. And Richard dreams; a dream repeats itself night after night, and he has a dream that liberates him. Richard discovers that the biblical story is his story. He experiences in it a kinship, a recognition of his life, his contingency, and who he is. And so the biblical story is able to set him free.

Richard must have been about 26 years of age when I first met him. I was a junior prison pastor, he was an experienced jailbird. He grew up in one of the nineteenth-century quarters of Amsterdam Old West, moving later to New West. He comes from a broken family. He never knew his father well and lives with his mother most of the time. Richard is a jailbird with a reputation. He and his buddies have contributed their share to insecurity on the streets and to the crime figures in Amsterdam. It was not only vandalism and so-called common petty crimes that were included in their repertoire, but also robberies and hold-ups and they were not afraid to use the force of guns. Feelings of remorse were never under discussion. Richard explains with pride that his friends refer to him as 'a great madman'. Also in the penitentiary institutions, where he spent most of his young life, he is perfectly able to look after himself. He does not deny that his stay in jail is difficult, but he knows how to conquer his negative feelings by making himself 'at home' as much as possible. All efforts to get Richard on 'the straight and narrow path' fail. He argues that he can only live the way he does, and he considers prison sentences and detentions as a sort of 'business risk'.

During his last but one detention Richard is serving his time for a very serious offence: murder. And not just murder, but the murder of his best friend Frankie, his brother in crime. Even during his stay in the Arrivals Department of the prison the story about this crime is spreading round the whole institution. The first conversation Richard has with the pastor is not about the offence, but about the fact that several wardens congratulated him on his deed. Frankie had a bad reputation in penitentiary Holland, and everyone is happy they have got rid of him – thanks to Richard! But Richard finds this unbelievable. To him it remains murder, the murder of his best friend, and for him this is difficult to come to terms with.

After two or three conversations Richard brings himself to tell the pastor exactly what happened. During a night out joyriding in a stolen car, Richard, Frankie, a friend and a girlfriend, under the influence of alcohol and amphetamines, are involved in a fight. Along a motorway they turn off and a knifing follows, in which Richard kills Frankie. According to the investigators' reports it happened with a knife half a metre long. On Frankie's body there were 59 stab wounds. Despite it happening in the early hours, dozens of car drivers must have witnessed the events, but nobody stopped. Once Richard told the pastor this story, he was able to tell it to his lawyer and he made a full confession. Richard calls this conversation with the pastor his 'confession'.

For Richard there is quite a lot to cope with. He has a murder on his conscience, and the victim of this murder is his best friend. He will have to go through a process of coming to terms with his guilt and he has to mourn, for the two cannot be separated. But there is more. He is irritated by the way others have reacted to what has happened; all those car drivers who just drove by, for example. And the police who name a(n) (arbitrary) number of 59 stab wounds – how did they come to this number? It does not fit in with his own recollection of the knifing. And the reactions inside the jail, from staff and inmates: approval, and respect for a killer who matters apparently – Richard does not want this. Richard has much to deal with, but his experience of what has happened (his inner world) does not correspond with the reactions he gets from the outer world.

An important first step is the confessional conversation with the pastor and the full confession to the police. Once the Prosecution Counsel has made their case there is room for a second step in the twofold process of dealing with what he has done. Richard dreams. And he dreams repeatedly, every night, the same dream.

He only has to close his eyes and he looks at Frankie, who looks at him. In the dream Richard tries to explain to Frankie what has happened, to give an explanation or to justify what he has done. But he fails. Frankie keeps looking at him, and remains silent.

During the talk with the pastor Richard says: 'It was bound to happen. It just had to happen at one time. It was him or me. Well, finally it was him . . .' When the pastor keeps on asking about the nature of their friendship, seen in the light of this remark, Richard admits that he and Frankie were very close. So close that Richard's mother had once said they might as well marry each other! The pastor makes an inner note that a slight measure of (latent) homosexuality could have played a part for one of them. No matter how, Richard tells that if one of the two would pay too much attention to a third person, for example by going out, this would be seen as strong rivalry. It would always lead to tension and quarrels. Something of the like must have played a part on the night of the murder, regarding a girlfriend in their company. But Richard insists that this was no more than a provocation, but certainly not the cause of the knifing. The real cause lies in the fact that they were so close. After several conversations the pastor increasingly gets the impression that those two were so close, and looked after each other so often, that Richard especially could not handle it any more: the strong friendship turned into a blazing urge to destroy.

Richard's recurring dream seems to confirm this. The picture of Frankie, the image of Richard's consciousness, talks to him silently, again and again. Richard's answer is always the same: It was inevitable; it finally just had to happen. It was me or you. Well, it became you! But it could just as well have been me. Please forgive me, please . . . But the dream keeps coming back, which means that this way Richard will find no forgiveness for his deed. His subconscious tells him that the excuse he is trying to make is no real excuse. His conscience keeps accusing him, more so every time in the vision Frankie keeps silent. Richard cannot ignore the dream, or silence his conscience. Richard asks, consciously or unconsciously, for justice, which he cannot give himself. Then something remarkable happens . . .

The Passion of Christ and how life really is

Palm Sunday draws near, the day we traditionally read the Passion of Jesus Christ by Matthew. The pastor has also planned to read this text during the prison service, but not on his own as it is too much text for one person. He asks Richard and a fellow inmate (jailed for homicide) to help him. They will read aloud a part of the text in turn. The pastor has chosen these two men for their reading skills, and he knows them both well enough to be sure that they will not make a 'mess' of it. In retrospect the service turns out to be a very special occasion for all involved.

The organization of the service that Sunday was plain. In the middle of the church was a life-sized wooden cross. There were no other ornaments or symbols that would divert the attention of the community. The pastor and the two detainees read the Passion. After that follows a short meditation by the pastor, the intercessory prayers and a modest communion service. During the service the atmosphere is loaded: all present know Richard, his reputation and the offence for which he has been locked up. The fact that he, of all people, dares to stand in front of the troops and read from the Bible makes a deep impression.

Afterwards, the reaction of Richard is remarkable. The pastor compliments both men and both, independently, answer the same: 'It was heavy. You picked for me exactly the parts of the text that referred to my situation!' The pastor denies this, claiming he divided the sections according to how it was printed. Still, he notes that apparently both men have recognized something in the text and that there is a matter of identification. These thoughts are confirmed ten days later . . .

A meeting of Catholic and Protestant prison ministers takes place. The pastor decides to make the celebration of Palm Sunday the topic of discussion of this meeting. In consultation with his colleagues he invites both detainees to join the meeting. Again during this event it is noticed how much both inmates recognize themselves in the story of the sufferings of Jesus Christ. Important items are Judas' betrayal, the denial by Peter and the fact that Jesus had been deserted by his friends. In this context Richard says something remarkable: 'I would have liked to be Jesus' friend . . . but I am afraid I would have turned out to be his Judas!' This is for all present something to think about.

One of the colleagues regrets the fact that the pastor limited himself to the Passion: should he not have pointed towards Easter, the triumph of life over death? Richard's reaction is vehement: 'You professionals are always too quick with your answers, that all will be fine again and so on. But let it just be said for once how life really is!'

It is striking how Richard identifies himself with the biblical story. Reading out loud he undergoes the text as something that refers to him: treason, denial, being left alone, being killed, dying . . . it had become his story. And by reflecting out loud he becomes aware of himself and his acts. He was Frankie's best friend, and became his Judas. But in this self-awareness, this guilt-awareness, he is no longer alone, for the biblical story turns out to be his ally. And his invitation to the other participants to become also his ally is fierce. By not coming too soon with answers, victory, resurrection and Easter – 'Let it just be said how life really is!' – Richard asks us emphatically to stand next to him, to be serious about his sufferings and . . . to his guilt. Only those who dare to stand next to him will be able to join him in his search for forgiveness, reconciliation, towards Easter.

Dreaming about sunflowers

The first step has been made. Some days later Richard has a second dream:

> He sees enormous sunflowers. The flowers carry the faces of his friends and girlfriends. The face of Frankie, however, is not among them.

Richard feels that somehow this dream tells him something important. At first sight it seems easy to explain the meaning: boyfriends and girlfriends mean life, light (sun) and growth (flowers). When the pastor suggests this, Richard does not fully agree, though he agrees to think about it. Maybe the positive sunny side of life that is offered in this dream is still premature for Richard. A new solidarity of girlfriends and friends, the human world, society, is perhaps too soon for Richard. Perhaps one day he will see himself in a dream as a sunflower.

Nevertheless a step has been taken: the repetitive dream, of a non-speaking conscience that could not be silenced, is now gone. From this point on Richard can be assisted by the pastor on his way towards justice, forgiveness and reconciliation. However, it is not a path without obstacles. Some weeks later Richard receives his final sentence. He has been found guilty by the judge and is sentenced to five years of imprisonment. It is notably little for such a serious crime. Evidently Richard is happy not having to do many years in jail, but at the same time he considers this sentence as unjust. He suspects the judge has been influenced by the thought that the victim also had a heavily criminal past, and maybe must have thought something like 'Good riddance to bad rubbish'. But on the other hand it is possible that the judge had listened to Richard's lawyer, who declared at the trial that Richard had strong regrets and was having great difficulty coming to terms with the loss of his best friend. No matter how it transpired, the sentence is not in keeping with Richard's sense of justice.

Finally, Richard is transferred to a penitentiary institution. The pastor is no longer there to accompany him on the journey on which such an important first step has been made. The day before his departure Richard gives the pastor the address of his mother, where he himself always lived when he was free. 'If ever you hear about me, that I am getting married or whatever, please get in touch. Would you do that for me?' The pastor agrees but suspects that it is not marriage that Richard is thinking about, but a possible act of revenge by Frankie's family or friends. Is Richard thinking of his own death and funeral? Has he, in the silence of his heart, pronounced his own death sentence?

Years later the pastor meets Richard again in the house of detention. This time it is for a much smaller crime. The first thing he says to the pastor: 'Sorry, but I just had to spend more time in prison.' Apparently the five-year sentence for murder had not been enough . . .

Conclusion

What have we witnessed here?

Richard has been confronted by the boundaries of being human: the death of his friend has broken the ties with his fellow humans, and it rests on his own conscience. How final in the first instance this can be is made clear by the repetitive dream; every effort to ask for explanation, forgiveness or reconciliation, every demand to restore friendly bonds and social coherence, is met with silence. Out of this existential loneliness (a loneliness enforced by the reaction of the wardens and his fellow-inmates, the drivers on the highway, the report of the police and the sentence of the judge), Richard calls for solidarity. This solidarity he finds in recognizing himself in the story of the Passion of Christ, and he poses his question to the pastor and his colleagues: do not come too quickly with answers, but let it just be said how life really is!

This existential call for solidarity, human bonds and friendship appears in a second dream: a dream of sunflowers with the faces of his circle of friends. This dream acts as a vision in which Richard is invited to go the way of penance (maybe shaped in the form of a subsequent imprisonment, for which he committed a lesser crime), and finally forgiveness and reconciliation. The pastor can accompany him on this journey up to the point where Richard finds the strength to travel on his own.

Does this mean that Richard's guilt receives forgiveness, and that he can go on with his life bearing this guilt, and that from this present situation he will be able to join again the human world?

In my opinion Richard has met with yet another personal limit. 'I would have liked to be Jesus' best friend . . . but I am afraid I would have turned out to become his Judas,' he says. Is Richard truly capable of friendship, solidarity, faithfulness? He longs for it, but the one who comes too close, has had it! How free is he? This applies to all men and women. How hard it can be to live as truly free human beings . . . The ancient stories of the Bible know everything about it . . .

PART 2

Dreams and Religion:
Empirical Data, Theory and Reflections

5

Varieties of Religious Dreaming

Some Explorations from the Point of View of Descriptive Psychology of Religion

BARBARA KONING

Introduction

This chapter explores the prototypical situation of 'a religious person who is sharing a dream', and offers reflections for pastors. It is a contribution from the science of psychology of religion to the larger field of descriptive empirical practical theology (Van der Ven 1998).

Dreams are a universal phenomenon. Every day when people sleep they dream several times, irrespective of whether or not they remember this imagery on waking. When it comes to dreams, particularly in caregiving contexts in the western world, the primary point of view is that they may express emotional dynamics. The question of the individual's meaning-making system, and how clients personally deal with their life situations and emotions, may go unnoticed. In this chapter I acknowledge that dreams may reveal emotional dynamics, but reverse the emphasis. In the background I trust pastors will understand their professional role when it comes to dealing with emotions. For now I want to bring the presumed religious frame of reference of a client to the foreground and explore some of the possible interfaces with dreams. I aim at identifying – in a method-ical way – some of the basic phenomena in this area as an orientation for pastors. I offer this as a working model I have developed during the course of years of working with dreams in settings of practising pastoral counsel-ling and spiritual direction.[1]

As the author of this chapter I assume the beneficial potential of paying attention to dreams. In this book as a whole and in reports throughout the literature on dreams, we find many indications of such beneficial effects resulting from dream work. These include the expansion of the meaning system, structural qualitative shifts in personality dynamics and an overall

---

1 See also my website listing resources: www.dreampilgrims.com.

higher quality of life (cf. Rossi 1985). In addition I make use of auto-biographical reports of people working with their own dreams.

I discern and explore four different types of interfaces between reli-giosity and dreams, with illustrations, and conclude with comments on including dreams in pastoral conversations.

Religious elements and themes in the characteristics of shared dreams

Starting with a singular dream, as a first interface with religiosity, we can easily recognize the possibility of religious elements appearing in the contents or style forms of the shared dreams. For example, in the dream characters we may meet a priest, monk, member of the dreamer's congre-gation, mother Mary, angels, and many others. Settings or objects may appear in dreams that are needed to perform all kinds of religious rituals in waking life, such as a church building, a baptistery, a candle, a cross, a hymnal and more. Or we may recognize elements that traditionally belong to saints in the history of the Church or relate to Bible stories, like the heart of St Francis of Assisi or an up and down movement resembling that of the angels climbing the ladder to heaven in Jacob's dream (Gen. 28.12). Also in the storylines and plots of the shared dream we may recognize a theme closely related to religious motifs and motivations, like 'forgive-ness', 'longing for union', 'travelling to a destination', and more.

Using scientific terminology here can be helpful for a more systematic methodical approach. We will consider the conceptual aspects of content and style form separately.

Categories for the possible contents of dreams

At the most elementary level of possible contents of single dreams the Hall/Van De Castle coding system[2] – which treats a dream report as a story or play – has identified the following 12 categories:

1 *Characters*, such as animals, men and women, friends, strangers and mythical beings.
2 *Social interactions*, such as aggression, friendliness and sexuality.

---

2 Source: www2.ucsc.edu/dreams/Info/content_analysis.html.

3 *Activities*, such as thinking, talking and running.

4 *Successes and failures.*

5 *Misfortunes and good fortunes.*

6 *Emotions*, such as happy, sad and embarrassed.

7 One or more *Settings*, such as indoors vs outdoors, and familiar vs unfamiliar.

8 *Objects*, such as chairs, cars, streets and body parts.

9 *Descriptive modifiers*, such as tall, fast and crooked.

10 *Temporal references.*

11 *Elements from the past.*

12 *Food and eating references.*

All categories allow for connotations to religiosity.

Examples of religious contents of dreams

Some casuistic examples follow. In this chapter as a whole, those dreams mentioned without a literature reference stem from personal communications and are being cited with permission of the dreamers.

> I am sitting in a circle of people around my minister who is leading a celebration. Suddenly he is giving me a kind of musical instrument: I understand I will have to accompany the worship. The instrument is broken and it doesn't work properly. I can't fulfil the task given to me and I feel embarrassed about that. (Woman, aged 47)

> I am in India and meet an Eastern monk. I feel humble, for I know he is a holy man. He says: 'You will get whatever you need and know: whatever you don't get, you won't need.' (Man, aged 50)

> I am entering a room on the first floor of a large building. I will be joining the church service that is going to be held here. Suddenly I realize I am lacking my hymnal. I start walking around to find it, but I can't. (Woman, aged 42)

Categories for the semantic characteristics of dreams

Alongside the characteristics of content, we can look at the characteristics of the semantics of shared dreams. To a certain degree dreams can become construed as a narrative – but let us keep in mind that this need not necessarily be the case. As story-like expressions we then may recognize dynamic connections between content elements such as an *exposé* given at the start; *developing storylines*; one or more *crises*, each with one or more plots and resolutions; or merely dead ends with abrupt changes in settings and casts; *metaphors* captured in picture-language; and/or main *themes* and *motif(s)* around which elements of the composition somehow appear to be arranged.

Example of a potential religious core motif of 'not able to reach the criteria for acceptance' in the storyline of a dream

> I am on holiday in a foreign country. A bus arrives which is going to take us home. I find myself not acceptable. To undertake the journey, I will need to get washed and dressed up first and also then take care I will have had a meal . . . (Man, aged 67)

The story continues that when he tries to do so, he fails and gets stuck in a bunch of complicating difficulties; but we leave those details out.

Pastoral exploration of religious elements in dreams

Here, we don't need to make any premature speculations about the question of whether or not – after a process of interpretation – the religious elements as such turn out to convey a religious meaning for the dreamer. From this viewpoint we simply want to notice the *possibility* of finding religious content in the imagery, motifs and narrative dynamics in the dreams of religious as well as secular clients (for further reading see Hall 1993; Bulkeley 1995; 2009). We suggest that pastors choose a strategy for conversations that allows for some space to tentatively explore these elements further. For example, Bulkeley and Bulkley (2005, pp. 46–51) suggest that pastors ask 'specifying questions' about the various elements of dreams.

The effects of religious ideation

For our inquiry we move on to consider the dreamer and their specific religion and style of religiosity. Here we find two possible interfaces with dreams, discriminating the effects in two directions.

To begin with, for religious people from all kinds of religious traditions their beliefs can influence their attitude towards dreams and dreaming (Bulkeley 2008; Kelsey 1978). Among other themes, answers to questions such as the following can play a role.

- Given the fact that dreams can be considered as meaningful, are dreams divinely inspired?
- Can we perceive them as a channel through which God speaks to us?
- And if we answer this with a yes, is this the case with every single dream or with only some dreams – and how can we know the difference?

Further, we can note that certain religious practices closely related to core beliefs can heighten the susceptibility for remembering dreams. People performing an evening prayer may be 'incubating' a dream (Delaney 1991). People who are fasting may be withholding temporarily from certain regular foods and drinks that can affect their consciousness (like alcohol or caffeine) and then may find they are remembering more dreams than usual.

So within this configuration we would want to take a closer look at the way in which religious ideas and beliefs (including related practices/ experiences) affect ideas and beliefs about and sensibilities with respect to dreams (including practices and experiences).

Examples of religiously motivated ideation affecting dreams and dream life

Focusing on the array of possible Christian views with respect to topics such as the type of authority of the Bible, perceptions of God's indwelling presence and of human nature, and theological understanding of secular culture, we can find a variety of answers. To mention a few, these include the evangelical author Greg Cynaumon (2002, pp. xviii, xix), who was on the staff of a mainstream evangelical Bible-teaching church. He considers that 5%–10% of the dream cases he has studied to be examples of divine intervention. In his opinion the other dreams originate from the human unconscious, but he still considers those as worthwhile to attend to as well, especially for reasons of promoting mental health. In contrast, the Roman Catholic Benedictine monk Anselm Grün (1993, p. 5) clearly states: 'there are three spheres . . . through which God meets us . . . and speaks to us; there are our thoughts and feelings, our body and our dreams . . . Above all . . . on the spiritual journey we have to consider the three spheres in

95

order to perceive God's word personally.' Grün suggests that for any dream Christians can put the question into words in a prayer asking what it is God is wanting to show to them.

Faith as the domain of application

Conversely, provided that a dreamer takes the messages from their dreams seriously, the interpretation attributed to dreams concretely can influence elements within their religiosity-as-lived on a daily basis.

In this type of inquiry we first purposely distinguish between the religious and secular domains of an individual's life. We acknowledge that these may permeate one another all the time, but for now we want to focus selectively on the possibility of direct applications to the more narrow domain of lived religion. As a next step we differentiate the concept of 'religiosity'. This characteristic can cover a wide variety of different concrete elements. With a well-trained view, many of these can be grouped together and then accumulated as belonging to one of the following four psychological dimensions:

1 *Cognitive.* Elements are derived from several sources of religious knowledge – like creeds, Bible texts, informed knowledge about the background and history of the tradition, clear moral guidelines, such as the Ten Commandments.
2 *Behavioural.* Elements are related to performance of collective and individual religious rituals and practices, whether prescribed or voluntary – like attending worship services, or private prayer before bedtime or meals, or applying religious ethical standards.
3 *Experiential.* Elements are sensed experientially as religious in character, such as having found a sense of purpose and meaning in life, a feeling of belonging, direct mystical experiences and revelations, moral emotions, ecstasy or trance.
4 *Social.* The practising of religion in one way or another will take place within a matrix of relationships, whether engaged in profoundly or superficially – like the sharing with individual fellow practitioners, forms of participation in small subgroups, and identification with the larger religious community.

With the help of this differentiation we then are able to ask ourselves specific sub-questions about how the interpretation of a specific dream can be applied to these domains of religiosity.

We find casuistic material that discusses the following questions throughout this book, and the chapters that illustrate the points are cited to direct readers to them. Can dreams and how our clients live and work with them foster or challenge a personalized understanding of creeds or background knowledge which is foundational for the dreamer's religious tradition (see Graham and Creaven, Chapter 7; Haden, Dream Narrative 1, about understanding call and vocation)? Can dreams enrich individual or communal religious practices like prayer life, reading the Bible (Nelson, Chapter 11), moral decision-making (Korthals Altes, Dream Narrative 6); contribute to an enlivened experience of divine presence in everyday life (Koning, Dream Narrative 4) and deepened interpersonal relationships with members of the religious community (Haden, Dream Narrative 1; Nelson, Chapter 11; Parker, Dream Narrative 5)?

Examples of applying the interpretation of a certain dream symbolism to one's faith

Behavioural domain – enriching the practice of prayer

The Jewish author Vanessa Ochs describes the following dream from her own experience, together with an interpretation (Ochs and Ochs 2003, p. 50), from which I select some fragments:

> Once again I have my recurring dream. I am living in a house and, while walking through, discover there is an entire wing I have not even noticed before . . . It's all mine and it's all wonderful, and I am happy to have it.

> . . . When I try to interpret this dream, I decide it links my soul to a teaching of the Hassidic master of the Baal Shem Tov, who taught that each day holds at least a hundred opportunities to express gratitude for what we have. How little we need to wish for when the most valuable treasures we have are already ours: the qualities of our character, the gift of our body, the many people we are connected to, and the bounty of things that sustains us and gives us joy. My dream puts me in touch with a primary spiritual goal: to be vigilant about noticing my blessings and expressing my gratitude for them.

Experiential domain

The episcopal priest and Jungian counsellor John Sanford (1968/1989, p. 30) shares the example of a woman named Margaret who was dreaming about a shower of white square papers coming down from heaven like snow. She carried with her an emotional burden of severe feelings of guilt for something she had done. So far in the pastoral sessions she had not felt confident that she had been forgiven by God. The pastor felt he was allowed to say: 'Well, maybe God wants to show to you in the dream that your sins have been washed white as snow.' And now she finally could accept the message. Through the dream she could accept that God had forgiven her. Through the interpreted dream, the conceptual knowledge of 'forgiveness' changed into a lived experience.

Mystical fruits

Within the context of the last configuration we now take a closer look at the fact that people who are doing dream work may recognize certain kinds of qualitative shifts in their state of being – whether incidental experiences or structural changes – which are felt to be of an intrinsically mystical character, stemming from a Divine Source. Along their journey of doing dream work, they may find themselves in a process of self-confrontation and making fundamental changes to the way they live their lives – a process of purification and *metanoia* (cf. Johnson 1991) – perhaps becoming healed, being guided, purified, renewed and transformed (cf. Barash 2000; Sanford 1978). Let us call this interface 'mystical fruits'.

Before giving some examples, we note the difference with our previous interfaces. These mystical fruits can be recognized by dreamers even if the dreams themselves do not contain religious content (our first configuration). Neither is this type of experience realization of having transcended a former state of consciousness or physical condition, reserved for people who practise a religion (our second configuration), as one example below will show. Nor is it required that the interpretations of separate dreams be applied to one's religiosity (our third configuration): the meaning found in dreams can be applied to domains of 'secular meaning', like one's attitudes to friendships or being more creative or any other domain. But, of course, the chance that a label such as 'religious' will be attached to these fruits is probably somewhat more likely when a dreamer already has a basic religious outlook on life and experiential sensibilities.

For a terminological instrument the classic work of Evelyn Underhill (1990/1919) offers a helpful tool. Underhill discerns and explores three cyclic processes of development involved in the Mystic Way: awakening, purification and illumination of the self. Empirical examples as discussed here suggest that dreams may somehow relate to these dynamics.

Two illustrations of mystical fruits

Sanford (1978) shares a series of eight specific dreams of his client Martin, and the interpretations that arose during the pastoral conversations. As a result of the whole experience, Martin was radically renewed (1978, pp. 122–3). 'His religious feeling and orientation returned. He was able to find a spiritual home in his church and became once more a practicing Roman Catholic. The changes in him that his dreams helped bring about have proved to be lasting.' A variety of images is discussed by Sanford in his presentation of the series of dreams, among which we recurrently find images of changing places and a core motif of 'being on a journey'. Concrete examples of symbolism, in chronological order of the sequence of the dreams, included leaving the house of his parents, being on sacred ground in the desert, hitchhiking on a journey, building and furnishing a new house in a new place, travelling by motorbike.

Kathleen Sullivan (1998) wrote a personal 'dreamography', about a process of 35 years of restoration of her life through the workings of the dream (1998, p. xi). After a highly disturbing nightmare which she considered to be a wake-up call, she started to keep records of all her dreams. Among her many dreams, a recurrent image captures her attention, which unfolds in two series, described in her book. In the 'Reunion' series her dreams are determined to let her know that she will reunite with someone, a person without a clear name whom she only vaguely remembers from her high-school years. The 'Victor Biento' series, a simultaneous set, presents her evolving relationship with that 'someone', who provides guidance that eventually leads to a major transformation. All domains of her existence were affected and restored or renewed: body, emotions, convictions, relationships, spirituality. I limit myself to mentioning her bodily healing from a chronic bacterial infection and its upsetting facial outbreaks (Sullivan 1998, p. 105). The final recovery resulted from working with symbolism that healed her lack of self-esteem by being tenderly embraced by Victor Biento (29 May 1991). 'My willingness to show my authentic uncovered face in public in this dream was reinforced by the deep compassion and total acceptance of Victor, that energy so long sought for and so highly valued' (1998, p. 106). When the author incubated another dream to ask for specific guidance in the process of further physical healing, her following dream raised the issue of making amends to someone named Paul whom she had betrayed 30 years before (1998, p. 114). This mission she put into concrete practice in daily life through writing letters and meditating. Taken together, her dream experiences of being guided and healed and renewed change her perspective on human existence. Having an atheistic worldview at the start, she later consciously adopted a spiritual-religious outlook on life.

Some concluding remarks

When it comes to the emotional dynamics revealed through dreams (the dominant perspective in western situations of caregiving), people don't expect their pastors to be master-interpreters of underlying unconscious structures. And likewise pastors should not assume that they need a very specific, highly developed expertise for that type of conversation. It is already of great value when a pastor is present to people's life stories in a supportive way, and to the feelings and experiences the dreamer wants to share: by listening intently, being an interested and empathic witness and helping to explore what's on the table by means of open questions.

But what religious clients do expect from their pastors, and also long for, is that they highlight, understand and can put into words the ways in which religious life is involved and is making sense. Aspects of the dream as told can offer opportunities for a very meaningful sharing concerning the faith of the client. Religious elements that were part of the dream content, or tentatively recognized in the motifs and structure of the story, can be explored (our first configuration); religion may have shaped a frame of reference, or the attitudes towards and sensibilities with respect to dreams, and evoked the remembrance of dreams (our second configuration); the interpretation of a dream can have consequences for some part of the dreamer's faith (our third configuration); and sometimes profound life changes brought about by dream life may be the area where faith essentially and dynamically is being experienced as a lived truth (our fourth configuration). When we change terms like faith, religion and religiosity into 'worldview' or 'meaning system', these ideas can be applied to secular clients, too. Dreams can be a portal to very meaningful sharing about matters of existence.

We can claim space for such a pastoral conversation when we take into consideration that there is not *one* true interpretation of a dream – several interpretations are possible at the same time, meaning that all can be true (Hebbrecht in this volume). And for such a type of counselling ministers have a well-trained ear to offer and have often undergone a thorough grounding in explaining texts and narratives. According to Bart Koet, in the past the interpretation of Scriptures and of dreams were related; and nowadays the same hermeneutics still count and are being put into practice (e.g. Koet 2006, and his chapters in this volume). For an excellent demonstration of the simultaneity of many layers of meanings of dreams, see Taylor (2009, Chapter 2).

Leaving the topic of dreams solely to psychologists is like leaving a sacred piece of the garden of the soul completely untended, as psychologists often do not engage religiously with dreams at all. Dreams deserve the warmest interest of pastors.

References

Barash, M. (2000), *Healing Dreams: Exploring the Dreams that Can Transform Your Life*, New York: Riverhead Books.

Bulkeley, K. (1995), *Spiritual Dreaming: A Cross Cultural and Historical Journey*, New York: Paulist Press.

Bulkeley, K. (2008), *Dreaming in the World's Religions: A Comparative History*, New York: New York University Press.

Bulkeley, K. (2009), 'The Religious Content of Dreams: A New Scientific Foundation', in *Pastoral Psychology* 58, pp. 93–106.

Bulkeley, K. and Bulkley, P. (2005), *Dreaming Beyond Death: A Guide to Pre-death Dreams and Visions*, Boston: Beacon Press.

Cynaumon, G. (2002), *God Still Speaks Through Dreams: Are You Missing His Messages?* Nashville: Thomas Nelson.

Delaney, G. (1991), *Living Your Dreams: Using Sleep to Solve Problems and Enrich Your Life*, New York: HarperCollins.

Grün, A. (1993), *Dreams on the Spiritual Journey*, Schuyler: BMh Publications.

Hall, J. A. (1993), *The Unconscious Christian: Images of God in Dreams*, New York: Paulist Press.

Johnson, R. A. (1991), *Owning Your Own Shadow: Understanding the Dark Side of the Psyche*, New York: Harper One.

Kelsey, M. (1978), *Dreams: A Way to Listen to God*, New York: Paulist Press.

Koet, B. J. (2006), *Dreams and Scripture in Luke-Acts: Collected Essays*, Leuven: Peeters.

Ochs, V. L. and Ochs, E. (2003), *The Jewish Dream Book: The Key to Opening the Inner Meaning of Your Dreams*, Woodstock VT: Jewish Lights Publishing.

Rossi, E. L. (1985), *Dreams and the Growth of Personality: Expanding Awareness of Personality*, 2nd edn, New York: Brunner/Masel.

Sanford, J. A. (1968/1989), *Dreams: God's Forgotten Language*, New York: Harper San Francisco.

Sanford, J. A. (1978), *Dreams and Healing: A Succinct and Lively Interpretation of Dreams*, New York: Paulist Press.

Sullivan, K. (1998), *Recurring Dreams: A Journey to Wholeness*, Freedom CA: Crossing Press.

Taylor, J. (2009), *The Wisdom of Your Dreams: Using Dreams to Tap into Your Unconscious and Transform Your Life*, New York: Tarcher/Penguin.

Underhill, E. (1990/1919), *Mysticism: The Preeminent Study in the Nature and Development of Spiritual Consciousness*, New York: Image Books.

Van der Ven, J. A. (1998), *Practical Theology: An Empirical Approach*, Leuven: Peeters.

6

The Wonder of Dreams
How Dreams Advance in Contemporary Miracle Stories

ANNE-MARIE KORTE

Introduction

Between spring 2003 and autumn 2007 the Dutch Catholic Broadcasting Company (KRO), part of the Dutch public broadcasting system, invited people to send in stories about self-experienced miracles, and presented a selection of these stories in a television programme entitled *Miracles Exist!* In the filmed versions a staged reconstruction of the wondrous event was presented and the story tellers were interviewed and invited to recount the story in their own words. When studying this extensive collection of contemporary miracle stories, further detailed below, I found that dreams play a remarkable part in these narratives. This finding makes these stories of interest for a more systematic exploration, as presented here. In some of these miracle stories, dreams even feature prominently, as is the case in the following three examples:

Mother saves child (filmed dream story from KRO collection)

Since she was 12 a women now in her thirties has had a recurring dream. She sees a child slowly disappearing under water in an unknown place located outside. The surface of the water then becomes completely still. She is strongly aware that she cannot do anything to help. This dream has made her afraid of approaching water in outdoor situations: she always passes quickly over bridges and keeps away from the water's edge. As an adult woman and mother of a three-year-old daughter the dream has made a deep impact on her. One morning she takes her child to the neighbours to play. Her little daughter rides her tricycle. Back home the woman feels a great anxiety. While she is busy at home, she is suddenly drawn to the bedroom window. She feels that something or someone forces her to go to the window. She looks outside and sees her daughter on the tricycle riding into a pond between the houses. The child disappears under water and the water closes above her. 'It really happens to me, it really does,' she screams. She runs out and pulls her child out of the water, dragging her from under the tricycle, and saving her life. Her dream never returned.

Forecasted death (filmed dream story from KRO collection)

When he is ten years old, a boy has a wondrous dream about his grandfather, who was an alcoholic living somewhere in a Salvation Army shelter at that time, and who died suddenly a short time later. The boy always wondered what this dream meant, in which he saw so many details of his grandfather's 'home'. Almost ten years later, as a young man he has the opportunity to visit the shelter, where the dream and reality come together. Although he has never been there before, he is able to tell the exact story of his grandfather's last night in the Salvation Army house, as he saw it in his dream ten years earlier. Now he can also come to terms with his grandfather's sad fate: 'He did his very best but I think life was just too heavy for him.'

Recovered sled (filmed dream story from KRO collection)

A young man of 29 tells how as a boy he lost his sled when playing outdoors one winter. He assumed that some other child had taken his sled, but his attempts to find it were not successful. Aware that his parents had little money, he felt very concerned about the lost sled and he cried himself to sleep that night. The same night he saw in a dream the sled standing behind a green gate in the garden of a large house. The next day he went searching again and when he recognized the green gate of a villa in his village he opened the gate and went into the garden. There he found his sled, with his own name tag on it, in the backyard of the house, just as he had seen in his dream.

The programme in which these stories were presented was made by the entertainment division of the Catholic Broadcasting Company, which meant that it did not fall under institutional religious supervision, and it did not have to serve educational aims. For the programme makers, the focus on contemporary miracle stories made it possible to honour the public's interest in emerging and more personalized forms of spirituality (see Partridge 2004; Lynch 2007; Smith 2008), as well as recall the positive connotations that miracles have within classic Roman Catholic spirituality. Actually, the attractiveness and exceptionality of the story and the credibility of the story teller were touchstones for selection and broadcasting. Stories from all kinds of religious backgrounds were told in the programme, but most stories, as illustrated in those mentioned above, do not have a classic religious frame of reference or refer to religious ideas, texts or practices.

The programme was extraordinarily successful and ran for five seasons. More than 2,500 wondrous experiences were collected by the programme makers, and about 130 of these reported events were filmed and broadcast. The programme had an interactive website where the televised stories could be viewed and discussed; a book was published with a selection of the most popular stories of the series; and a huge congress was organized where the public could meet programme makers, story tellers and researchers from different disciplines studying miracles.

Because of my previous research as a theologian into classical Christian miracle stories and my involvement in interdisciplinary religious studies (see Korte 2000; 2004), I was invited by the Catholic Broadcasting Company to conduct an explorative study into these miracle stories. The files of the programme, based on telephone calls, letters and additional research, were at my disposal for this purpose, and the complete collection of filmed versions was made accessible for this research. A database of 1,700 stories was created and comparative surveys of the narratives were conducted. I described their common traits, and discerned inductively several patterns and typologies in these contemporary miracle stories. This research was inductively conducted and consisted of comparative discursive analysis of the narratives. I also related the narratives to actual cultural and religious developments (see, among others, Houtman and Mascini 2002; Sengers 2005) and to the style and content of the classical miracle stories of western religious traditions (see Walker Bynum 1997; Cavadini 1999; Woodward 2000; de Nie 2003; Goodich 2007). I studied a selection of filmed versions and compared them to their written originals. My overall aim was to discuss the phenomenon of the miraculous in late modern western society on the basis of this collection of narratives. I published a series of articles in which I systematically discussed a number of aspects of this unique collection of narratives to answer questions such as: what do people today call a miracle, which cultural and religious patterns can be found in contemporary self-acclaimed wonder stories, and what do these stories and their common patterns tell about wonderment and belief in modern secularized settings?

The most important common characteristics of the miracle stories in this collection, according to my research, are the following:

- *Individual* (no communal or institutional) *setting.* The stories are predominantly situated in daily and family life; they are often small in scope and very personal in their meaning.
- *Participant's perspective.* The stories are in almost all cases told from the perspective of the person who is addressed and helped by the miraculous event (as distinguished from a neutral or outsider's position).
- *Situation of crisis.* Most stories mention a situation of crisis, such as illness, (imminent) death, endangerment, being lost or abandoned, and report a wondrous (unexpected, amazing, surprising, unheard of) way out of these difficulties.
- *'Restoring' content and effect.* The stories centre around experiences of amazement and disclosure; they often result in the regaining of trust or faith, and in a substantial amount of cases the outcome is that the story tellers feel strengthened, relieved, safe or grateful in a more or less lasting way.

The stories are told by people from various backgrounds, lifestyles and interests. Most story tellers do not mention having a religious affiliation or background (or not having one), and only very few of them state explicitly that they belong to a religious community. Comparing story patterns and discursive characteristics, I identified three main interpretative frameworks in which these stories are told: the story tellers refer to classic religious traditions (15%); they make use of self-constructed spiritual interpretations (63%); or they do not refer to any religious framing at all (22%).[1]

The key words of these narratives – induced by the call of the KRO to send in 'miracle stories' – are *miracle* and *wonder(ment)*, and the story tellers use a variety of expressions and phrases to state what they mean by this. Almost all narrators point to the exceptional and unique character of their wondrous experience and state that the event happened against and above all normal expectations. Many story tellers experience the event as a precious and astonishing gift that is directly addressed to them, as detailed by Copier (2014).

---

1 This classification is constructed with reference to Heelas and Woodhead (2005), Hume and McPhilips (2006), Lynch (2007) and Tweed (2006).

Dreams that warn, predict, announce, reveal or instruct regularly appear in these stories. In about 4% of these miracle stories (studied in three cohorts of 500–600 narratives) dreams fulfil a central role (actually in 73 out of 1,700 cases). The KRO, after finishing the television series on miracle stories, created a separate series for people to tell their dreams and have them explained by a professional dream interpreter (KRO's *dream doctor*). But this series stopped after only a few airings and was much less popular than the one on miracles.

In this chapter I focus on the 73 dream stories in the KRO collection of contemporary miracle narratives. Three of these stories, together indicative for the variety in this category, were presented above. I aim to answer the following questions: what characterizes these dream stories as a genre of contemporary miracle narratives, and do they stand out as a particular group within the KRO collection? What can we learn from debates about the interpretation of biblical miracle stories for the understanding of these contemporary dream stories? And what does it mean that these contemporary dreams are actually regarded as *miraculous*?

The dream stories as a group within KRO's collection of contemporary miracle narratives

A comparative investigation, built on my earlier research into this collection, shows that the dream stories as a group differ in several respects from the other contemporary wonder stories in the KRO collection, namely (1) interpretative frameworks, (2) types of wondrous events, and (3) gender patterns. I will outline these differences and discuss their implications. First, the proportion of dream stories told without any reference to religious discourse or practice is far greater than the average number of stories without these references in the whole collection (see Table 1).

Dreams rarely occur in the miracle stories with explicit reference to classic religious frameworks (Catholicism, Islam, etc.), and they are also less

Frame of reference	Dream stories	Total collection
Classic religious	4% (3 out of 73)	15%
Non-religious	47% (34 out of 73)	22%
Contemporary religious	49% (36 out of 73)	63%

Table 1: Dream stories as a group.

present in miracle stories recounted in terms of a rather general spiritual-izing interpretation (for instance: 'it was an angel that was sent to rescue me'), a category I have labelled 'contemporary religious frame of reference'. An example of a dream story from this latter category is the first one in the introduction to this chapter: here we find a recurring 'warning' dream in combination with the experience that 'someone or something' forces the story teller to look out of the window at the crucial moment.

The two other examples in the introduction are dream stories recounted without any religious reference. In these stories the dream – about the grandfather's shelter and the sled behind the gate – solves a problem. These dreams are experienced as surprisingly meaningful and for their narra-tors they are very precious: they still remember them in detail many years later. The tellers of these stories are not inclined to use religious terms and interpretations in their account, in common with a considerable number of narrators of dream stories more generally. This is probably due to the fact that the personally meaningful dream is a relatively independent and acknowledged narrative genre. In modern western societies a story about a significant dream is not dependent on religious contexts or suppositions for its understanding and recognition. It can stand by itself, and its mean-ing can be grasped without additional explanations – telling your dreams has become a respectable part of therapeutic discourse,[2] as I will discuss further on. But on the other hand telling and sharing personally meaning-ful dreams *publicly* is not very common in modern western societies. Not many arenas offer the opportunity to present and discuss dreams openly, and this also could explain the interest in sending dream stories with no religious references to the KRO programme.

But I think there is another reason why so many dream stories in KRO's miracle collection have a non-religious frame of reference. I propose that the personally meaningful dream functions as a parallel to the experiences of miraculous intervention that many miracle stories relate. Where in sto-ries without dreams this intervention is ascribed to God, saints, angels, deceased family members, or 'a benign power', in stories that centre around a dream the dream takes over this role. The dream itself becomes experienced as a wondrous intervention – although not explicitly iden-tified as such. This could explain why so many dream stories without any religious references have been presented in answer to KRO's call for

---

2 Since Sigmund Freud's book *The Interpretation of Dreams* wash published in 1899, dream interpretation and the subsequently termed dream work is an important part of psy-chotherapeutic practice. See, for example, van Eeden (1913), Flanders (1993), Hill (2004) and Schredl and Wittmann (2005).

contemporary miracle stories. It shows that in the absence of an established context of interpretation and discussion of dreams, the meaningful dream itself tends to become 'wondrous'.

Second, the types of wondrous events related in the dream stories differ in various ways from the typology ascertained in the collection as a whole. The general pattern of the types of miracles is shown in Table 2.

In the dream stories most of these types of miracles are present. The dream, however, creates an extra instance or medium in these stories, in terms of both time and content. The dream does not coincide with the wondrous outcome but announces or affirms this event, or prepares the narrator for it. Warnings, predictions and instructions are part of the dream and the dream provides the narrator with knowledge, insight and clues. The actual outcome of the wondrous event in the dream story resembles those in the other miracle stories of the whole collection: rescue, guidance, signs of deceased loved ones, retrieval of cherished objects, etc. However, miraculous healing, which forms the core of 10% of all the miracle stories, seldom takes place in the dream stories. This type of wonder is very prominent in miracle stories recounted in a classic religious framework. Wondrous healing abounds, for instance, in stories of people who have been on pilgrimage to places such as Lourdes or Mecca (see Korte 2000; 2004; 2014).

Typology of wondrous events	Frequency in total collection
Miraculous rescue	20.0%
Special sign (of guidance)	15.4%
Contact with/sign of deceased person	15.2%
Forecast, premonition	10.4%
Miraculous healing	10.0%
Retrieval (of lost person or object)	7.6%
Miraculous fulfilment of urgent wish	7.4%
Apparition (person, angel, vision, etc.)	5.8%
Contact with 'other reality'	4.8%
Performance as wonder worker	2.4%
Other	1.0%

Table 2: Types of wondrous events.

The dream stories in turn report a type of wonder that is almost absent in the other miracle stories of this Dutch collection. Six dream stories relate predictions about (own or nearby) pregnancy and birth, announcing or revealing the pregnancy itself, the birth date, the gender or the name of the child. This I find notable because anthropological and historical research has demonstrated that in many cultures dreams are the vehicles of announcement of new life and death *par excellence* (see Hume 2002; Keen 2003; Mohkamsing-den Boer 2005; Doniger O'Flaherty 1984; Doniger and Bulkeley 1993).

So it might be no coincidence that precisely in the dream stories of this miracle collection this type of wonder takes the upper hand: almost 40% of the dream stories concern predictions of birth and death of close kin and beloved persons. The second example above, the boy's dream about his grandfather in the shelter, is one of them. The young man's unease in discussing his dream openly for so many years shows again that there is a general lack of opportunity for sharing and discussing dream stories publicly.

Third, the dream stories have particular characteristics when it comes to gender patterns. In the collection as a whole the wondrous events are reported by about 55% women and 45% men. The types of miracles they recount form gendered patterns: male story tellers tend to prevail in wonders of 'rescue', and they have a slight upper hand in stories of 'contact with another reality' and 'performing as miracle worker'. Women predominate in miracle stories of 'contact with the deceased' and 'retrieval of lost objects and persons'. They are also in the majority with 'predictions and appearances', and are slightly more numerous in 'wish fulfilment', 'guiding signs' and 'wondrous healing'. Taken together, ensuring safety and averting danger occur more often in the miracle stories of male narrators, while those of women more often concentrate on fostering enduring relationships and finding spiritual guidance (see Korte 2014).

These patterns, generally speaking, also apply to the group of dream stories. The dream story resulting in a rescue is primarily a male narrative, and the one with clues about pregnancy and birth a woman's story. But in addition the dream stories tend to corrode the rather conventionally gendered patterns in this collection, especially in the case of male narrators. In their dream stories men tell of contact with deceased loved ones and recover lost objects, as shown in the examples above. Also the male tellers demonstrate their competence in various forms of forecast. So it seems that the dream story offers male narrators in particular the opportunity to express publicly their 'extraordinary' (intuitive, non-rational, non-normative masculine) experiences and capacities. This corresponds to the fact that dream stories often have a non-religious frame of reference, in which the share of male narrators is significantly greater than in the other two frameworks. But the dream story, by virtue of its eye-opening and preparatory working, might also offer women a stage to transcend normative gender expectations, by preparing and empowering them to become active and effective in averting danger and threat, for instance, as we encounter in the example of the woman who saves her child from drowning and simultaneously overcomes her fear of smothering water masses.

Contemporary dream stories in the light of the interpretation of biblical dream and wonder stories

In mainstream Christian reflection the religious relevance of dreams is primarily discussed and acknowledged in the context of Bible interpretation. The fact that the biblical literature contains many dream stories, mostly prophetic (predictive) or symbolic (meaningful, educational), has led to the recognition that dreams are an important way to receive divine instructions and advice. In Genesis, for instance, the patriarchs Jacob and Joseph receive many clues and insights about their religious calling via dreams. Dreams are in particular valued in their contribution to the individual growth of faith of the leading male biblical characters: their calling, crisis, renewal and eventual abdication go hand in hand with major dreams. But the possible delusive and misguiding effect of dreams can be found as well. Experiencing religiously inspired dreams can, in biblical texts, become associated with pagan origins and locations – their potential threat for 'true' faith then is palpable. The patriarch Joseph becomes famous for his dreams and dream explanations only when he is under foreign rule in Egypt; his engagement with dreams is described as part of his 'adaptive' survival strategy in a hostile and superstitious environment. Joseph's portrayal also implies that authoritative interpretation by an expert is crucial for the right handling of dreams.

This ambivalence towards the (religious) status and trustworthiness of dreams in biblical texts can also be found in the ensuing Christian stance towards dreams.

Divinely sent dreams were certainly interwoven into the religious fabric and language of Christian religious culture from early times, but they were not the subject of a fully articulated dogma, nor was dream interpretation by the clergy institutionalized in any way.

Dreams have never acquired an established role in the belief or religious ritual of Christian tradition. Dreams do not equal an established or guaranteed way to get in touch with God, and their (authoritative) status and trustworthiness has become increasingly dependent on other authoritative instances, such as formal doctrine, authorized Bible interpretation and ecclesial authority (see Koet 2009).

In the light of this state of affairs two substantive differences in the nature and appreciation of dream stories can be articulated concerning the group of dream stories in the KRO collection. First, noticing that about half these stories are told without any religious reference at all, it is no wonder that the idea of dreams as revealers of divine truth and instruction does not emerge in these dream stories. Contemporary dreams can mediate extraordinary messages, and are often experienced as personally directed at the receiver, but the narrators do not speculate about their sender – their origin does not seem to be of great interest to them. Second, no story teller assumes that professional dream interpreters or religious authorities should be sought to explain these dreams: the narrators consider themselves fully able to understand their own dream. The genre of the contemporary dream story thus at first glance seems to have little in common with its biblical forerunners.

However, contemporary debates on the interpretation of biblical wonder stories offer hermeneutical insights and tools that could be of interest when applied to the study of contemporary dream stories. Current Christian interpretation of biblical wonder stories, both Protestant and Catholic, is increasingly inclined to deploy a strong psychological point of view. This aligns with the cultural tendency to understand religion in western secularized societies primarily as an individually oriented and introspectively anchored practice. In this perspective, miracles belong to the field of individual experiences and inter-subjective events. The relevance and meaning of miracles, then, should be preferably explained in connection to inner or psychic reality and the individual search for orientation in life. Eugen Drewermann (1984), spokesperson for this trend and theologian and psychoanalyst, has strongly advocated the reappraisal of dream, myth and legend in biblical stories to counter the over-rational interpretations of Christian faith in late twentieth-century theology. Drewermann sees the miracle stories of the New Testament as a kind of still life. He compares them in their compactness and wealth of images with dreams: their explanation depends on a very detailed reading and an associative completion. The psychoanalytic approach to dreams informs his exegesis. Following this programme, Drewermann discovers in many biblical miracle stories great inner conflicts related to processes such as coming of age and taking personal and social responsibility. For example, the daughter of Jairus, according to the Gospel of Mark raised by Jesus from the dead, is painted by Drewermann as a girl on the verge of adulthood, who needs to be freed from the grip of her parents' obsessive care. The girl is not really dead – she was only so stifled that she could not continue living. 'Give her something to eat,' Jesus says at the end of this story, and Drewermann (1993) translates: let her grow and mature; do not keep her small and dependent any longer – a message addressed to the parents of the girl and to all overprotective and possessive parents. With this profound psychologizing interpretation of biblical miracle stories Drewermann challenges the modern embarrassment over miracles that has become inherent in western rationalist secularist worldviews. The miracle story is recast as a dream or a movie that offers therapy for the soul, a deeper, better, healed self and possibly also renewed religious involvement. But the question is, does this interpretation also do justice to the uncomfortable and unruly aspects of miracle stories, to the unsettling 'wonder' of biblical and contemporary miracle stories?

The dream stories in the KRO collection could be subjected very well to the psychologizing interpretation that Drewermann proposes, but they are, in my view, more than polite suppliers of life guidance and seismographs of inner turmoil. The dreams announce future events, address fate and destiny, and tell about disasters and horrors that are still to come. The very fact that these narrators find their dreams 'miraculous' shows that there is more to it than just the unlocking of self-knowledge and life's wisdom. The stories reveal something of extraordinary significance. These dreams not only tell something about our unconscious suffering, our deepest desires, our actual self, as Drewermann argues with regard to the biblical miracle stories. The biblical and contemporary dream stories also speak about the as yet unknown future and the always unpredictable social world that surrounds and transcends us, as is evidenced by the large number of dream stories in the KRO collection that contain announcements of birth and death.

Conclusions: The wonder of dreams

Above I noted that the contemporary dream stories in the KRO collection confront us with a paradox: almost half of them are recounted with no religious reference (which is a much higher rate than the average in this large collection) and hardly any narrator speculates about a transcendent origin or meaning of the dream itself. But all tellers of dream stories in this collection do esteem their experience 'wondrous' or 'a miracle'. Of course, this interpretation is invoked by the call of the KRO to send in 'miracle stories'. But in my view several other factors contribute in a substantive way to this labelling.

The fact that these narrators see their experience as miraculous is in the first place related to the status and function of dream stories in contemporary western culture. As we saw, Christian religious institutions did not cultivate the telling of significant or extraordinary dreams by lay persons, and a western secular worldview only recognizes the relevance of personally meaningful dreams as part of therapeutic discourse. Telling and sharing extraordinary dreams *publicly* is not very common in modern western societies. With the lack of a narrative and interpretative cultivation of significant dreams, apart from the therapeutic context, the occurrence of these dreams, in ordinary life tends to become very special and elusive, and makes them look more exceptional than they probably are. The absence of public visibility of open debate on extraordinary dreams stimulates the idea that these dreams are 'wondrous'.

Second, the particular content of these dream stories contributes to this interpretation. The qualification 'miraculous' marks the sensation of a surprisingly felicitous or reassuring outcome, in almost all cases of a problem, deep concern or crisis, an outcome that could not have been reached by conventional means. All narrators talk about experiencing an event that is partly beyond their influence and power: it just happens to them, it comes to them as a gift. The fact that they feel helped or guided and often also personally addressed by the unexpected event underlines its 'wondrous' character, in particular against the background of the modern western emphasis on the individual's responsibility for their own fate (see Beck, Giddens and Lash 1994; Ricoeur 2005; Taylor 2007). Moreover, as stated, I believe that the personally meaningful dream actually functions as a parallel to the experiences of miraculous intervention that many miracle stories relate. Where in stories without dreams this intervention is ascribed to divine or other benign instances, in stories that centre around a dream the dream takes over this role. The dream itself becomes experienced as a wondrous intervention – although not explicitly identified as such.

Third, I argue that the label of 'wonder' might function as a playground for non-normative gendered positions and behaviour. The dream story offers male narrators in particular the opportunity to express publicly their 'extraordinary' (intuitive, non-rational, non-normative masculine) experiences and capacities, but the dream story, by virtue of its eye-opening and preparatory working, might also offer women a stage to transcend normative gender expectations. This could for some be an attractive aspect of telling 'miracle stories', including dreams, as means to negotiate gender roles in the public arena (Korte 2000; 2004; 2014).

Fourth and lastly, the miraculous aspect of contemporary dream stories probably lies in their potential prophetic aspects. The fact that these narrators find their dreams 'miraculous' could mean that these dreams offer them more than an introspective exploration and confrontation, the position taken by Eugen Drewermann in his hermeneutics of biblical miracle stories. These dream stories do more than that: they announce future events, address fate and destiny, and tell about disasters and horrors that are yet to come. Here lies, in my view, the most critical meaning of these dream stories. Psychological approaches take dreams as opportunities to process and relive impactful events. But dreams, as ethnographic research shows, have a broader range of workings. Dreams 'prepare your emotions' and make it possible to act effectively towards both change and acceptance of change. Dreams play an important role in 'rites of passage' and in other significant changes in human life, because they make present the still unknown future and the always unpredictable social world that surrounds and transcends us.

References

Beck, U., Giddens, A. and Lash, S. (1994), *Reflexive Modernization: Politics, Tradition and Aesthetics in the Modern Social Order*, Cambridge: Polity.

Cavadini, J. C., ed. (1999), *Miracles in Jewish and Christian Antiquity: Imagining Truth*, Notre Dame: University of Notre Dame Press.

Copier, J. (2014), 'More Between Heaven and Earth: Awareness of Transcendence and Intentionality in Contemporary Religious Miracle Accounts', Master's Thesis Religious Studies, University of Amsterdam.

Doniger O'Flaherty, W. (1984), *Dreams, Illusion and other Realities*, Chicago: University of Chicago Press.

Doniger, W. and Bulkeley, K. (1993), 'Why Study Dreams? A Religious Studies Perspective', in *Dreaming* 3(1), pp. 69–74.

Drewermann, E. (1984), *Tiefenpsychologie und Exegese (Teil I. Die Wahrheit der Formen: Traum, Mythos, Märchen, Sage und Legende; Teil II. Die Wahrheit der Werke und der Worte: Wunder, Vision, Weissagung, Apokalypse, Geschichte, Gleichnis)*, Olten: Walter-Verlag.

Drewermann, E. (1993), *Hij legde hun de handen op: De wonderen van Jezus*, Zoetermeer: Meinema.

Flanders, S., ed. (1993), *The Dream Discourse Today*, The New Library of Psychoanalysis, Vol. 17, London and New York: Routledge.

Goodich, M. E. (2007), *Miracles and Wonders: The Development of the Concept of Miracle*, Aldershot: Ashgate.

Heelas, P. and Woodhead, L. (2005), *The Spiritual Revolution: Why Religion is Giving Way to Spirituality*, Malden: Blackwell.

Hill, C. E., ed. (2004), *Dream Work in Therapy: Facilitating Exploration, Insight, and Action*, Washington: American Psychological Association.

Houtman, D. and Mascini, P. (2002), 'Why Do Churches Become Empty, While New Age Grows? Secularization and Religious Change in the Netherlands', in *Journal for the Scientific Study of Religion* 41 (3), pp. 455–73.

Hume, L. (2002), *Ancestral Power: The Dreaming, Consciousness, and Aboriginal Australians*, Melbourne: Melbourne University Press.

Hume, L. and McPhilips, K., eds (2006), *Popular Spiritualities: The Politics of Contemporary Enchantment*, Aldershot: Ashgate.

Keen, I. (2003), 'Dreams, Agency, and Traditional Authority in Northeast Arnhem Land', in R. I. Lohman, ed., *Dream Travellers: Sleep Experiences and Culture in the Western Pacific*, New York: Palgrave Macmillan, pp. 127–49.

Koet, B. J. (2009), 'Divine Dream Dilemmas: Biblical Visions and Dreams', in K. Bulkeley, K. Adams and P. Davis, eds, *Dreaming in Christianity and Islam: Culture, Conflict and Creativity*, New Brunswick and London: Rutgers University Press, pp. 17–33.

Korte, A. M., ed. (2000), *Women and Miracle Stories: A Multidisciplinary Exploration*, Leiden: Brill.

Korte, A. M. (2004), 'Miraculous Women: Miracles, Religious Authority and Gender', in M. Poorthuis and J. Schwartz, eds, *Saints and Role Models in Judaism and Christianity*, Leiden: Brill, pp. 415–32.

Korte, A. M. (2014), 'Signs from Heaven: Figuring the Sacred in Contemporary Miracle Stories', in A. Berlis, A.-M. Korte and K. Biezeveld, eds, *Everyday Life and the Sacred: Re/configuring Gender Studies in Religion*, Studies in Theology and Religion, Leiden: Brill.

Lynch, G. (2007), *The New Spirituality: An Introduction to Progressive Belief in the Twenty-First Century*, London: I. B. Tauris.

Mohkamsing-den Boer, E. (2005), *Dreams and Transitions: The Royal Road to Surinamese and Australian Indigenous Society*, dissertation, Radboud University Nijmegen.

de Nie, G. (2003), *Word, Image, and Experience: Dynamics of Miracle and Self-Perception in Sixth-Century Gaul*, Aldershot: Ashgate.

Partridge, C. (2004), *The Re-Enchantment of the West*, Vol. 1, Alternative Spiritualities, Sacralization, Popular Culture, and Occulture, London: Clark International.

Ricoeur, P. (2005), *The Course of Recognition*, Cambridge MA: Harvard University Press.

Schredl, M. and Wittmann, L. (2005), 'Dreaming: A Psychological View', in *Swiss Archives of Neurology and Psychiatry* 156, pp. 484–92.

Sengers, E., ed. (2005), *The Dutch and Their Gods: Secularization and Transformation of Religion in the Netherlands since 1950*, Hilversum: Verloren.

Smith, James K. A. (2008), *After Modernity? Secularity, Globalization, and the Re-Enchantment of the World*, Waco TX: Baylor University Press.

Taylor, C. (2007), *A Secular Age*, Cambridge MA: The Belknap Press of Harvard University Press.

Tweed, T. A. (2006), *Crossing and Dwelling: A Theory of Religion*, Cambridge MA: Harvard University Press.

van Eeden, F. (1913), 'A Study of Dreams', in *Proceedings of the Society for Psychical Research*, 26, pp. 431–61.

Walker Bynum, C. (1997), 'Wonder', in *American Historical Review* 102, pp. 1–26.

Woodward, K. L. (2000), *The Book of Miracles: The Meaning of the Miracle Stories in Christianity, Judaism, Buddhism, Hinduism, Islam*, New York: Simon and Schuster.

7

Psychosystemic Engagement of Dreams

LARRY KENT GRAHAM AND

SHYAMAA CREAVEN

Introduction

This chapter brings pastoral dream work into conversation with Larry Kent Graham's psychosystems model of pastoral care and counselling. It expands the individualized interpretation of dreams by means of a relational pastoral ontology, which has been developed by Graham as a general framework for pastoral care and counselling. Graham calls his model a 'psychosystemic approach', which is a basis for putting what is commonly known about dreams into a comprehensive interpretation of the person–world relationship and for fashioning modes of engagement that link the dreamer in creative new ways to larger social and ecological forces impinging on their lives. Looking to dreams from this viewpoint reframes their potential with a new appreciation. Dreams are messages addressed uniquely to the dreamer, which arise from the dreamer's multiple transactions with the complexly ordered universe in which they reside. Dreams create a new energy in the dreamer and disclose hidden but significant realities in the dreamer's world. Dreams also skirt danger. They threaten as well as enliven. They spiritually empower.

The conversation between psychosystems thought and pastoral guidance will be illuminated by the psychospiritual clinical work with dreams practised by Shyamaa Creaven with her clients. Influenced by the dream work approach of Gestalt Therapy Theory, Jungian Depth Psychology and Dream Yoga, Creaven works regularly with the psychospiritual and systemic dimensions of dreams in her private practice. Together we present a theory and practice for ministers to work productively with their own dreams and with the dreams of those to whom they minister.

Meaning of psychosystems

The term 'psychosystemic' integrates individual psychological and social experience and articulates the multiple relationships between them. 'Psycho' refers to the dynamics of human personal identity and development in its known and unknown, conscious and unconscious, dimensions. 'Systemic' refers to the patterned interconnection between persons and their social milieus, beginning with our families but including culture, nature, and extending even to God (whether understood as a cultural construct and/or metaphysical influence). Psychosystemic theory, in short, is the theory that attempts to map the reciprocal interplay between the psyche of individuals and the various social, cultural, and natural contexts in which individuals reside. A full description of the theory, which combined process and liberation theology with psychodynamic and analytically oriented therapies and family systems psychotherapy, is detailed in Graham (1992).

Psychosystemic theory posits that all reality is interconnected or relational and that it is organized in relatively stable configurations oscillating between continuity and creativity, or homeostasis and change. Dreams arise and take on significance in this relational milieu. The model posits six structural elements, and five connectors between the structures. The six structural elements are the actual occasion of experience underlying all subsequent experience, followed by person, family, society, culture, nature, and God. The five psychosystemic connectors are Contextual Continuity, Contextual Creativity, Di-Polar Power, Contending Values, and Reciprocal Transactions. Structures and Connectors interact at both a conscious or public level, and an unconscious, private, or out of awareness level. A psychosystems map is presented in Figure 1 to visualize the psychosystemic model.

A psychosystems map

Contextual Continuity (located at 9:00 or left-middle position on the graphic) is the capacity of a system, and each entity or subsystem within the larger whole, to regulate itself and to preserve its core values, power arrangements, transactional patterns and organized identities. Contextual Creativity (3:00 or right-middle position), or finite freedom, is the capacity for the system and its parts to change its organizational patterns and for something new to come into place.

Di-Polar Power (12:00 or top-centre) is a central category in psychosystemic theory. Understood as the capacity to influence and to be influenced,

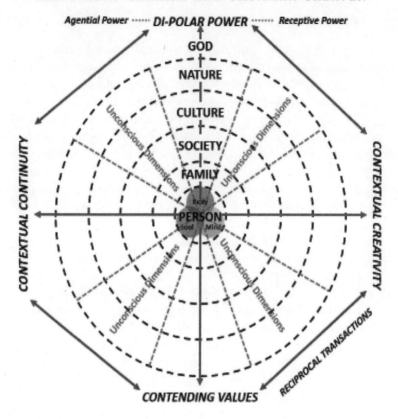

Figure 1: Psychosystems map.

power is conceived as a duality, with agency comprising one pole and receptivity the other. Agential power is understood as the dynamic capacity to influence the environment. Receptive power is the capacity to be influenced by the environment. Without the power to receive and preserve influence, Contextual Continuity is impossible; things would fall apart. Without agential power change would be limited and the system stagnant or atrophied.

Because the interactions of people and systems are so power-laden and dynamically interconnected, issues of Contending Values (6:00 or lower-centre position) are always present. A value is a desired outcome. Desired outcomes vary by context, motivation and aims, and are therefore contested at all interactional levels. Contending Values in psychosystemic terms are delineated by the concepts of beauty vs evil. Beauty, as derived from process theology, is understood as the most favourable relationship between intensity and harmony of experience. Intensity is vital agency working to create new reality, often at the expense of established harmony. Harmony is the capacity to creatively order the greatest degree of contrast, and channels agency towards desired ends. Evil, the value that contends with Beauty, is its opposite. Evil is conceived as discord and triviality. Put another way, discord is disharmonized intensity, and triviality is harmony without intensity. Translated into Christian moral reflection, Beauty is best expressed in terms of love of self, God and neighbour, a just social order and ecological vitality. Evil is expressed in terms of lovelessness towards self, God, and neighbour, unjust social arrangements, and ecological rapaciousness.

Reciprocal Transactions (graphically represented by solid arrow-tipped diagonal, vertical and horizontal lines) are the processes by which power, values and creativity are exchanged within and between entities in the psychosystemic milieu. Transactions are multiply directed and always influential, with consequences of their interactions occurring throughout the psychosystemic milieu.

The concept of God is central to the psychosystemic model presented here. It is developed from the process theology and philosophy of Alfred North Whitehead and Charles Hartshorne, as interpreted through John Cobb and David Ray Griffin. Briefly, God is present in every moment of existence, influencing and receiving, but not controlling, what happens in the becoming of the universe. In every moment of becoming, God preserves the past (including evil as well as beauty) and envisages particular options for the next moment in time. God is pervasively present and unfailingly active as both receptor and agent of what is taking place in the universe (see Cobb 1969; Graham 1992, pp. 67–9; Mesle 2008).

To summarize, the psychosystemic matrix in which we will interpret dream work is 'the totality of the network of actual entities, persons, families, societies, cultures, nature and God as these are contextually organized consciously and unconsciously by contending values, Di-polar power arrangements, reciprocal transactions, and creative potentialities' (Graham 1992, p. 262).

Relational context of dreams

As the authors initially conversed about our work with some of our own dreams we realized that we were laying the foundation for much of what follows in this chapter. We will begin our linking dreams to psychosystems thought by presenting a portion of that conversation.

[S] [Shyamaa] I am wondering how the dream you shared about your psychosystems book might help us present this chapter more powerfully.

[L] [Larry] The dream took place when I was bogged down in the theory-building that led to the book, *Care of Persons, Care of Worlds* (Graham 1992) where I lay out the psychosystemic pastoral ontology. I had come to the point where I thought it was not possible to accomplish this and was considering terminating the project. It felt like I was stuck in a huge impasse.

At that time I had a dream about returning to a setting in Southern California where I had grown up:

> I came across a small shrine I had erected as a little kid in a remote area near my house. The shrine, forgotten, was a shambles but still recognizable. As I stood there, an angel-like being appeared in dazzling colours, surrounded by light. Stern and quite angry, he said, 'This is your shrine and you have neglected it. You are going to die!' I was stunned. I had no idea that this shrine was so important and that I had such a responsibility towards it. I defended my innocence and pleaded for more time to repair it. The angel gave me the time to try, but he was furious and sure that it was beyond saving.
>
> As I frantically put the stones into place, I had an awful realization. All parts of the shrine were there but one: the keystone, the piece that held it all together. I began to panic. Suddenly I noticed that one of my respected colleagues was standing nearby, watching, with his hands behind his back. I knew immediately that he had the missing stone.
>
> I approached him with determination. 'You have the stone I am looking for. I want it back.' He replied with a gentle smirk, 'I don't have it.' I said, 'You do have it, and if you don't give it back you will die.' We were both stunned by the ferocity of my words.
>
> After a short time he smiled and handed me the keystone from behind his back. I placed it in the shrine. Instantly the shrine transformed from a scattering of rocks to a resplendent, gem-filled sacred place. The angel reappeared and was obviously very pleased with what had happened. I felt grateful to be alive! And I had a sense that I could now leave that place bearing its beauty and a sense of destiny and spiritual accountability that I had not realized before.

[L] When I pondered the dream afterwards, I realized that my calling was to be a pastoral theologian, not some other kind of theologian or scholar. The colleague I had challenged in the dream, an esteemed scholar whose standards set the norms for most theological scholarship, was a man to whom I had always looked for validation. Suddenly I no longer harboured an inferior sense of social location and professional valuation. This dream became the source of the inner strength and vision I needed to continue to articulate my expanded way of seeing the world through the psychosystems prism I was trying to formulate. Indeed, my very life and its ultimate worth depended on such a change taking place!

[S]   I continue to be moved by the beauty and intensity of your dream. It seems to be a great example of a numinous dream. Numinous dreams are terrifying and put us face to face with our ultimate destiny in extremely concrete and personal terms. There is no escaping a response and a decision when these dreams confront us, and they have everything to do with how we will live out our lives in the world.

Not all dreams are numinous dreams, nor are numinous dreams the only ones that convey strong spiritual and influential messages.[1] Psychosystems thought illuminates many types of dreams and speaks to many spheres of living.

[L]   Maybe you have a dream that is of a differing systemic impact that we might share.

[S]   One came immediately to mind as you invited me to think about dreams with you. My dream is indeed of a different quality from yours yet also had a distinct impact on both my relationship to agency and creativity and my sense of place in the world. It occurred when I was 30 years old, on pilgrimage in India:

> In the dream I sat on the bank of the Ganges river in early morning as a rugged old dog was sitting nearby, trying to get my attention. A wise woman meditating near me said plainly, 'That is your father and he is calling you home.'

[L]   That is very compelling. What meaning did you make from it at the time?

[S]   I took it as a call to action. The Ganges is a place of spiritual vision and a place people go to die. I felt that the dream was an imperative to seek out my father, a person I had only ever met three times in my life, before he died. So, I booked a ticket to Florida to visit him. I should point out here that while dreams invite action, they are rarely literal and generally require translation. Still, some dreams can give a direct clue as

---

1 Note that there are considered to be a wide range of different types of dreams that connect to psychosystems thought, including Existential dreams, Daydreams, Sacred/Numinous Dreams and Grief dreams, to name but a few. See Bulkeley (1994) for a fuller discussion.

to what is to be done in waking life. I took a risk that this dream was as much literal as symbolic, something only the dreamer can safely determine, often with the help of a dream dialogue. My trust that God had a hand in this dream dawns on me now as I study how psychosystems thought and dreams work together.

[L] The fact that you were on pilgrimage when you had the dream seems directly connected to adventure. The 'principle of adventure' is a psychosystems concept that refers to the way life pushes and is drawn forward into new combinations of experience, new configurations of past and present tending towards the future (Graham 1992, pp. 47–8). My dream created a similarly strong energy in my life. Notice that as you and I share these dreams a new relational bond has grown between us. Until you invited me to describe my dream in relation to this project, I had not considered the influence of my dream on the actual creation of my theory. Your insight enriched the power of the dream for me. Tell me, does my response to your dream have any impact on your insights into it?

[S] Yes. Your relaxed attention and kind prompting has given me space to encounter this dream anew. While this dream fits into a larger sequence of dreams that unfolded as I met my father again, the important thing to point out here is that following the wisdom of this dream led to a transformation of impasse energy between my father and I that had bound up my womanhood in significant ways. I am grateful to see this as I sit here with you.

[L] I am very moved by this dream. I wonder what it feels like for you to be telling me your dream in the context of our writing this chapter.

[S] Until I shared it with you now, I did not quite put together just how pivotal that moment of dreaming was in my life. I can now see larger systems at play. This dream served as multiple turning points: in my relationship with my estranged father; the family system between my mother, my father, and me; my relationship with my partner; and ultimately my agency as a woman.

[L] My response to your dream, then, was important in your telling it. As we had the conversations about each of the dreams, it seemed that something significant happened that we can draw upon to help the reader understand working with dreams from a psychosystemic orientation.

[S] The quality of your presence as respectful of my own narration and interpretation of the dreams, as well as your curious receptivity rather than analytic stance, has greatly enhanced my own relationship to these dreams and to you now. A powerful feature of your approach is your attitude of dialogue – what you refer to in your theory as 'reciprocal transactions' (see Graham 1992, pp. 262ff for a fuller account of the concept).

[L]   The psychosystems perspective apprehends our experience in more complex relational terms than are often disclosed on the surface level of dream interpretation. And I think that you and I have just discovered that the process of working with dreams psychosystemically is thoroughly relational and continues to unfold. For example, our relationship with the editors of this volume at the outset stimulated us to think about dreams in pastoral work from a psychosystemic point of view. Then, sharing our two dreams was a reciprocal transaction that generated deeper understandings of our own histories and opened us to greater awareness of how the power of our dreams influenced our lives. And, maybe most importantly, sharing our dreams together created a strong and promising relational bond between us!

As we hope to show as this chapter proceeds, a psychosystemic approach to dreams offers the view that working with dreams and their powers is always a relational process as well as a personal or intrapsychic activity relevant to multiple systems of our lives and often coaxing us towards new creative responses in our intersecting contexts. Dreams may appear as personal and private, but in the relational context of sharing dreams they take on deeper and wider significance. This came alive for us as we reflected together on our dreams and what we hope to convey about the alive dynamics of dream work.

Psychosystems theory posits that all reality is interconnected, whether recognized or not, and therefore relational transactions are the foundation of everything else that happens. When applied to dreams, the character of the relational transactions between the pastor or spiritual guide and the dreamer will have a significant impact on what is co-created from the interaction they have with one another and the dream. We examine below some of the most compelling features of psychosystemic dream work.

Psychosystemic features of dreams

While all elements of a psychosystemic approach relate to dreams, some features are most salient for the work of the pastor and spiritual caregiver. We will highlight three features of dreams most relevant for pastoral engagement: transactional effectiveness, increasing beauty, and liberating creativity. Put succinctly, being receptive to the power of dreams and joining their agency has creative consequences for negotiating the psychosystemic matrix in a manner that moves towards an increase of beauty in the form of love, justice and ecological harmony.

Dreams as transactional effectiveness

To begin with, the dream itself mediates a transaction between the dreamer and various dimensions of the dreamer's life-situation, including the dreamer's conscious and unconscious relationship to their family, society, culture, natural order and God. One of the core concepts of psychosystems thought is 'reciprocal transactions'. If systems are interconnected there must be a theory of exchange and influence and some way of accounting for stasis as well as creativity between entities. Persons often seek spiritual care because they feel that they are at a 'transactional impasse' within themselves or between themselves and their environments. This was the case for Larry at one point in the research and writing, and for Shyamaa in relation to her father and larger situation as a woman in the world. Dreams emerged as powerful transactions between our deeper selves and the world in relation to which we were stuck. These dreams, when received and integrated, became a source of transactional effectiveness in which we were able to feel empowered to understand and act.

The spiritual caregiver, then, does well to explore how dreams reveal transactional impasses, at the same time providing clues about how to access the agency of the dream to more effectively interact with the dreamer's context. Shyamaa recounts her work with the dreams of a South American pre-med student in which various important transactional elements within the dream itself only later translated into systemic effectiveness on other levels of the psychosystemic world of the person. The dream of one of Shyamaa's clients may be a vivid example of the multiple transactional dimensions of a dream.[2]

Ms S, a female client from Columbia, South America, shared a dream of an old immigrant woman screaming in terror in a foreign language while a young, white American doctor tried to sedate her. The dream was not only expressing a transactional dynamic between two aspects of her psyche, her Columbian self and her American pre-med student self; she was also touching upon the dynamics of discrimination and misunderstanding that she faces in American culture. Her dream, then, linked contending values in her psyche, but also contending values and disharmonies in her social and cultural milieu. It also reflected the current transactional impasse between her mother and herself and her relationship to the elders in her various communities, including the Santeria community of her native spirituality.

---

2 All the dreams reported in this chapter are presented with permission of the dreamers, whose identities remain anonymous.

Our dialogue about these various transactional dialogues brought the various dimensions of the dream to the foreground one at a time from the dreamer herself. This was also the first time that this young medical student began to address racial discrimination with me, her white, American therapist, enriching and deepening our relational transactions as well. Our relational context allowed for shared relational power, both of us as agents and receptors to one another, which addressed the inequalities in privilege between us and allowed for fruitful transactional healing through relationship across cultural lines. The transactional effectiveness between us provided for her a partial empowerment to engage more effectively with the injustice that was causing impasses and more effective transactional roles in the subsystems comprising her larger world.

In working with dreams, the pastor and caregiver must pay close attention to the reciprocal transactions between them and the dreamer. It is our aim to create a mutual dialogue in which we are receptive to the dream and its many dimensions rather than forcing the dream into our agency. The dream has various meanings to convey to us; these meanings come from the dream and the dreamer and from the conversation between the pastor, dreamer and dream. This is why a psychosystems approach to dream work does not rely on pre-codified dream interpretation resources. The power in the dream is lost if we do not explore it with curiosity and allow its contextually creative voice to first affect us and then to take on new dimensions as we engage with it reciprocally. Those pastors who work closely and productively with their own dreams will be best positioned to work with the dreams presented by others.

Dreams as the power of beauty

The highest value in psychosystems thought is beauty (12:00 lower centre in Figure 1), understood as the greatest combination of intensity and harmony of experience, expressed through love of self, God and neighbour, relational justice and ecological synergy. Larry's dream unified a divided self, brought creativity and harmony out of discord, and contributed to the construction of a novel theory of pastoral care and counselling. Shyamaa's dream sequence reunited her with her father, enjoined their love and commitment, and changed the balance of power in relation to her role as a woman in the world. It is God's intention that the universe increase in beauty; through dream work, the care seeker engages the creativity of the dream and thus engages God's active power in life.

Dreams are of many kinds with different significance and purposes, yet each dream, as an enlivening transaction between unconscious and conscious awareness, represents a form of creativity. Shyamaa recounts how she and her client, Clark, explored a dream that illuminates creativity out of impasses and intensity and harmony arising from discord and triviality.

I am in an early spring mountainous landscape. I approach a small, swampy lake. As I get closer I see that the lake is stagnant and full of muck, tar-like and thick. It scares me and I am both compelled to see my reflection in the water and repelled by the thought of getting closer. Two mallards are swimming around the surface as if it was clean and flowing water. I am happy to see them. On the bank is a giant bulldozer that has been displacing earth and further dirtying the water. I feel rage and fear when I see the bulldozer. The mallards are looking at me and when I focus on them I know I must approach the devastation of the water and look at my own reflection. The mallards get more cheerful and begin to dance playfully with one another as I look into the water. I see my face and begin to weep. I am so terribly upset and sick to my stomach until I hear the mallards causing a joyous raucous. Somehow I get the message that the lake can be rehabilitated if it is left to nature, that deep within is clean water and healthy algae. I feel utterly grateful, as if my own life depends on this possibility. In the morning I felt sick and renewed – sort of a strange combination of purpose and anxiety about the meanings in this dream.

As Clark reflected on this dream with Shyamaa, he became more aware of the contexts in his life that the dream speaks into and of the culture of comfort he has bought into. This striving for material comfort keeps him from looking closely at the pollution within and around him. In the dream dialogue Shyamaa became aware of a few contexts in Clark's life where discord and triviality were eroding his espoused value of environmental justice and ecological harmony. His job at a company that is actively destroying the everglades made him a very comfortable living but contributed to environmental discord rather than harmony. In reflecting on the dream he concluded that his multiple sexual relationships in a polyamorous community and his draw to strip clubs and internet porn further 'polluted' the inner waters of his life. While being aware of the dominant theme of pollution in his dream, Clark was drawn to the mallards and the possibility of renewal. The mallards represent hope in the midst of devastation and also serve as a guiding presence, filled with creative resilience or contextual creativity. Clark came to the realization that he was not living in accord with his deepest values and that he was polluting his inner world, as well as contributing to the very devastation of the natural world. The transactional impasses within Clark's inner world, between his contending values and his conscious choices, led him to a life where he did not want to look at his own reflection. Taking the step to look into the water was a very creative moment for Clark. Incorporating the power of this dream into his life has helped him to move from discord and triviality into a new harmony and intensity of personal living, environmental justice and relational care.

Clark's dream work illustrates the power of beauty coming into being through reciprocal explorations with a pastoral or spiritual guide. We see in this vignette that the human psyche is an active centre of synthesis of all its interrelations with the environment, and can best be understood in the context of the multiple worlds from which it draws and to which it contributes. The dream can stand in relation to the environment in many ways. Hence the dialogue between the dreamer, the dream and the pastoral caregiver can explore various combinations of power and value operating in the dreamer's intrapsychic and social-cultural-natural world.

The values of beauty and evil are contending values (see 6:00 on Figure 1) and these contentions are frequently transmitted through dreams. Though beauty is a positive aesthetic value, dreams sometimes are discordant, trivial and ugly. Whether positive or negative, the intense aesthetic value of the dream is to be respected even when it seems 'scary', 'weird' or 'disjointed'. In fact, the most seemingly discordant or confusing dreams can be a profound effort towards harmony and the most harmonious dreams will fade into fiction or triviality without the intensity that brings a real opportunity for active engagement. Because discord and harmony are psychosystemically connected, it is entirely possible that the most discordant or alarming dreams can reveal or generate hidden harmonies and be a complex expression of beauty. To support the emergence of such creative potential, context, curiosity and care are all key ingredients to be integrated into the dream dialogue between the dreamer and dream worker.

There is a special category of dreaming that comes into focus at this point. We call it 'the waking dream of the world'. The waking dream of the world, like dreams appearing from the unconscious during sleep, comes unbidden as threat and possibility for the dreamer. But, unlike dreams appearing (usually during sleep) from the unconscious, these imaginative phenomena combine conscious, unconscious and social energies into a new set of possibilities for the dreamer and for the world's becoming. These waking dreams of the world conjure the aspirations and hopes of a culture, of a people, at a given point in time. They come to us in many ways. A leading example in the USA is the Revd Dr Martin Luther King Junior's prophetic dreams as living documents of power and hope expressed so famously in his 'I Have a Dream' speech, in which he gives expression to the powerful dream of a nation coming into fuller self-realization.

The waking dreams of the world transcend the psychic processes of the dreamer and of the limits of the sleep state where we traditionally look for dreams, though they might emerge from them. In the broadest sense of the use of the word 'dream', there is active power to craft and contribute to an unfolding future for a person and the world along the lines of increased love, justice and ecological vitality. For instance, in the USA, rampant school violence has led families and community groups to change gun control laws and develop more effective mental health resources. In this way a dream of justice and peace can birth a movement. To this end, there is the dream of a particular individual person expressed in the subjective aim and hopeful desire of the person in his/her context, but the inspiration for the dreams arise from a variety of influences and possibilities in the family, culture, nation, ecology and God.

These waking dreams of the world are agents and mediators of our best intentions towards the future. And they become, for good or ill, the dreams of a society, culture and era. When faced with these waking dreams of the world, the spiritual guide does well not to dismiss them as idealism, ideology or political cant, but explore their links to the dream energy found in sleep dreams. Other potential forms of waking dreams are drawn from such activities as active imagination, intention-setting, guided visualization, forms of meditation, free association, journal writing, story writing and symbolic artistic creation. These additional aspects of dream work are to be welcomed and explored. Thus, dreams evoke a new set of values and possibilities for personal living as well as for creatively transformed social structures and ecological policies and practices. Put succinctly, much goodness in personal living and social change begins with a dream.

With respect to beauty, then, the aim of a psychosystems approach to care is to increase love, justice and ecological partnership through the ministry of care. Dreams as creative acts in themselves contribute to liberation in either direct or coded form by prophetically calling forth what is needed, or by illuminating the sources of internal oppression, stagnation and vitiation. They have great potential to move us and the world from the evil of triviality and discord to creative constellations of intensity and harmony in the concrete situations of our lives.

Dreams as liberating creativity

In psychosystems perspective the dream conveys dynamic creative power in the life of the dreamer. That creative power is not wholly bound to the inner workings of the individual human psyche. The dream frees and even liberates contextually creative potentials for promoting novel agency and receptivity in the larger milieu as well as in the life of the dreamer. In dreams and in the dream dialogue between the dream, the dreamer and the caregiver we discover a formative locus where God's lure can meet subjective personal aims that together move towards a more intense and harmonious experience. In working with dreams the care provider assists in liberating contextual creativity in the life of the care seeker, enriching the person and the immediate world. From a psychosystemic standpoint all past experiences are synthesized with the divinely engendered lure of creative possibility that allows for the next moment of the self and world to be genuinely novel, intense and harmonious. Dreams are one medium for this novel and creative partnership between God and the world to take place.

Pastoral work with dreams can lead to a more dynamic conscious/ unconscious synergy as well as point the way to a more creative synergy in life. When dream work is on track, synergy can be felt in the room! Creative synthesis is a dimension of beauty. A dream can function to expand a fixed identity through the emergence of unconscious aspects of self, asking us to include more in our identity and experience of the world, and to co-create something unique and powerful. Thus, when Larry, Shyamaa, Clark or our pre-med student remembered a dream and shared it with each other, a new thing of beauty came into place.

Dreams do more than mediate contextually creative potentials for the dreamer and the dreamer's world. They also create new meanings and dynamics between the dreamer and the caregiver. Shyamaa and Larry found new appreciation for one another and new insight about our respective lives through the reciprocal transactions that emerged as we shared our dreams. This creativity had positive outcomes in our subsequent commitments elsewhere. The pastoral caregiver will do well to recognize that creativity is contextual, when understood psychosystemically, and that the transactions between the caregiver and care seeker will have a variety of values for each and for the way they participate in their worlds beyond the ministry context.

Pastoral work with dreams

How do the elements of transactional effectiveness, empowered beauty and liberated creativity play out in the reciprocal dialogue between a care seeker and a care provider attending to dreams? To listen to a dream requires receptive power in the form of active openness to receiving the unknown by the care provider. Reciprocally effective transactions are required for the relational power of dreams to be handled well. The balance of receptive and agential power in the dream dialogue between the care seeker and the care provider may become a dance of attuned harmony and intensity, or a thing of beauty in psychosystemic terms. Within this reciprocal transactional dance, we suggest a few basic guidelines for the care provider and the care seeker.

We begin our guidelines for responding to dreams reminding the reader of five steps or stages in working with dreams commonly practised in the psychotherapeutic field (see Bulkeley 1994; Koning 2014). Following from that brief overview we identify some specific questions to explore dreams from a uniquely psychosystemic standpoint.

Common stages in psychotherapeutic dream work

The first stage involves entering the territory of the dream. This involves setting a tone of welcome and expectation. It requires emotional readiness to enter the dream energy dialogically and collaboratively. Meditation, deep breathing, attunement and visualization are common means of crossing the dream threshold and entering an arena of creativity and mystery. Telling the dream begins here.

The second stage is to ask about the context of the dream: inquiring about what was happening in the dreamer's life that gave rise to the dream and what particular challenges and opportunities are being faced by the dreamer. Exploring the type of dream, antecedents for it, and how it picks up familiar themes as well as discloses unique alternatives is part of understanding the dream's context.

The third stage is dialogue with the dreamer, letting the dreamer's thoughts, images, feelings and speculations range as they will. In this stage the dreamer is elaborating and working with his energies; the care provider remains connected and receptive, acting agentially to explore but not to guide or force the direction of the conversation or possible interpretations and behavioural implications. The care provider assists the dreamer to dialogue with the dream and each of its parts, including the feelings and psychospiritual energy and thoughts associated with the dream.

The fourth stage is the contextually creative stage where the dreamer and care provider explore possible connections to the dreamer's inner life and the salient elements in the psychosystemic milieu. The minister may ask, 'Does the dream suggest a direction or action you should take?' 'Does the dream support or change your values and ways of thinking?' In this stage the care provider may muse or wonder about various elements of the dream and their connections to the dreamer and the dreamer's life in the world.

The fifth stage focuses on integrating the dream into the dreamer's identity and actions, or closing the dream by imagining alternative endings. At this point the dream becomes an empowering agent in the dreamer's life and integrates the personality as well as confirming or redirecting a course of action in the dreamer's world.

Within this structure of dream discourse several psychosystemic elements come into focus. Exploring these elements may provide depth and dimensionality to what caregivers already do.

Psychosystemic exploration of dreams

To connect with the di-polar power elements in a dream the caregiver might ask, 'What power do you receive from this dream and how might it impact your world?' and 'Is God's power touching your life through this dream?'

To explore the way the dream negotiates the line between contextual continuity and contextual creativity, the care provider might ask the dreamer, 'What is your dream setting free inside you and beckoning you to address?', 'How does the dream re-establish your commitments?' and 'How might the dream release you to explore new ways of being in community?'

To examine the way the dream mediates contending values within the dreamer and impinging on the dreamer from his milieu, the minister might ask, 'Does this dream help you set right anything in your life?', 'What value conflicts or moral distress does the dream disclose and what guidance does the dream provide to understand and resolve them?' and 'If you act on the dream, how will your life become more intense and harmonious?'

To examine the power of reciprocal transactions mediated by the dream, the caregiver might ask, 'How does this dream speak to any stuck places in your life?', 'Does the dream offer you a way through the conflicting relationships you face?' and 'How does this dream speak to the ups and downs in your relationship with God?'

All of these modes of engaging the dream imply that something positive will occur. And in our experience such is usually the case. But some cautions are also in order. As we have noted, dreams can be dangerous territory for the dreamer and the dream worker. They can destabilize and dis-integrate. They may become part-processes that are cut off from integrated personal and social functioning, requiring more sustained professional help. They may be attached to behaviours that are discordant and trivial, and link to unjust and ecologically rapacious movements or practices. They may offset rational faculties and integrated selfhood, leading to fanaticism, obsessive thought processes and compulsive action. Dreams may become terrifying nightmares rather than holistic syntheses of experience. Vigilance and accountability are essential professional dimensions of dream work. Supervision and referral options are essential backdrops for any kind of contracted caregiving, and become especially important for entering the territory of dreams. It should be noted that this chapter does not cover traumatic dreams and the unique approaches required of them.

Summary and conclusion

This chapter has suggested ways that ministers might help others to increase the love of God, self and neighbour; promote a more just social order; and enhance the ecological vitality of the universe through employing a psychosystemic theory of pastoral psychology to engage the relational energy generated by dreams. The main insight from a psychosystems standpoint is that dreams are not just individual products of a closed psyche, unrelated to the actual world. Rather, the dream is best understood as a source of power and creativity that brings us into intense and harmonious reciprocal transactions with all elements of our existence. In their sleeping, waking and communal-contextual dimensions, dream processes can also contribute to the clarification and alignment of our subjective aims or contending values with the creative input of God, since 'the basis for creative contextuality lies in God's agency as liberator and lure to creative advance' (Graham 1992, p. 181).

References

Bulkeley, K. (1994), *The Wilderness of Dreams: Exploring the Religious Meanings of Dreams in Modern Western Culture*, Albany NY: State University of New York Press.

Cobb, J. B. Jr (1969), *God and the World*, Philadelphia: Westminster Press.

Graham, L. K. (1992), *Care of Persons, Care of Worlds: A Psychosystems Approach to Pastoral Care and Counseling*, Nashville TN: Abingdon Press.

King, M. L. Jr, 'I Have a Dream'; the speech is available at http://abcnews.go.com/Politics/martin-luther-kings-speech-dream full-text.

Koning, B. (2014), www.dreampilgrims.com.

Mesle, R. C. (2008), *Process-relational Philosophy: An Introduction to Alfred North Whitehead*, West Conshohocken PA: Templeton Foundation Press.

8

Rabbinic Dream Work

An Introduction to the Dream Discussions in the Babylonian Talmud (Berachot 55a–57b)[1]

BART J. KOET

Introduction

The aim of this chapter is to present a specific model of dream interpretation. It is a special approach: the rabbinic approach, as found in an old text on dreams, the rabbinic dream book Berachot 55–57, from the Babylonian Talmud. Although Sigmund Freud said that he took his inspiration for his book *Traumdeutung* from the Greeks, some scholars doubt it and refer to the similarities between rabbinic hermeneutics and the hermeneutics of Freud, when dealing with interpretation of dreams (cf. Frieden 1990). After a short introduction about the rabbinic dream book and its place in the Talmud and rabbinic tradition, some texts in translation are presented together with a commentary.

Dreams are often used to promote religion or to propagate an interpretation of religion. As we have seen with the Bin Laden tapes, dreams are also sometimes used to bring political ideas to the fore using a religious disguise.

However, religion also promotes dreams. In classical times and cultures, and also in some contemporary cultures, paying attention to dreams is a means of receiving divine guidance (Koet 2006). But for rabbinic and Christian scholars in the past, not all dreams were of religious value. However, for some rabbis, even those dreams that were not seen as coming from God could still be important. Although there are quite a few sayings about dreams in rabbinic writings, by far the most important text is the quite elaborate passage dealing with dreams in the Babylonic Talmud: Berachot 55a–57b. It is sometimes known as the 'rabbinic' or 'Talmudic dream book' (for an extended collection of rabbinic statements

---

1 An earlier, slightly different version of this chapter was published as 'Over droomuitleg bij de Rabbijnen', in *Collationes* 29, 1999, pp. 27–47.

about dreaming, see Kristianpoller 1923). In an article on this passage Peter Alexander (1995, p. 230) argues that it is also the natural starting point for any discussion of the rabbis' view on the subject.

This passage is significant not only because it gives insight into the rabbinic view on dreaming, but also because it deals with interpretation of dreaming. For these reasons this text is a most important window into the rabbinic art *par excellence* of interpreting (Frieden 1990; cf. Niehof 1992). Thus, this passage deserves scholarly attention not only for the content, but also for the way it came into being and even for the fact that the theme of 'dreaming' was afforded such an extended discussion in the Talmud.

Because this chapter appears in a handbook and not in a study devoted to rabbinic hermeneutics, the technical and historical investigations of this passage are not dealt with here. Instead, we present a few texts from this rabbinic dream book, introducing some of the basic principles the rabbis used when interpreting dreams. We give some preliminary information about the Talmud and rabbinic literature and the structure of the rabbinic dream book. In the next sections we discuss passages with the themes 'dreams as wisdom' and 'seeking the positive message of each dream', and ask: 'Are dreams coming from God?'

What is the Talmud?

In the Tanakh, the Jewish Bible (Husser 1999), in Flavius Josephus' writings (Gnuse 1997) and in the writings of the New Testament (Koet 2006) we find dreams functioning in narrative texts, but in the Talmudic dream book we also find elaborate reflections about the nature of dreams.

It is well known that the Talmud is a fairly unique collection of books. It is no law book, but rather a collection of discussions. In his column of the *Jerusalem Post*, international edition, on 24 May 1986, Pinchas Peli compared the Talmud to James Joyce's *Ulysses* and its technique of 'stream of consciousness'. This is a series of thoughts connected by discussions. These associations are ordered in the form of a commentary on an earlier collection of Jewish oral law, the Mishnah. The Mishnah and the later Talmud are part of collections of orally transmitted sayings. The form in which the oral doctrine has been written down would nowadays be called notes. This oral character was largely preserved when these laws and rules were at a given moment edited and standardized. The final edition of the Mishnah is dated to the end of the second or the beginning of the third century.

The statements in the Mishnah resemble shorthand, and as such they require explanation; and this explanation was given in the form of the Talmud. In the order of the sections of the Mishnah the Talmud gives an account of rabbinical discussions through the centuries. Mostly following the text of the Mishnah, there comes a stream of thoughts: a usually small but sometimes large collection of debates, statements and stories. The extent to which the Talmud is a compilation is shown by the fact that two languages are used next to each other. Thus the Talmud in many ways resembles an old building. The building may form of different styles from different periods: one may be able to distinguish Romanesque and Gothic elements, sometimes with baroque decorations. And still it is one building. Similarly the Talmud consists of pieces of wisdom from different generations that have been given a certain unity. The final edition begins in the fifth century.

The fragments of text are usually connected by means of mnemonics, the art of training the memory. In a time when books were expensive and rare, remembering texts was one possible way to share common wisdom. For example, a certain rabbi is quoted in the Mishnah. After he has been quoted, and been recalled, this memory technique is used. Advantage is taken of the opportunity to express a few of his other statements or to tell a story about him. Alternatively, the subject quoted is elaborated and a few other rabbis' statements about the same subject follow. In this way a scholar from the first century seems to enter into discussion with a teacher from the second or third century. One can imagine how things went in an academy in Babylon. Following the citing of a Mishnaic text, one student/ teacher quotes a statement from his teacher about a statement of *his* teacher. Then a series of statements of the same teacher follows.

The fragment about dreams is also in a passage that has clearly been structured with the help of mnemonics. We find a list of various matters, each introduced by: 'there are three things that . . .' In a culture without computers, newspapers and even books as we know them, these were devices for storing pieces of wisdom that could only be saved thanks to a trained human memory.

The Talmud concerning dreams: Babylonian Talmud Berachot 55–57

The passage discussed here can be found in the Babylonian Talmud in discussions commenting on and circling around the first Mishnah book, Berachot. This book deals with the benedictions (in the Hebrew Berachot).

Benediction is related to praying and because of that subject Berachot is an important book. For this reason the discussions are fairly extensive. The passage examined here is part of three pages in the Talmud, and its structure is relatively straightforward.

Discussing the ninth chapter of Berachot (= Ber) of the Misjna (= m) in the Babylonian Talmud (= b) one can find a number of folios with discussions and associations. Our piece is part of three (b.Ber 54a–57b) comments on the first sense (of the Misjnah):

> He that sees a place, where miracles have been wrought for Israel he should say: Blessed be those wonders did for our fathers at this place. (m.Ber 9,1)

In the first pages there is a discussion about the wonders that Israel could experience, both concerning individuals and concerning the community (54a–54b). As a result of such a wonder, rabbi Yehouda is introduced. This rabbi introduces four types of people who have to be thanked. These ways of categorizing using numbers are the basis for several other judgements by the same rabbi where he uses lists. This time records of three items are given using the same formulation: 'three matters'. Rav Yehouda said in the name of Rav that the three matters needing mercy are a good king, a good year and a good dream. Although first the discussion is finished, the word 'dream' is an occasion for an elaborate discussion about different aspects of the dream phenomenon.

Alexander (1995) indicates that a detailed analysis of the Talmudic dream book was still a desideratum, but his division is insufficient for our purposes. Alexander divides it into three parts, each covering a different literary genre. In the first part there are discussions about theoretical questions about dreams. In the second part there is a narrative about dream interpreters and the ethics involved in such a profession. The last part is a collection of different 'dream images' and their possible meaning when one sees them in a dream. In this chapter we present some more 'theoretical' passages.

It is very important to note that the texts of the Talmud are in fact a reflection of discussions: open discussions. These discussions raise central questions about the origin of dreams, interpretation methods, the role of the interpreter, payment for dream interpretation, good or bad dreams, or whether or not there are only worthwhile dreams. As expected, different opinions are expressed in the Talmud. There is no one truth; there is only one way of looking for the truth and that is focused on 'learning discussions', always with nuances. For a modern reader an analogy with a cocktail party is useful: there are many voices, different voices. One can notice magical statements alongside rational or psychological ones. Such a cocktail party may be inspiring for the post-modern reader: discussions with staccato arguments; oppositions; points of dispute and sometimes harmony . . . but not too often.

Some selected texts[2]

1 *A dream which is not interpreted is like a letter which is not read*

Rav Hisda said: Any dream rather (*than one after*) a fast.

Rav Hisda said (*too*): A dream which is not interpreted is like a letter which is not read.

Rav Hisda said (*too*): A good dream is ever wholly fulfilled nor a bad dream is ever wholly fulfilled.

Rav Hisda said (*too*): A bad dream is better than a good dream.

Rav Hisda said (*too*): The sadness caused by a bad dream is sufficient for it and the joy which a good dream gives is sufficient for it.

Rav Joseph said: Even for me the joy caused by a good dream nullifies it.

Rav Hisda said: A bad dream is worse than scourging, since it says, 'God has so made it that men should fear before Him' (Eccl. 3.14).

Rabbah son of Bar Hanah said in the name of Rav Johanan: This refers to a bad dream (Babylonic Talmud Berakhot folio 55a = b.Ber 55a).

This is the first fragment in this Talmud tractate, Berachot, which deals with dreams. In the circle of rabbis the software of the memory was quite impressive. Before the fragment quoted above their search machine was dealing with the number three. The last sentence of this 'search' is:

There are three things for which one should supplicate:
A good king, a good year and a good dream.

Because the word 'dream' is mentioned, the rabbinic search machine starts with a new search. Now the word 'dream' is the catchword. It is the

---

2 I use – sometimes with some modifications – the translation into English with notes and glossary by M. Simon and edited by I. Epstein (*Hebrew–English edition of the Babylonian Talmud*, London: Soncino Press, 1960–94).

beginning of a whole passage dealing with dreams. It is as if each rabbi in the circle of learning contributes to the search. The first statement sounds totally incomprehensible today: 'Any dream rather (*than one after*) a fast'. The reason for this is partly due to the rabbinic style: stenographic and apodictic. However, in those days everybody would have understood it. It is an indication that the rabbis resented dream incubation as part of their project of the rejection of revering other divine beings. Dreaming after fasting was, for example, a regular phenomenon in the cult of the god of medicine, Asclepius. In Hellenistic circles fasting was part of dream incubation. The ritual in Asclepian temples consisted of going to the temple of Asclepius, not eating, receiving dreams during the night, then having these dreams interpreted by the priests in order to predict the health of the dreamer. For the rabbis, that practice was idolatry and thus dreams were excluded from their discussion.

Now that it is clear which dreams people were allowed to pay attention to, the real argument starts. Here is a quote from Rav Hisda: 'A dream which is not interpreted is like a letter which is not read.'[3] This sentence is often referred to in popular literature about dreams. The obvious meaning is that a dream, like a letter, contains a message and thus one has to listen to one's dreams. This is an explicit statement about dreams, indicating that dreams are important and that people can learn something from them. That idea is further developed in the subsequent statements, again sayings attributed to Rav Hisda: 'A good dream is never wholly fulfilled, nor a bad dream ever wholly fulfilled.' Thus, Hisda divides dreams into two categories: bad dreams and good dreams; but the fact that he identifies these two categories is not the most important element. He adds that a bad dream is better than a good dream. Why? One suggestion could be that a bad dream is a warning that a person can learn from.

He argues that although people have to listen to their dreams, they have to realize that a dream – that riddle-like phenomenon of the night – is never wholly fulfilled. In the following passage, Hisda turns to the emotional side of dreams. Dreams affect the psychical state of mind of the dreamer. Bad dreams bring sadness and good dreams bring joy. The final point of this passage refers to the value of bad dreams. Bad dreams are comparable to divine punishment, but the aim of such punishment is that ultimately somebody becomes a better person.

---

3 Rav Hisda was an important Jewish teacher from Babylon, who is believed to have died in 320.

In this passage we hear several opinions from Rav Hisda about dreams. Each statement is debatable, but for us the most important remark is that ignoring dreams is as incomprehensible as not reading letters. We should realize how important letters were in those days; they were the only tool for communication between people in different places.

2 Although you to listen to dreams, you have to reckon with the fact that they do have a nonsense factor

A prophet that has a dream let him tell a dream:
and he that has My word let him speak My word faithfully.
What has straw to do with the wheat, says the Lord. (Jer. 23.28)
What is the connection of straw and wheat with a dream?
Rabbi Johanan said in the name of Rabbi Simeon ben Yohai:
  The truth is, that just as wheat cannot be without straw,
  so there cannot be a dream without some nonsense.
Rav Berekiah said: While a part of a dream may be fulfilled,
  the whole of it is never fulfilled. (b.Ber 55a)

In this passage, directly following on from the previous piece, without any introduction and thus also without any rabbinical authority, a text is borrowed from the prophet Jeremiah who relativizes the value of dreams (Jer. 23.28; cf. 23.9–40; Deut. 13.1–5). In the passage from Jeremiah the opposition to dreams as a means of communication with the divine is clearly voiced. This is in opposition to visions on dreams elsewhere in the Old Testament (for more discussion about this 'divine dream dilemma', see Koet 2009). Crown witness is Numbers 12.6–7, which argues that God speaks in dreams with the prophets (but see also Gen. 41.15–25).

The rabbis had to cope with the dream scepticism tradition. Thus, a very old tradition is cited (see **A** below) to relativize this prophetical text of Jeremiah. Simeon ben Yohai was one of the most important teachers of the second century. The observation made in this tradition is a beautiful example of searching for the meaning of dreams and it shows how the rabbis could relativize a biblical pronouncement and adapt it to their own conceptions. Simeon says that of course dreams also contain some non-sense, but in the meantime nevertheless there is in them – like in wheat – some quite valuable material. Therefore, in dreams one can find nonsense (straw) besides wisdom (wheat).

3 Always interpret a dream positively

A Rav Huna son of Ammi said in the name of Rav Pedath who had it from
Rav Johanan:
   If one has a dream which makes him sad
   he should go and have it interpreted in the presence of three.
B He should have it interpreted!
   Has not Rav Hisda said:
      A dream which is not interpreted is like a letter which is not read?
      Say rather then: He should have a good turn given to it in the pres-
      ence of three.
C Let him bring three and say to them:
   I have seen a good dream; and they should say to him,
   Good it is and good may it be.
      May the All-Merciful turn it to good;
      Seven times may it be decreed from heaven that it should be good and
      may it be good. (b.Ber 55b)
         They should say three verses with the word *hapak* [turn], and
      three with the word *padah* [redeem] and three with the word *shalom*
      [peace].

But when the dream combines wheat and straw, how can one find this
wheat in an unpleasant dream? The rabbinic answer is given in this passage, which I have divided into three parts. In the first part (A) the problem
is stated: what should be done with bad dreams? The second part (B) is a
short comment on that problem. The first step is to interpret a bad dream;
this advice was given at the beginning of the Talmudic dream book, thus it
is not surprising that that statement is repeated here. One has to interpret
dreams like one has to read letters. However, this statement is explored
further. One has to choose to give a *good* turn, a positive interpretation,
to the unpleasant dream. In (C) one can learn how to do it. If a person
has an unpleasant dream, they must go to 'three'. These three resemble
in their number a law court. The dreamer must tell them that they had a
good dream. This is more than a definition; it is a principle and a choice.
With that it becomes clear that the unpleasant dream must be explained as
good and transformed from a bad dream into a 'good' one. Furthermore,
an unpleasant dream has to be a good dream. The 'court' must confirm
this observation with much emphasis and explicit repetitions of the positive intention. They confirm that the dream is good in four different ways
and so they exorcize the negative content of the dream. Afterwards they
quote nine biblical verses. The common denominator of the first three is

the term 'to turn'. The common denominator of the second three verses is 'redeem' and the last one is 'shalom' (peace). Hence the programme is clear: the dreamer has to turn from the negativity, and in doing so can be redeemed and thus can find peace.

The ritual is therapeutic and didactic and reveals to the dreamer implicitly that they can choose their own interpretation and even to a certain extent also their own feelings. One can battle fear, especially fears that are derived from dreams.

4 Divine dream dilemma

When Samuel saw a bad dream,
he used to say, 'The dreams speak falsely.' (Zech. 10.2)
When he saw a good dream,
he used to say: 'Do the dreams speak falsely?'
It is written, 'I [God] do speak with him in a dream.' (cf. Num. 12.6)
Raba pointed out a contradiction.
It is written, 'I do speak with him in a dream',
and it is written, 'The dreams speak falsely.'
There is no contradiction;
in the word it is through an angel,
in the other through a demon. (b.Ber 55b)

It is argued by the great Jewish scholar, Abraham Joshua Heschel, that Jewish thinking and living can only be adequately understood in terms of a dialectic pattern, containing opposite or contrasting properties. As with a magnet, the ends of which have opposite magnetic forces, opinions are opposite to one another and exemplify a polarity that lies at the very heart of Judaism.

When we look at the various views on dreams and visions in biblical traditions we also detect such polarities. It is often argued that in biblical traditions dreams are seen as having a divine origin. This seems to me not always true. Some dreams (maybe even most) are a result of the business of the day (see Eccles. 5.2, or 5.3). But some of the dreams were recognized as more important (e.g. as prophecy) (Koet 2009).

So, where do dreams come from: from God or from man? Are dreams valuable or worthless (see fragment 2)? When we listen to the judgements in b.Ber 55–7 (and also elsewhere in the Talmud or in Judaism) categorized then we find a sliding scale of answers. On the one hand there are rabbis who suggest that a dream can have a divine origin, on the other hand there are those who say that they come from people. In this passage Samuel plays with several possibilities. Dreams can come from God; dreams can be false. The origin of a dream coincides with where it comes from. Samuel declares that a bad dream is nonsense, but he considers good dreams as coming from God. This dovetails preceding fragments in which the rabbis urged to choose a positive interpretation of dreams. Samuel discharges that by taking only good dreams seriously. Raba's opposition seems to nuance the freedom of Samuel's interpretation.

5 *The dream follows the explanation*

Rav Bizna son of Zabda said in the name of Rav Akiba who had it from Rav Panda who had it from Rav Nahum, who had it from Rav Biryam in the name of a certain elder, Rav Bana'ah:

> There were twenty-four interpreters of dreams in Jerusalem.
> Once I dreamt a dream and I went to all of them
> and they all gave different interpretations,
> and all were fulfilled, thus confirming that which is said:
> All dreams follow the mouth.
> Is the statement that all dreams follow the mouth Scriptural?
> Yes, as stated by Rav Eleazar.
> For Rav Eleazar said:
> Whence do we know that all dreams follow the mouth?
> Because it says, and it came to pass,
> as he interpreted to us, so it was.
> Raba said:
> This is only if the interpretation corresponds to the content of the dream: for it says, to each man according to his dream he did interpret.
> When the chief baker saw that the interpretation was good.
> How did he know this? Rav Eleazar says:
> This tells us that each of them was shown his own dream and the interpretation of the other one's dream. (b.Ber 55b)

From the long list of rabbinic teachers it is clear that a very old tradition is quoted here. An important principle of b.Ber 55–57 is introduced. In whatever manner one explains a dream, that explanation always gives direction to what follows. This pronouncement is the key for the narrative that follows this passage, but the narrative is too long to quote here. It concerns Bar Hedya who was an interpreter of dreams. He would give a favourable interpretation to people who paid him, and an unfavourable interpretation to those who did not pay. The story shows that people are affected by such interpretations. The argument is that 'all dreams follow the mouth'. The interpretation of the dream is partially fulfilled. There is thus a connection between the word and what is going to happen. Thus dream interpreters have a certain power. The rabbinic narrative argues that having power means having responsibility.

The passage shows how the interpretation of a dream gives power and responsibility to dream interpreters, who have to be as honest as possible. However, implicitly, it is again clear that people themselves can also choose how to explain their dreams. As illustrated in fragment 3, the rabbis strive for a positive interpretation, meaning that there is no need to fear one's dreams, for one should always look for a positive explanation. For the rabbis, the art of dream interpretation is 'always look for the bright side of life'.

6 Only one-sixtieth part of dreams prophecy

(Mnemonic: *Five, Six, Ten*)
Five things are a sixtieth part of something else: namely, fire, honey, Sabbath, sleep and a dream.
Fire is one-sixtieth part of Gehinnom.
Honey is one-sixtieth part of manna.
Sabbath is one-sixtieth part of the world to come.
Sleep is one-sixtieth part of death.
A dream is one-sixtieth part of prophecy. (b.Ber 57b)

In this saying, five things can be seen as one-sixtieth part of something that is bigger. The rabbis know that a man is only shown in a dream what is suggested by his own thoughts. However, the rabbis do know that in Scripture it is said that God speaks with his prophets in dreams and visions (Num. 12.6–7). According to this statement, this possibility is very limited: only a very small number of dreams are prophetic.

Conclusion

Since Freud, dreams have primarily belonged to the psychological realm; today they also belong to the neurological field. In the world of the rabbis we meet wisdom from the past. They have a keen eye for the complexity of dreaming, for their absurd side and also for the possibility to find wisdom in them.

Their first rule seems to be that you have to pay attention to dreams. Do not ignore them, but take them seriously: a dream that is not interpreted is like a letter that is not read. The second rule is that you should always focus on the positive aspect of dreams. Even dreams that seem to be negative have a positive influence: you could learn from them. The rabbis even invent a ritual to transform dreams that provoke fear into dreams that give rise to positive feelings. It is an interesting and realistic perspective. On the one hand they take dreams so seriously that you have to listen to them. On the other hand the dreamer (or the interpreter of the dream) gets the freedom to choose a positive interpretation of the dream and as such is lord of the dream. The rabbis know that the outcome of a dream follows the interpretation and that it is thus important and realistic to choose a positive interpretation. Thus, interpreting dreams in a positive way produces a positive outcome.

This is one of the ways in which the rabbis seem to honour the complexity of the dream phenomenon, while at the same time they seem to inspire dreamers not to be afraid of their dreams. In contrast with what some people may expect, the rabbis do not attribute the origins of dreams automatically to the divine realm. Most dreams come from the dreamer. Knowing the Bible, the rabbis know that it is not impossible that some dreams are from God, and are prophetic. Rabbinic tradition seems again to be realistic. They argue that only a very small number of dreams are really prophetic. It is exactly because the rabbis honour the complexity of dreams that they can be inspiring for ministers when they encounter people who tell them their dreams.

However, the most inspiring element could be that the rabbis stress the fact that dreamers do have a choice. They do not have to be afraid of their dreams; it is always necessary to look for a positive interpretation, even of dark dreams. This practice of looking for the good side of dreamers and non-dreamers alike is something that no pastor should forget.

References and Bibliography

Alexander, P. S. (1995), Bavli Berakhot 55a–57b, 'The Talmudic Dreambook in Context', in *Journal of Jewish Studies* 46, pp. 230–48.

Flannery-Dailey, F. (2004), *Dreamers, Scribes and Priests: Jewish Dreams in the Hellenistic and Roman Eras*, Leiden: Brill.

Freud, S. (1986), *The Interpretation of Dreams*, London: Penguin.

Frieden, K. (1990), *Freud's Dream of Interpretation*, New York: State University of New York Press.

Gallop, D. (1996), *Aristotle: On Sleep and Dreams*, A text and translation with introduction, notes and glossary, Warminster: Aris and Phillips.

Gay, P. (1987), *A Godless Jew: Freud, Atheism, and the Making of Psychoanalysis*, New Haven: Yale University Press.

Gnuse, R. K. (1997), *Dreams and Dream Reports in the Writings of Josephus*, AGAJU 39, Leiden: Brill.

Gollnick, J. (1999), *The Religious Dreamworld of Apuleius' Metamorphoses: Recovering a Forgotten Hermeneutic*, Waterloo ON: Wilfrid Laurier University Press.

Handelman, S. (1981), 'Interpretation as Devotion: Freud's Relation to the Rabbinic Hermeneutics', in *The Psychoanalytic Review* 68, pp. 201–18.

Hanson, J. S. (1980), 'Dreams and Visions in the Graeco-Roman World and Early Christianity', in W. Haase, ed., *Aufstieg und Niedergang der römischen Welt* II, 23, 2, Berlin and New York: Walter de Gruyter and Co., pp. 1395–427.

Heschel, A. J. (1976), *God in Search of Man: A Philosophy of Judaism*, New York: Farrar, Straus and Giroux.

Husser, J. M. (1999), *Dreams and Dream Narratives in the Biblical World*, Sheffield: Sheffield Academic Press.

Koet, B. J. (2006), *Dreams and Scripture in Luke-Acts: Collected Essays*, Leuven: Peeters.

Koet, B. J. (2009), 'Divine Dream Dilemmas: Biblical Visions and Dreams', in K. Bulkeley, K. Adams and P. M. Davis, eds, *Dreaming in Christianity and Islam: Culture, Conflict and Creativity*, New Brunswick NJ: Rutgers University, pp. 17–31.

Koet, B. J. (2012), 'Introducing Dreaming from Hermas to Aquinas', in B. J. Koet, ed., *Dreams as Divine Communication in Christianity: From Hermas to Aquinas*, Leuven: Peeters, pp. 1–21.

Koet, B. J. (2012), 'Jerome's and Augustine's Conversion to Scripture through the Portal of Dreams' (Ep. 22; Conf. 3 and 8), in B. J. Koet, ed., *Dreams as Divine Communication in Christianity: From Hermas to Aquinas*, Leuven: Peeters, pp. 93–124.

Kristianpoller, A. (1923), 'Traum und Traumdeutung', in S. Funk, W. A. Neumann and A. Wünsche, eds, *Monumenta Talmudica* IV, Volksüberlieferungen, Teil 2 Aberglauben, Vienna/Berlin: Orion.

Levinas, E. (1981), 'Quelques vues Talmudiques sur le Rêve', in J.-J. Rassial and A. Rassial, eds, *La Psychanalyse est-elle une histoire Juive?* Paris: Le Seuil, pp. 114–28.

Oppenheim, A. L. (1956), *The Interpretation of Dreams in the Ancient Near East: With the Translation of an Assyrian Dream Book*, Philadelphia: American Philosophical Society, New Series, Vol. 46.

Niehof, M. (1992), 'A Dream which is not Interpreted is like a Letter which is not Read', in *Journal of Jewish Studies* 43, pp. 58–84.

Rice, E. (1990), *Freud and Moses: The Long Journey Home*, New York: State University of New York Press.

Stemberger, B. (1976), 'Der Traum in der Rabbinischen Literatur', in *Kairos* 18, pp. 1–42.

Stemberger, G. (1999), 'Griechisch-Römische und Rabbinische Hermeneutiek', in *Communio Viatorum* 61, pp. 101–15.

Weber, G. (2000), *Kaiser, Träume und Visionen in Prinzipat und Spätantike*, Stuttgart: Franz Steiner.

White, R. J. (1975), *Artemidorus Daldianus, The Interpretation of Dreams: Translation and Commentary*, Park Ridge NJ: Noyes Press.

9

Muslim and Freudian Dream Interpretation in Egypt

AMIRA MITTERMAIER

Al-Hagg Ahmad, an Egyptian in his eighties, once told me about his encounter with a group of German doctors. They said that all dreams are meaningless. 'You in the West are the children of Freud and of Nietzsche!' al-Hagg Ahmad responded. 'But we as Muslims *have* to believe in dreams. If you don't believe in dreams, you're not a Muslim.'

I begin with al-Hagg Ahmad's comment to highlight a widespread rhetorical insistence on a stark difference between 'West' and 'Islam'. In this chapter I seek to complicate such dichotomies by highlighting interplays and unexpected convergences. Drawing on 15 months of fieldwork in Cairo, I show how in a place where multiple traditions of dream interpretation coexist, the meaning of a dream is never stable but is always up for debate. At the same time I hope to illustrate that ethnographic attention to concrete interpretive moments can offer insight into the complex and fluid processes of meaning-making that bring into conversation dreamers, Muslim shaykhs and psychologists.

At first sight Freudian and Muslim dream interpretation indeed seem largely incompatible. Reviving the Aristotelian verdict that dreams have little to do with the Divine, Freud (1900, p. 608) famously hailed the interpretation of dreams as a 'royal road to a knowledge of the unconscious activities of the mind'. By contrast, classical and contemporary Islamic dream manuals contend that not all dreams originate in the unconscious. Rather, some dreams come *to* the dreamer, not *from* them. They are prophetic and provide ethical guidance. Underlying the two dream models are divergent views not only on the nature of dreams but also on human nature and on reality itself. Therefore, according to al-Hagg Ahmad, it is *either* Freud *or* Islam. There is no space for Muslims who are also informed by Freud or for interspaces that might be opened up when Freud's legacy comes into play with other beliefs and practices. On the ground, however, the boundaries are often blurry. In what follows I describe how western-trained psychologists in Egypt unwillingly can become caught in religious dream models, and how Muslim dream interpreters integrate Freud into their interpretive systems.

I draw on my fieldwork in Cairo in 2003–04, which involved speaking about dreams with Sufis, psychologists, dream interpreters, intellectuals and laypeople, observing dream tellings and dream interpretations, buying dream booklets, and watching dream interpretation programmes on television (see Mittermaier 2011 for further details). As I talked to people about the meaning of dreams, it quickly became clear to me that, far from subscribing to one fixed field of knowledge, my interlocutors often juggled different authoritative discourses, drawing on the Qur'anic text, hadiths (prophetic sayings), psychoanalytic interpretations, and modernist paradigms alike. For many, Islam does not stand in opposition to modern science, nor does it function as the predecessor of science or as its mirror image. Islam rather is articulated with, and through, modern science, just as science is articulated through religion.

Significantly, al-Hagg Ahmad's attempt to sort out the proper relationship between Freud and Islam does not speak to an exclusively modern dilemma. The question of how the Islamic tradition is to deal with non-Islamic knowledges has a long history. At the time of the revelation, the Prophet Muhammad had to distinguish his message from pre-Islamic thought systems, and Muslim scholars in the Abbasid period tried to negotiate the proper place for Greek philosophy within their tradition. The challenge of seemingly incompatible worldviews was posed in new ways with the rise of the natural sciences and preoccupied many Muslim reformers in the nineteenth and twentieth centuries. The Muslim reformer al-Afghānī, for instance, wrote a response to Orientalist Ernest Renan, who had argued in 1883 that a scientific outlook and Islam are entirely incompatible. While trying to refute Renan's claim, al-Afghānī (2002, p. 108) conceded, 'the Muslim religion has tried to stifle science and stop its progress'. The fact that Muslims still have not freed themselves from the yoke of tradition, in al-Afghānī's view, was ultimately the masses' fault because they dislike reason and fail to see the beauty of science. An alternative response to the challenge posed by modern science is the widespread claim of Muslim reformers that 'that's what we've been saying all along'. According to some reformist interpretations, the nature of microbes, the ozone layer, the shape of the moon's orbit around the earth, and human embryonic development are all already prefigured in the Qur'an. Not surprisingly, then, a modern Islamic psychology was developed in the latter half of the twentieth century, which equates Qur'anic concepts with their Freudian counterparts. In the Qur'an, *nafs* refers to the soul or human self. It moves through three stages. *Al-nafs al-amāra* (the commanding self) is controlled by passion and impulses; it commands evil (e.g. Qur'an 12:53). *Al-nafs al-lawāma* (the reproaching self) is torn between good and evil (e.g. 75:2). *Al-nafs al-mutma'inna* (the trusting self), which is the highest stage, is the self at peace (e.g. 89:27). When equated with their Freudian counterparts, *al-nafs al-amāra* becomes the id, *al-nafs al-lawāma* the superego, and *al-nafs al-mutma'inna* the ego. Mustafa Mahmūd, a prominent religious figure in Egypt, developed a 'Qur'anic psychology', and Muslim scholars in the Gulf States and Malaysia similarly have been active in working towards an Islamization of psychology, taking writings by medieval scholars such al-Kindī (d. 873), al-Tabarī (d. 923), al-Rāzī (d. 925), Ibn Sīnā (d. 1037), al-Ghazālī (d. 1111), Ibn Bajjah (d. 1138) and Ibn Tufayl (d. 1185) as possible starting points (Haquem 1997). (See also Abaza (2002) on the Islamization of the sciences more broadly.)

Regardless of whether Islam and modern science are described as incompatible or as fully compatible, they are both conceptualized as distinct entities. Yet, as Stefania Pandolfo (2000, p. 123) notes in her work on spirit healers and psychiatrists in Morocco, concepts of cultural authenticity that are embraced by Orientalists and nationalists alike 'obliterate the long history of exchanges and transformations in the shaping of those entities that are today called the Arab world and the West'. Diverging from al-Hagg Ahmad's claim about an inherent incompatibility and from reformist attempts at harmonization, I want to draw attention to interspaces, ambiguities, and the messiness that comes into play when actual dreams are told and interpreted in Egypt today. After a brief excursion into Muslim dream interpretation, I examine the interpretive work performed by two Egyptian men of roughly the same age: a psychoanalyst and a Muslim dream interpreter. As we will see, for Muslim dream interpreters the line between classical texts and imported psychological dream models can be highly porous. At the same time, sceptical psychoanalysts sometimes unwillingly get caught in religious idioms. The epistemes offered by the Islamic tradition and the secular sciences continuously inform and inflect one another.

Muslim dream interpretation

Ta'bīr, dream interpretation in classical Arabic, literally means 'taking across, making something pass over'. In Islamic traditions, the dream interpreter is a mediator between the divine and the human realm. Muslim dream interpretation goes back to the time of the Prophet Muhammad, who supposedly interpreted his followers' dreams and assured them that the only form of prophecy left after his death would come in the form of truthful dream visions.[1] The dream vision (*ru'yā*) is considered to be a divine gift, and classical dream manuals and contemporary dream interpreters distinguish it from two other kinds of dreams: those inspired by the devil or evil spirits (*hulm*) and dreams that reflect the dreamer's wishes and worries (*hadīth nafsī*). Because of their close relationship to prophecy, dream visions were highly valued in the Islamic tradition, and dream interpretation for a long time was understood to be an orthodox practice – see Fahd (1966), Kinberg (1994), Lamoreaux (2002) and Schimmel (1998) for more details on the history of Muslim dream interpretation. The Muslim oneiric tradition did not evolve in isolation but was greatly affected by Artemidorus's famous dream book, which was translated from Greek into Arabic in the ninth century (Lamoreaux 2002). More than a thousand years later another dream model entered into dialogue with the continuously reimagined Muslim tradition of dream interpretation. Around 1950 the Freudian legacy crossed over into Egypt, making it the first country in the Middle East to actively engage with psychoanalysis.

The importation of psychoanalysis was part of a larger endeavour concerned with enabling Egypt to 'catch up' with Europe. Since the early nineteenth century, Egyptian students had been travelling to Europe to seek knowledge, spurred by the urgently felt and constantly re-created need to help Egypt overcome its supposed backwardness. One of the many students who went to Paris in the early twentieth century was Mustafa Ziwer. Born in 1907, Ziwer had been among the first philosophy students at what is now Cairo University, and after graduating in 1927 he left for France, where he studied philosophy, medicine, chemistry, biology and applied psychology, and also underwent psychoanalysis. On his return to Egypt, he was appointed by Taha Hussain, then minister of education, to found the first psychology department in Cairo in 1950, and he came to be praised as the first Egyptian, or even first Arab, psychoanalyst. Whereas most of the people seeking Ziwer's help as an analyst came from elite backgrounds, Freudian theories travelled into Egyptian households by way of Ziwer's radio programmes. On Cairo's campuses, as an elderly Egyptian psychologist told me, 'Freud was like the Qur'an at that time.'

Referring to India, Ashis Nandy (1995, pp. 82, 138) has noted that psychoanalysis, after having become a 'positive science, an exportable technology, and an index of progress', was imported 'into the [so-called]

---

1 I use the term 'dream vision' to maintain some of the ambiguity that surrounds the term *ru'yā*. According to classical sources, a *ru'yā* can come in the form of a truthful dream or a waking vision. My Egyptian interlocutors sometimes did not specify whether they were awake or asleep when seeing a *ru'yā*.

savage world in the high noon of imperialism'. In Egypt, too, the importation of Freud's theories can be understood as part of a larger modernization movement. Freudian psychology arrived infused with claims to
truth, authority and expertise. It was a form of modern science that, in
Foucault's words (1988, p. 106), is a 'power that forces you to say certain
things, if you are not to be disqualified not only as being wrong, but, more
seriously than that, as being a charlatan'. Whereas the relevance of Freud
continues to be debated in the West (not to mention within and between
various schools of psychoanalysis) and whereas the rise of pharmaceut-
icals and biomedical models have undermined psychoanalytic explanatory
models in many places (Luhrmann 2001), my interlocutors in Egypt tend
to refer to Freud's model as *'ilmī* (scientific). By contrast, Muslim dream
interpretation is often called *fulklūrī* (folkloristic), *sha'bī* (popular) or
usūlī (traditional).

Contemporary Egyptians have a basic familiarity with Freudian concepts, but this does not mean that his theories are simply accepted as
true or even relevant. During my fieldwork I was repeatedly struck by the
ambiguous place western psychology holds in Egyptians' everyday dream
talk. Just like the Muslim reformers, laypeople sometimes claim that what
Islam says ultimately coincides with what modern science says. Others
draw on western psychology to prove that Muslim dream interpretation
is backward, outdated, unscientific and ultimately un-Islamic. Al-Azhar,
the authoritative institution of Sunni Islam, and key figures of the Islamic
Revival movement have decried dream interpretation as charlatanry in
recent years, and the Egyptian Ministry of Religious Affairs has claimed,
'there is nothing in the Islamic religion that confirms the idea of dream
interpretation'. Azharite and state-aligned critics sometimes reject both
Muslim dream interpretation and western psychological models. Still
others, such as al-Hagg Ahmad, defend the Islamic interpretive tradition
while claiming that Freud is mistaken or irrelevant for Muslim dreams.
'Freud is wrong,' an imam told me, 'because he relates everything back to
sex.' In any case, the imam continued, none of the people who go to the
mosque and pray regularly will ever need a psychologist.

Freudian psychology and Muslim reformism have by no means margin-
alized religious dream discourses in Egypt. On the contrary, there seems to
have been a revival of interest in dream interpretation in the wake of the
larger Islamic Revival since the 1970s. Muslim dream interpretation is mar-
keted today by way of cheap paperback books, newspaper and magazine
columns, TV programmes, websites and CD-Rom. This renewed, mass-
mediated interest in dreams does not exclude Freudian psychology but
often incorporates it. Next to the many new editions of standard Muslim

dream manuals, one finds in Cairo's street stalls booklets featuring titles such as *Dreams and Nightmares: Scientific and Religious Interpretation, Dreams Between Science and Belief* and *The Foundations and Principles of Dream Interpretation Between Freud and the Muslim Scholars.*

The very distinction between 'science' and 'belief', which gets recycled in these titles, is itself the outcome of a specific understanding of science that finds its roots in the Enlightenment. Yet on Cairo's streets, in every-day dream talk, and on Egyptian television this distinction often becomes blurry. A prophetic or divine sign in the eyes of some can be a hallucina-tory projection according to others. These debates are not necessarily pre-dictable along the lines of who is inside and who outside which tradition or who considers herself more closely aligned to it. Neither the Islamic nor the psychological dream episteme is a homogeneous, unchanging entity. Far from the Freudian legacy simply displacing the religious interpretive model, the two dream epistemes have come to mutually constitute each other in ways that are not always predictable.

To illustrate this process, I next turn to two interpretive moments that centre on terms widely associated with Freud: *desire* and the *unconscious*. As we will see, though seemingly Freudian, these terms carry within them multiple layers and possibilities of meaning.

Hungry people dream of bread

Dr Hakim (a pseudonym) is an Egyptian Lacanian psychoanalyst and one of Mustafa Ziwer's former students. At the time of my fieldwork he was retired. I visited him a number of times because I enjoyed his profound knowledge of European and Egyptian literature and his detailed memories of the early years of psychology in Egypt. He, by contrast, seemed some-what ambivalent about our meetings and my research. Although he was generally welcoming, he was critical of popular dream beliefs and seemed annoyed by my interest in the work of Muslim dream interpreters. 'They're all charlatans,' he said whenever I told him about the shaykhs I worked with. 'Dreams are not about prophecy at all; they're about desire (*raghba*).'

During one of our conversations I brought up a popular dream inter-pretation programme on Egyptian television that used to feature a shaykh and a psychologist.[2] On this show viewers called in to tell of their dreams, and the shaykh would discern what kind of dream they were recounting

---

2 'Shaykh' here refers to an Islamic scholar or authority figure.

and, accordingly, who should interpret it. The shaykh took on all divinely inspired dream visions; the rest he left to the psychologist. For many Egyptians this show was a perfect example of how 'science' and 'religion' could harmoniously be brought together. When I mentioned the programme to Dr Hakim, he told me that he once was invited to participate but declined the offer because he disliked the fact that the shaykh always had the last word on the programme. He added in passing that he used to run his own dream programme on a Saudi Arabian satellite television station in the late 1990s. Together with a colleague he interpreted dreams of viewers who called in to the show. Curious about the programme, I borrowed a stack of videotapes from Dr Hakim and watched them at home. Besides the décor, which featured the two psychologists on black leather seats placed on top of clouds – godlike, one might say – what intrigued me most about the programme was the complex interpretive field the psychologists were required to navigate. They had to respond to dreams such as the following, related by a woman calling from Qatar: 'I have recurrent dreams, spiritual dreams; I'm in contact with people. I'm afraid when I wake up. After my father died, I used to still communicate with him. The Prophet also comes to me in my dreams. At first I was not sure whether it was him, but then I prayed *istikhāra* to find out and I saw him again . . . Does that mean I'm clairvoyant?'

While only saying a few sentences, the woman evokes a range of potentially meaningful dreams. She refers to dreams of the dead, dreams of the Prophet, and *istikhāra* dreams. The latter are dreams seen after a prayer through which one seeks advice when feeling unable to decide between two permissible alternatives. A dream seen after this prayer is generally taken to be a divinely sent answer, a dream vision, a *ru'yā*.

Knowing Dr Hakim, one would expect a triple negation in response to the woman's questions: No, it's not really the Prophet you see; you only want to see him. No, *istikhāra* does not provide God-sent answers. And no, you're not clairvoyant. Wanting to see the Prophet and truly seeing the Prophet are separated by an insurmountable gap, from Dr Hakim's customary point of view.

Yet the religious colouring of the dreams (and the fact that the programme is broadcast on a channel based in Saudi Arabia)[3] makes such a

---

3 Wahhabism, an eighteenth-century reform movement and today the official doctrine of Saudi Arabia, aims at purging Islam of all 'superstitions'. Yet Wahhabi scholars are often ambiguous with regard to dream interpretation. Often they call the practice un-Islamic while acknowledging the possibility of divinely inspired dream visions. This partially explains why dreams and dream interpretations are not simply erased from Saudi-based TV programmes.

bluntly negative answer impossible. Dr Hakim diplomatically responds by quoting the well-known hadith (prophetic saying) that affirms that whoever sees the Prophet in a dream vision has truly seen him. Then he refers to another prophetic tradition that defines the dream vision as one of 46 parts of prophecy. Though not a Muslim dream interpreter, Dr Hakim seems to be caught in an authoritative discourse, which, as Bakhtin (1981, p. 342) has noted, 'demands that we acknowledge it, that we make it our own; it binds us, quite independent of any power it might have to persuade us internally; we encounter it with its authority already fused to it'. Though most probably not persuaded internally, Dr Hakim gives a religious response to what has been framed as a series of religious dreams. He adopts a religious discursive rationale to make himself heard and to authorize his discourse. Thus, not only modern science can force people to say certain things if they are not to be disqualified as being wrong or as being a charlatan, but, depending on the context, so can religious traditions.

Dr Hakim's colleague, another Egyptian psychoanalyst, jumps in to suggest that the dreams of the deceased father are clearly related to the woman's longing. This allows Dr Hakim to switch his interpretive mode and to emphasize that the woman's dreams are indeed a form of wish fulfilment. Before moving on to the next caller, the colleague adds a final word of psychological wisdom: 'Hungry people dream of bread.'

While this final statement seemingly reasserts the authority of the psychological explanation, the woman's own framing of her dreams as religiously significant and the psychoanalyst's initial reference to the prophetic tradition have already destabilized the universal explanatory power of psychology. Even introducing the concept of desire does not unambiguously close this opening because desire is itself an overdetermined term that is at home in multiple interpretive traditions and that can index very different conceptions of the real. The Islamic dream model recognizes the role of longing in evoking visions of the Prophet but the fact that dream encounters with the Prophet can be evoked does not mean that they are hallucinatory. In the Islamic model, rather, desire can pave the road for a divinely sent dream vision. Whereas the hungry fantasize about bread in their dreams but still wake up hungry, the religious dreamer might use her longing to invite a real visit of the Prophet or encounters with the dead.

The interchange between the Qatari woman and the two psychoanalysts problematizes the assumption that the secular sciences will always be the authoritative way to explain natural phenomena in today's world. It shows that, along with social contexts, the authority of interpretive approaches can shift, and that the same terms can underline the truth of very different conceptions of the real. Interpretations do not take place in empty space, but they are shaped by the social contexts in which they occur. What Dr Hakim says on television is very different from what he told me in his living room. Yet the fact that the psychoanalyst gives in to a religious authoritative discourse should not simply be understood as resulting from the necessity of hiding his 'true' views because he lives in a repressive society. This kind of playing into context occurs around the world, including in North America and Europe. Dr Hakim's invocation of a religious discourse on television is just one instance of how he uses different discourses in different contexts. In doing so, he changes the way he engages with his profession and, probably unwillingly, expands the meaning of *desire*.

The unconscious resignified

Along with the practice of psychoanalysis, Mustafa Ziwer imported a distinct Freudian notion of the unconscious into Egypt; a concept that is particularly complex, as Lacan (1978) and Ellenberger (1970) elucidate further. Although Freud (1900, p. 143) acknowledged that 'there is at least one spot in every dream at which it is unplumbable – a navel, as it were, that is its point of contact with the unknown', dominant under-standings of his theory take the origin of dreams to be limited to a faculty located inside the human subject. Adopting the belief that all dreams originate in this particular faculty, Egyptian psychologists tend to deny the possibility that dreams might offer insight into a metaphysical world. Rather than refute the existence of this metaphysical realm altogether, they often refer to Qur'anic verses that state that only God has keys to the unknown.[4] Although psychologists insist that dreams offer access only to the personal but not to a metaphysical unknown, psychological tropes can be picked up and resignified by religious dream interpreters. Like the concept of desire, the unconscious is heavy with cultural baggage but it is never a stable term. Far from being the sole and mechanistic source of dreams, it might become a medium of communication with a supernatural Elsewhere. This ongoing resignification of religious and psychological dream concepts can be illustrated through an interpretation offered by Shaykh Nabil, a Muslim dream interpreter in Cairo and one of my key interlocutors during my fieldwork.

---

4 For example, 6:59: 'For, with Him are the keys to the things that are beyond the reach of a created being's perception: none knows them but He' (Muhammad Asad's translation).

Dr Hakim and Shaykh Nabil were roughly of the same age but belong to different socio-economic classes. Shaykh Nabil lived in a working-class neighbourhood and Dr Hakim in an upper-middle-class one. Although both men interpreted dreams, they drew on different interpretive traditions. Whereas Dr Hakim's intellectual trajectory was shaped by his engagement with Freud, Lacan and Ziwer, Shaykh Nabil was the guardian of the shrine of Ibn Sīrīn, an eighth-century scholar who has long been considered the father of Muslim dream interpretation. The majority of dream booklets sold on Cairo's streets are ascribed to Ibn Sīrīn, usually offering updated and abridged versions of his classic manual. Shaykh Nabil, now deceased, spent most of his time at Ibn Sīrīn's small shrine, reading the Qur'an, praying, sleeping, smoking *shīsha*, receiving visitors and interpreting dreams. He liked to refer to himself as the 'little Ibn Sīrīn' or the 'modern Ibn Sīrīn'. Whereas other Muslim dream interpreters are dismissive of Freud, Shaykh Nabil had no problem with evoking Freud when interpreting dreams because he believed that Freud can help bring the tradition up to date. His understanding of Freud's theory is admittedly reductive yet it is simultaneously expansive as he applied Freudian concepts to divinely inspired dream visions as well.

Shaykh Nabil also interpreted dreams online but without actually ever touching a computer. A journalist printed out the dream texts that are sent to a website and dropped them off at the shrine on a weekly basis. In a stack of papers that the journalist brought to the shrine one day in November 2003 was the dream of a 22-year-old Egyptian woman named Huda who had written the following: 'I saw in my sleep one of my dear friends, and he was dead. In truth he's not dead. Twice a month I have this dream, and every time I wake up and find myself crying. I also cry in the dream.'

Other dreams in the stack were longer, others even shorter; some more vivid or more dramatic. Huda's dream was not exceptional in any way. Without a moment of hesitation Shaykh Nabil jotted down his response on the lower half of the page: 'The message is from the unconscious (*al-lā wa'y*) and it points to a happy future. It is a glad tiding (*bushra*) of the death of the past, of the beginning of the future, and of leaving behind hardships. The symbol of death in the dream is the death of the past. We die in the dream and wake up to new life. [The dream] directs you to a happy future.'

The effect apparently intended by Shaykh Nabil's interpretation was to dispel Huda's worries. According to his response, she had nothing to be concerned about. The dream that had troubled her turned out to be a foretelling of a not clearly defined yet happy future. That death symbolizes life and crying means release from hardship resonates with standard Muslim dream manuals. What is unusual in the shaykh's interpretation, however, is his use of the term *unconscious*. The exact word he uses is the Arabic word *al-lā wa'y*, a term borrowed from modern psychology and generally associated with Freud in Egypt. Shaykh Nabil's terminology is perplexing because it erases the line between a meaningful dream vision and a dream that merely reflects the dreamer's concerns and wishes. Many of my Egyptian interlocutors hold that dream visions are seen by the dreamer's heart (*qalb*) or by her spirit (*rūh*), which leaves the sleeping body and roams in an intermediary realm called the *barzakh* where it can communicate with the spirits of the dead. Others relate dream visions to a heightened perceptiveness of one's inner gaze (*basīra*), or they told me that dream angels transmit dream visions to the dreamer. The term *unconscious* seems out of place when speaking of prophetic dream visions.

I visited Shaykh Nabil a few days later to ask him to explain his interpretation of Huda's dream. How can a dream that comes from the unconscious tell Huda something about the future? How can it be a *bushra*, a glad tiding, which according to the Prophet Muhammad would come only in the form of divinely sent dreams?[5] Would not a dream that springs from the unconscious simply index Huda's wishes and worries? Where then does her dream originate: in her unconscious or in an Elsewhere?

Although Shaykh Nabil seemed irritated by my questions, he ordered tea for both of us from the street café facing the shrine, sat down with me, and explained, once again, that things do not have to be so black and white. The 'unconscious' (*al-lā wa'y*) and the 'inner mind' (*al-'aql al-bātin*), he told me, refer to the same thing. As he phrased it, 'It's like the sun that shines here and there but is felt differently in different places and called by different names.' He explained that the inner mind is located in the heart and that it is much stronger than the conscious mind because it has the capacity to read from the Eternal Tablet in heaven. The Eternal Tablet (*al-lawh al-mahfūz*) generally refers to an archetypical repository of the Qur'an, or more broadly to a heavenly tablet on which all human destinies are inscribed. The dream angels who transmit dream images to the dreamer are sometimes said to read the dream vision on the Eternal Tablet and to then deliver it to the dreamer, either by showing it to her inner gaze or by telling her the dream vision. In claiming that the unconscious

---

5 The term *bushra* is derived from the same root as *mubashshirāt* (glad tidings), which the Prophet Muhammad announced to be the only thing that would be left of prophecy after his death. When asked what glad tidings are, the Prophet answered, 'truthful dream visions' (*al-ru'yā al-sādiqa*).

has access to this Eternal Tablet, Shaykh Nabil turns the unconscious into a medium that offers insight not into the depths of the human mind but into a metaphysical Elsewhere. His interpretation contrasts sharply with that of Orientalists, who referred to the unconscious to suggest that the Prophet Muhammad wrongly believed that his revelation experiences originated outside himself. Deferring to the authority of 'modern advances in psychology and psychiatry', Maxime Rodinson (1980, p. 77) argued that the concept of the unconscious enabled us to understand the true nature of the Prophet's so-called revelation. Similarly, Montgomery Watt (1974, p. 17) remarked that the 'modern Westerner' realizes that what seems to the Prophet to come from 'outside himself' can really come from the unconscious and that Muhammad might have simply been a man with a strong 'creative imagination'. For Shaykh Nabil the imagination encompasses a much broader range of possibilities (including prophetic ones), and evoking the unconscious does not make the dream experience any less real or relevant. A dream that is received by the unconscious in his view can reveal a timeless truth and future events. The unconscious here is a prophetic medium.

Shaykh Nabil only seemingly locates the origin of the dream within the dreamer. Although he is familiar with Freud's notion that unconscious wishes motivate dreams, he subsumes the term under his own dream theory, which implies a less sealed model of the self than that underlying the Freudian paradigm. He agrees that most dreams arise from what one is preoccupied with, but according to his semi-Freudian interpretation, a dream can be a hope and a manifestation from God even at the same time. Thus, although modernity did not introduce subjective interiority to Islam, one might say that Freudian psychology has provided Shaykh Nabil and other interpreters with a new vocabulary for talking about the relationship between the religious self and an Elsewhere. For Freud the concept of the unconscious served as evidence that dreams *cannot* come from a metaphysical Elsewhere; Shaykh Nabil (maybe unknowingly) challenges these assumptions. For him the unconscious is the immediate source of the dream, but it ultimately belongs to God and is operated by His will.

Conclusion

I have described two interpretive moments in which the line between Freud and Islam becomes blurry. My ethnographic examples illustrate the fluidity and openness of both the Freudian and the Islamic tradition of dream interpretation as they are understood and enacted in Egypt today.

In the case of Dr Hakim, the disciplinary power of the Islamic tradition traps a sceptical psychoanalyst. In the case of Shaykh Nabil, a Muslim dream interpreter resignifies psychoanalytic vocabularies. By juxtaposing these examples, I hope to have complicated the notion that the secular sciences are always necessarily hegemonic. Islamic *and* secular discursive traditions can force people to say certain things if they want to be taken seriously, and only close attention to context can allow us to trace the shifting terrains of hegemony.

At times attention to interplay might run the risk of overlooking the power relations that frame, delimit and shape this very interplay. I opened my discussion with al-Hagg Ahmad's assertion that one is *either* a follower of Freud and Nietzsche *or* a Muslim, and I suggested that such claims to incompatibility can be made purposefully, not only by Orientalists or nationalist purists but also in the context of everyday, mundane encounters. Al-Hagg Ahmad makes his claim to make a particular point in a particular context and while talking to particular people: German doctors at first, and later me, a German-Egyptian anthropologist associated with a US institution at the time. In the current political climate it is easily understandable why al-Hagg Ahmad would want to construct a sealed Muslim identity and to assert its superiority. His utterance subverts claims to the inherent superiority of western knowledge systems.

Ultimately, which dreams are projections and which the result of divine inspiration often remains ambiguous in Egypt. The origin of Huda's dream is suspended between the unconscious and an Elsewhere, and whether the woman from Qatar truly saw the Prophet or whether she only wanted to see him is left an open question in the psychoanalyst's dream show. I have attempted to highlight this openness and ambiguity.

A focus on ambiguity can also alert us to the fact that the West is just as full of internal debates and contests for intellectual legitimacy as is Egypt. Even Freudian psychology itself is not a closed system. Through his rereading of Freud, Jacques Lacan (2002) has opened a space for alterity within Freud's theory, and James DiCenso (1998) argues that, besides the more widely known tendency toward closure in Freud's work, one can detect conflicting qualities that resist totalization. According to such readings, dream interpretation even in Freud's writings can be seen as a paradigm for an opening to alterity that has profound ethical implications. Maybe this openness and excess in Freud is more tangible in Egypt, where his theories are subverted, resignified and opened up not necessarily through a conscious act of resistance on the part of traditionalists but rather through an ongoing reimagining of what dreams are and where they come from.

References

Abaza, M. (2002), *Debates on Islam and Knowledge in Malaysia and Islam: Shifting Worlds*, New York: Routledge.

al-Afghani, J. al-D. (2002), 'Answer to Renan', in C. Kurzman, ed., *Modernist Islam, 1840–1940: A Sourcebook*, Oxford: Oxford University Press, pp. 103–10.

Bakhtin, M. M. (1981), 'Discourse in the Novel', in *The Dialogic Imagination: Four Essays*, ed. M. Holquist, trans. C. Emerson and M. Holquist, Austin: University of Texas Press.

DiCenso, J. (1998), *The Other Freud: Religion, Culture and Psychoanalysis*, New York: Routledge.

Ellenberger, H. (1970), *The Discovery of the Unconscious: The History and Evolution of Dynamic Psychiatry*, New York: Basic Books.

Fahd, T. (1966), *La Divination arabe: Études religieuses, sociologiques et folkloriques sur le milieu natif de l'Islam*, Leiden: Brill.

Foucault, M. (1988), *Politics, Philosophy, Culture: Interviews and Other Writings, 1977–1984*, ed. L. D. Kritzman, New York: Routledge.

Freud, S. (1900), 'The Interpretation of Dreams', in *The Standard Edition of the Complete Psychological Works of Sigmund Freud*, ed. J. Strachey, London: Hogarth.

Haquem, A. (1997), 'Psychology and Religion: Their Relationship and Integration from an Islamic Perspective', in *American Journal of Islamic Social Sciences* 15(4), pp. 97–115.

Kinberg, L. (1994), *Ibn Abī al-Dunyā: Morality in the Guise of Dreams*, Leiden: Brill.

Lacan, J. (1978), *The Four Fundamental Concepts of Psychoanalysis*, ed. J.-A. Miller, trans. A. Sheridan, New York: Norton.

Lacan, J. (2002), *Ecrits: A Selection*, trans. Alan Sheridan, New York: Norton.

Lamoreaux, J. C. (2002), *The Early Muslim Tradition of Dream Interpretation*, Albany: State University of New York Press.

Luhrmann, T. (2001), *Of Two Minds: An Anthropologist Looks at American Psychiatry*, New York: Vintage.

Mittermaier, A. (2011), *Dreams That Matter: Egyptian Landscapes of the Imagination*, Berkeley: University of California Press.

Nandy, A. (1995), *The Savage Freud and Other Essays on Possible and Retrievable Selves*, Princeton NJ: Princeton University Press.

Pandolfo, S. (2000), 'The Thin Line of Modernity: Some Moroccan Debates on Subjectivity', in T. Mitchell, ed., *Questions of Modernity*, Minneapolis: University of Minnesota Press, pp. 115–47.

Rodinson, M. (1980), *Muhammad*, New York: Pantheon.

Schimmel, A. (1998), *Die Träume des Kalifen: Träume und ihre Deutung in der islamischen Kultur*, Munich: Verlag C.H. Beck.

Watt, W. M. (1974), *Muhammad: Prophet and Statesman*, London: Oxford University Press.

Dream Narrative 3

Renewed Through an Invitation
to Dance my Life

ANNETTE DUBOIS-VAN HOORN

Translated by H. A. M. Zwemmer

The month of November in the year 2009 was a barren period in my life. I had been trying to recuperate from a burn-out. It had become clear to me that I did not want to continue my life in the way I had done before. I was still searching for an answer to the question of the way in which I wanted to change my life. During this period I had a dream to which I gave the title 'Three tests'.

Three tests

The dream begins with me entering a classroom in order to take a test. In preparation for this test I had studied an article. I am surprised to see that all chairs have been placed in a circle. I sit down, as do several other people, all unknown to me. A group discussion follows. The question is put to me: 'What is praying?' My answer is: 'To be silent.'

Again I am to take a test but this time in a different classroom. The test has been composed by my husband Harry. The subject of the test is 'wave and flow'. Or is it 'weave'? I cannot quite see whether it is 'wave' or 'weave'.

Finally I have to take a third test. This time I have to go to the Dom Cathedral. I walk towards this church with my friend from primary school, H., her daughter and another child. H. shows me the way; she seems to be quite at home here. Her daughter opens the little door of a box pew so I can take a seat. In the meantime many people have gathered in the church. All start singing together:

In the beginning the earth lay lost,
In the beginning there was darkness.

God spoke his word
And light was born,
Light which is still our day up to now.

After this song a baldachin is carried into the church with loud bell-ringing. I am curious, get up and intend to get a closer look. As I walk it gets pitch-black in the church. I cannot see my hand in front of my face. I can only go by the sound of the bells. What I do see is the bright white dress of the priest. The baldachin makes its journey round in the church and I follow until I find an empty space on a bench and take a seat. From somewhere my name sounds three times, loud and clear. I am frightened and nervously look at my neighbour. Fortunately, it is an old friend, C.; we studied together at the school for kindergarten teachers. I explain to her how I could not find my initial place and thus had decided to sit down next to her.

The dream continues. I see how a dance forms part of the service. We have to practise all the steps before we will be able to perform really well. The teacher is dressed in white. I do not succeed in mastering the steps but I really have to. There is no other solution than to practise the steps again exclusively with the dancing teacher. First he tells me to bend my knees three times with the rhythm of the music; after that I have to remain still and feel what lives inside me. Subsequently we practise seven times. I have to feel the rhythm in my body. When I woke up I still felt the music and the rhythm in me.

How to interpret this dream?

It certainly helped that during the time of this dream I took part in a group in which people told each other about their dreams and their possible meanings. When I wrote down my dream I noticed how often the number 'three' occurred: three people dressed in white, three locations, three tests, three times I am called by my name, and dancing three times. In the Bible the third day is the day of the resurrection. This helped to find a direction in which to find the meaning of my dream. It confirmed my feeling that this had not been just another dream . . . The text of the song, 'In the beginning the earth lay lost', also points in this direction. The Light, the opposite of the earth and the pitch-blackness, still comes along with the day.

In the dream group we elaborated these themes. The tests are special. I was not asked to show my knowledge but I am invited to surrender myself to the flow and to be taken by the 'wave'. Surrendering to the flow is not self-evident to me. I need assistants. They are welcome to be intertwined ('weave' in the dream) in my life.

The child in me could be such an assistant. She evokes a feeling of wonder in me. Her innocence and naivety help me to cross the bridge to find the way inside. Her presence helps me not to think too much but just to experience how I am allowed to stand here, to be and to go.

The baldachin sets me in motion. The bell-ringing announces that something important is about to happen. It sounds like bliss. Three times my name is being called. In the church, when I have found a place next to C., I apologize: 'Lord, I am not worthy . . .' But I am, as it later turns out.

Part of the liturgy is a dance. I do not succeed in mastering this dance. I have to practise and am given private tuition. The baldachin transforms, becomes the priest. This is no coincidence; I am to be initiated. A preparation for this initiation is that I discover how praying can mean to be silent. Silent like Mary, who weighed all the words in her heart when the angel Gabriel had spoken to her.

The priest turns into the dancing teacher. He helps me to learn the dance. Not only with my head, but I learn with my whole body. I am allowed to stand for something, I am upright, standing up. To stand up means: I am here. That is the dance in the end. With it I give an answer to the voice that had called out my name. This dance could have been the answer to the healing of the crippled woman in the Gospel according to St Luke (13.10–13).

The dance is presence in full glory. The dance allows me to show myself. God has incarnated in me. Long after the dream I still feel how I went on my knees, how I surrendered myself to my vocation and to the one who called my name.

The dream and after

This dream will travel with me for the rest of my life. Most of this dream was one impressive affirmation: I am on the right track! To receive such an indication during a barren time in your life is an enormous stimulus.

During the time described above I attended classes to make a change of career. In one of the classes I made a painting, a symbolic map that represented my country, the place where I would function optimally. This map showed clearly how my future would be to work in my own practice and to accompany and coach clients on their life path. No longer would I be part of an institution but I would work as an independent person. I would shape my own dance. After this course I rounded off my activities in the institution I worked for and started my own office. From the moment I had made my decision to start my own practice the work just offered itself. In the dream I discovered how learning was not just a matter of the head, the brain; in the same way now I saw how there had been no need to direct my life beforehand. If I find the courage to show myself, I will meet with all that is meaningful and essential to my life. This makes me a free person. In this connection the dream implies a mission for me: I will have to take care not to let the dance in me be broken.

Recently the theme occurred to me again. Spontaneously I was repeatedly drawing people dancing. I wondered what this dance in my artistic expressions meant. While I was drawing I felt how I shrank back from presenting my plan for a writing workshop to a healthcare organization. Drawing the dance helped me cross that bridge. It helped to make me stand for what I am, what I can do and what I want.

A woman who dances, a strong lady who is not afraid to show her strength. More and more I become the woman who stands up for frail men and women. From deep inside I know what it is like to be fragile and vulnerable. It is my challenge to bring these people back in contact with their own strength. These people cross my path with a request for individual coaching or course that I teach.

Also in the appeal to buddy up with someone or to be a volunteer aid, I can bring my strength into my action. In this way my dream has become a permanent mandala. A way to go inside myself, become still and go out again, show myself and dance my life.

Dream Narrative 4

Guidance Through Dreams and Synchronicities at a Major Turning Point in Life

BARBARA KONING

In this narrative I recount a dream followed by a series of accompanying synchronicities. In faith I have come to value this particular golden thread of interrelated experiences as divine guidance to find my soul's and my life's destination at a major turning point in my life.

Biography

During the course of my life, it suddenly occurred to me that the concrete themes of a specific time of prayer in my young adulthood – during which I had formulated a sincere vow to God – had been materializing in various ways and at various times, without myself having originated them. This was a moment of awakening. I became aware that I had been living immersed in a series of multiple empirical events that had been 'meaningfully coinciding but not causally determined'. Such events, which are a-causally connected through meaning, have been entitled 'synchronicity' by Carl G. Jung (1978). I started to read books on this phenomenon (to mention only a few, these included Jaworski 1996; Joseph 2002; Mansfield 1995; Moss 2007; Rockwood Hudson 2000; Rushnell 2002; Bolen 1979; Sparks 2007). And much of what I understood sustained me in taking my life's synchronistic experiences very seriously. This phenomenon is widespread, perhaps even universal. I also gained much support when I found that it is honoured by Christian authors too (e.g. Rockwood-Hudson 2000; Rushnell 2002).

Following advice given by Joseph, from 2004 on, I put into practice the keeping of two parallel journals – one on synchronistic events and another on nightly dreams. I was inspired by his remark that sometimes the two diaries will coincide – when dreams and events in waking life are synchronizing – a case that will offer special divine guidance (Joseph 2002, p. 156). From that moment on a new world of discoveries opened. Smaller lessons have prepared me step by step to receive all the more consciously those gifts that were brought through synchronicities. I could offer several examples, but I will select one.

This series of meaningfully interconnected incidents took place over the course of 14 months. At first hummingbirds turned up in a dream. A few months after that dream, hummingbirds showed up in graphic form in two successive days at several times and places. In that same year great turmoil was taking place at work, demanding me to make some radical new choices. And then, completely unexpectedly, a living hummingbird suddenly crossed my path. That little being, very alive and very concrete and so near to me, appeared to me as being a tender message from God letting me know that I had made the right choices during what was a difficult and major turning point in life. To me this meant that I could anticipate a very meaningful future. Let me give you the detailed version of my story.

Hummingbirds showing up in a dream

Date: Summer 2007. The next scene is part of a much longer dream.

I am among a large audience that is situated outdoors. In front of the many rows of our chairs, a stage has been set up. During a break everyone's attention is somewhat distracted and people are chatting and walking around and so on. I have stayed seated. As I occasionally glance in front of me, I turn out to be watching something very special. It happens within in a split second and goes by unnoticed by most of the other spectators. Above the stage I see a small group of beautifully coloured tiny birds. They are flying from the left to the right. It strikes me how their positions appear to be arranged geometrically during their flight in space, looking a bit like a squadron, as if they have been tamed in a way and love to show their abilities in this aesthetic performance. Before I realize what it is that I am looking at, the show is already over.

As I wake up I am pretty sure that I have been watching hummingbirds. It is a species that does not inhabit the part of the world where I am living, in Western Europe. At that time I can't catch the meaning of this dream. Even when looking up some dream symbols in dictionaries, the words do not make much sense to me.

Meaningfully connected appearances of hummingbirds in graphic form

Two months later, on a Friday morning, I visit a kinesiologist, hoping to find an answer about a health issue through her method of Touch for Health. This involves a specific way of lightly touching the arm while asking a question. The tone of the muscles which follows the touch is interpreted as a direct reply of the organism, indicating either 'yes' or 'no'. The rational mind is passed by. At a certain moment, within the larger series of questions, the practitioner poses the question: 'May we ask for information through a divination card?' and the answer of my body is: 'Yes.' Then the therapist points one by one to several boxes containing different card decks (such as Tarot, Fairy Tale, and Angelic cards). Without my eyes having read the titles my body several times says 'no' and then suddenly a 'yes' is the reply when the therapist points to the box containing bird cards (Toerien and Dobben 2007). The next step is choosing between the 55 cards. Repeatedly the set is divided into two halves, of which one is chosen by my body, and then finally the remaining card is turned over. We are looking at the picture of the hummingbird. Of course, I immediately remember my recent dream and I feel alert when seeing this specific card. What message could it be conveying to me?

We read the written words: 'Full of joy I accept that a new time will start. I thank the all-encompassing consciousness of the hummingbird that it lets me know what is. Now I know that I have passed through my old limitations and that happiness is welcoming me.'[1]

When I am driving home I wonder what to make of it. I pray to God: 'If this is meant as a sign for me, can you confirm this by making another hummingbird appear to me?' Later that day I can hardly believe my eyes. I turn the television on – looking for some distraction for a few minutes before I have to leave the house for an appointment. *Exactly* at that moment a hummingbird appears in a commercial. And again, the next day, I see another depiction of a hummingbird. At around noon I am standing on the platform of the train station, about to travel to a meeting for a spontaneous appointment made earlier that day. While waiting there my eyes cannot miss the huge colourful picture of the hummingbird on the billboard near to me. Inwardly I surrender, willing to accept that somehow a message is being conveyed to me. But which one? At that time I have no idea.

---

1 Translated to English from the Dutch version.

Transitioning in waking life

Between autumn 2007 and June 2008, a difficult situation at work begins to escalate. With the help of some wise counsellors I decide to quit my job. I experience the whole process as a very tough time. There are no hummingbirds to bring a smile to my face during these nine months. And I don't recognize in any way the phrase 'happiness is welcoming me', which had been given to me on the divination card. I close the door behind me on 1 June 2008. That same summer I decide to enter the Dream Leadership Training of the Haden Institute (North Carolina). The financial bonus I received when I quit my job offers the means to fund the course.

Meeting a living hummingbird

In autumn 2008 I am participating in the first intensive session of the programme. I am taken by surprise when hummingbirds emerge as a topic in casual conversation. Hummingbirds . . . in this part of the world? Had you asked me before, I would have guessed these birds generally live in tropical areas. I instantly and vividly remember my dream and its accompanying synchronicities in the past year. But over the four days my group and I seem to be scaring away any birds whenever we walk around the grounds.

Then, on the afternoon of the last day, three hours of silence are prescribed to us all. This is meant for Sacred Time, to do soul work and process everything that has been received from the lessons and dream work. Afterwards we will gather to share what we have learnt. For some hours a stillness is everywhere, widening and deepening. It is a beautiful day and I am sitting in the garden with my journals and my notes, writing and reflecting. Suddenly I understand the meaning of one of the symbols from the dream I had shared with my classmates that same morning. It is symbolizing my former job. A part of me still longs to get rid of all the difficulties I had been going through in my work setting and have the former situation restored.

Wow, what striking timing . . . suddenly – yes, exactly at that moment – a hummingbird is flying right before my eyes, at a close distance: I estimate about three feet in front of me. There it is, hanging in the air, getting nectar from one of the flowers. I hold my breath and keep quiet. If I should reach out with my hand and arm, I could touch the bird. After a few seconds the bird is gone, as quickly as it came.

I mentally shift to a different state of consciousness, a mode of being somehow out of sync with earthly linear time. In my mind's eye all the hummingbird appearances flow into one another, intensifying and amplifying their meaning. Fourteen months ago, during the summer of 2007, before troubles at work reached their climax, I had that intriguing dream with beautiful hummingbirds flying together in such spectacular formation. Then two months later this bird appeared on a divination card. Having prayed about it, the two synchronistically related appearances within the next 24 hours had made a huge impression on me. And now, having changed my core business, a living hummingbird manifests itself at exactly the moment I am considering my longing to return to the old situation . . . I very clearly understand, inwardly, that these manifestations are giving me one consistent message. They want to encourage me to fully surrender to a completely new path in my life. Although I cannot rationally comprehend the purpose of it all, these miraculous signs apparently seem to be telling me to trust the whole course of events.

From that moment on I was able to invest commitment in following the whole process and the programme, trusting that I had found the right track for the next course of my life and daring to give full attention to my soul's calling. And the words written on the divination card have now achieved their full expression: 'Full of joy I accept that a new time has started.'

References

Bolen, J. S. (1979), *The Tao of Psychology*, New York: Harper and Row.

Jaworski, J. (1996), *Synchronicity: The Inner Path of Leadership*, San Francisco: Berret-Koehler Publishers.

Joseph, F. (2002), *Synchronicity and You: Understanding the Role of Meaningful Coincidence in Your Life*, London: Vega.

Jung, C. G. (1978), 'Synchronicity: An Acausal Connecting Principle', in *The Structure and Dynamics of the Psyche: Collected Works*, Vol. 8, Princeton NJ: Princeton University Press, p. 419.

Mansfield, V. (1995), *Synchronicity, Science, and Soul-Making: Understanding Jungian Synchronicity through Physics, Buddhism and Philosophy*, Chicago CA: Open Court.

Moss, R. (2007), *The Three 'Only' Things: Tapping the Power of Dreams, Coincidence, and Imagination*, Novato CA: New World Library.

Rockwood Hudson, J. (2000), *Natural Spirituality: Recovering the Wisdom Tradition in Christianity*, Danielsville GA: JRH Publications.

Rushnell, S. (2002), *When God Winks: How the Power of Coincidence Guides Your Life*, New York: Atria Books.

Sparks, J. G. (2007), *At the Heart of Matter: Synchronicity and Jung's Spiritual Testament*, Toronto: Inner City Books.

Toerien, J. and Dobben, J. (2007), *Bird Cards: The Healing Power of the Bird Kingdom*, Haarlem: Altamira-Becht.

PART 3

Dreams and the Practice of Pastoral Care

Dreams in Everyday Pastoral Care

WIM REEDIJK

In this chapter I share some thoughts and experiences as a Protestant pastor serving in an average parish in the Netherlands. My contribution to this book is to offer a personal introduction to the subject for ministers in everyday pastoral community care. This I do by giving two examples taken from my own practice, stressing the fact that the people involved gave me their kind permission to use their stories for further study and publication. I conclude the chapter with some advice to keep in mind if you want to pay attention to dreams in the spiritual guidance of your parishioners.

Preliminary words on theological awareness

Twenty-five years ago, the Dutch exegete and pastoral theologian Coert Lindijer (1986) wrote an excellent book on dream work and pastoral care. It still serves as a beacon in the Dutch language, although, unfortunately, it has been out of print for years. But, one must be honest and confess, albeit with hindsight, that in reaching out to pastors, Lindijer's book explained a lot about dreams, their interpretations and psychology, but it did not explore the theological potentials and assumptions. Neither did it balance dream work alongside other more traditional means of Christian counselling. Lindijer did not go into questions such as 'Are dreams as revelatory as the Word of God is?', 'Are all dreams sent from heaven?' and 'In what way do my dreams contribute towards a Christian life that yearns to believe that, as Paul wrote, "it is no longer I that live, but Christ living in me"?' (Gal. 2.20, World English Bible 2002).

As I will not be answering these intricate questions in depth, I will neatly sidestep this area of interest, but not without stressing that one has to have a theological awareness of what one is doing as a pastor, no matter how tentative. I consider spiritual guidance an important aspect of my pastoral concern, and it is important that I, and other pastors, should keep thinking through what dreams and their meaning add to growth in Christian belief.

Dream 1: Mother burying her children

Let me start with an elderly woman's dream. She is in her nineties now. Two of her children live nearby, one lives abroad. She has grandchildren and great-grandchildren. She has been bedridden for more than two years. Because of Parkinson's disease she cannot walk. Every day she is put in a wheelchair for a few hours. Sitting in her condition is patently agonizing. She needs help with everything. Her eyesight has seriously deteriorated in a very short time, so that she cannot read any more. Her world has become very small indeed. She is on the whole unassuming and undemanding. Notwithstanding her severe physical handicaps, she rarely complains. One day she told me the following dream.

> I am driving a car. My three children are with me. We have an accident. The car smashes into a tree. My children are killed instantaneously. The next moment I am standing next to their graves. I witness their burial.

A dream with such a horrific sequence is not something that people tell gladly. The content is disturbing. The fact that previous conversations with me about dreams had soothed her had encouraged her to tell her current dream. She also knew that I am interested in dreams, and so she did not mind telling me this one.

I asked her if she had any idea what this dream meant. She said that she didn't. I came up with the following tentative suggestion. Considering her age and condition, it would be normal to assume that she would be the first to pass away, long before her children. She is surely the first in line to go. Her children will lose her. But you can also take this loss the other way round: that in death, she is losing them. This is exactly what happens in the dream: she loses her children. Is it perhaps her own fear or death that troubles her? She shook her head. No, she was not afraid of death; this I already knew from previous visits. But still, I felt the need to raise the issue. The only thing she feared was that she would lose her family.

I asked, 'Are you afraid that when you die, your children will stop seeing each other, and as a family will disintegrate? Are you afraid that without you, they will stop behaving as siblings? That only through you they will stick together, and it is you, or your death, or death itself, that will drive them apart?'

This thought was a real worry for her, and all of a sudden she could see this message in her dream. Losing the children, burying her children because of her 'doing'; it all made sense to her. This doing was played out by imagining herself behind the steering wheel of the car, but not having the life of her children in her control.

Talking about the dream, but even more about her worries, came as a relief for her. I could also reassure her that her worries were very natural for a mother. Being well over ninety does not make you any less a mother. Besides, I was aware from their behaviour towards each other that her fears were far from unrealistic. Her children were not eager to see or speak to each other, or to consult together about the best possible care for their ageing mother. All this suggested that her worries were not unfounded.

Apart from that, we could go deeper into the question that she cannot hold the reins for ever. Her children are grown-ups. They carry their own responsibilities. She, as their mother, cannot 'control' their lives. She has to let go. The dream carried a lesson. And I was her aid to assist her in hearing the criticism as well.

Having been her pastor for some years now, I know this lady pretty well. She never asked anyone for psychological or therapeutic help. She just lived the life she lived, and managed quite well. But now she was struggling with old age. Existential questions about motherhood and about unfinished and unsolved issues were hovering over her sickbed.

This dream example shows that a pastor can not just listen to a dream but also be of help to clarify it, and, if need be, confront the dreamer supportively with possible truths; although only the dreamer can make the final decision. As a pastor I want to be near people, listen to their problems, give them advice, pray with them, helping them to see their lives in the light of the living God. People should know that they can share even their most distressing thoughts with a pastor.

Dream 2: The psalm-singing woman

The second dream was dreamt by a woman in my parish who was very musical. It was obvious how important music was for her. Music was definitely her vehicle of expression. In her dreams she often found herself singing. The first time I visited her, she played on her organ, accompanying herself while singing a psalm.

Once you know what is important for someone, you may also be able to understand their dream idiom. It is not only the words but also the imagery that explains something of the inner thoughts, feelings and emotions of the dreamer.

In the case of the psalm-singing woman we explore another sort of dream, with a different setting from that of the first type. Whereas the first dream (with the car accident) was realistic, this dream uses other means of expression. The first dream enabled me to think about the critical function a dream can have. This second dream is different.

Just before she had this dream, I talked with her about her trepidation of reaching the age of 80. For her being 80 meant that she was really old. It confronted her, for example, with the certain knowledge that she was no longer interesting in the eyes of men. She had been divorced and since then had hoped for a new and more rewarding partner than her previous husband. Approaching old age and death brought her to a state of anxiety. We talked about this, and she told me that she did not sleep well. When she did sleep her dreams made her restless. I suggested that she write down her dreams. 'Will I sleep better then?' she asked. 'You will be amazed,' I answered. So she did. The next time I saw her, she came up with this dream, which she had jotted down in a notebook alongside other dreams.

> I am looking for the way when I suddenly meet a woman. She is half blind and asks for directions. We walk along, and with us is God. He walks in the middle. In the meantime I sing a hymn: 'And where the road seemed lost, we were allowed to start in faith all over again.'

She was very happy with this dream. She could not figure out what the woman symbolized, but she immediately felt comforted and at rest. God was with her, and with the other woman, and she was singing these beautiful lines from a well-known Dutch hymn. She tried to remember for a moment from which hymn in the old hymn book these lines were taken, but the number of the hymn just slipped her mind. I could not help her out with the number either.

I asked her if she was aware of any associations. She said she was not. I suggested that the woman who was partially blind resembled her situation. She did not know how to deal with the shortcomings of old age. The woman needed help, and was asking for directions. Like the woman in the dream, she also struggled with a kind of blindness. Still she took the woman by the hand. And she was definitely not alone.

'Do you think that the fact that God is with you in your dream has an important meaning?' 'Yes,' she said, 'I think it says that I should not be afraid any more, because he is with me. I am not alone. And that I should not lose my faith in what lies in store for me in the near future.' Later in this chapter we return to the dream and give more attention to the half-blind woman.

80 and other numbers

It is interesting to point out what happened when I returned home. I wrote about the dream and our conversation, and just to be sure I looked up the hymn in my hymn book. This hymn happens to be number 305 and is composed by Jan Wit, a minister and poet who was born blind. Perhaps a coincidence to note, that the words came from a blind poet. But more intriguing and even electrifying was that the number 305 presents an arithmetical sum. Taking the 3 and the 5 together makes 8. And adding the 0 as a number visualizes the number 80: the exact number of years that filled the dreamer with so much anxiety.

Jung wrote interesting things about juggling with numbers and calculations in dreams, and I think that this is an excellent example of such a number dream (Jung, 1961a). The dreamer was familiar with her hymn book and without mentioning the number the dreamer unconsciously used the hymn, its imagery and its number, to succinctly convey an elaborate message. At the same time the number also revealed, to me at least, her ongoing occupation with pending old age.

No censorship as pastoral attitude

When I visited her at a later stage, I did not bring this detail to her attention. I kept this knowledge to myself, because I did not feel that mentioning it would be to her advantage. She was not worried any more thanks to this dream. Why should I rub in the aching truth that old age still worried her? Why should I spoil the consolation already received? Hymn 305 helped her to see that old age can mean that not everything is lost: with faith the road to walk can be found again.

In fact the hidden language of our dreams is perhaps a sign of the gentleness or sensibility of our spirit working through our unconscious. The spirit brings a strong message in a detached and innocent-looking way, as if spoken in a soft tone of voice. This could be very pastoral! Also, in faith language, God is said to work through his Spirit in us, including perhaps the covert or hidden way dreams tell us more about our destiny.

This sheds a different light on what Freud took to be the result of some inner faculty of harsh censorship. Something in us tells us what not to think or to long for. Freud is rather severe and even critical about this censor from within. But, as I see it, you can also take it the other way round. This faculty, which I attribute to the Spirit, dims the light of the glaring sun of truth, and by blurring our view, gently guides us through the shady path of life. It makes the truth bearable and clears the path that redeems the soul. 'Even though I walk through the valley of the shadow of death, I will fear no evil, for you are with me. Your rod and your staff, they comfort me' (Ps. 23.4, World English Bible 2002).

Freudian or Jungian

It goes without saying that thinking about dreams brings us immediately to the question of which approach one should adopt. I gladly confess my belief in being as flexible as possible. One should not adhere exclusively to one doctrine. Freud and his followers help me to appreciate that people unintentionally and unconsciously cover up their real urges and preoccupations in dream images and dream scenarios. Things and people are not always what and who they seem. Dreams contain hidden and forbidden longings, shielded by images that direct our attention towards other, more innocent and seemingly harmless directions and explanations. Of course, Jung, like Freud, knows that things can stand for other things. But Jung and his followers are less suspicious, cynical or distrusting than Freud. Jung's example of the difference between his approach and Freud's is telling. Freud, Jung says, will go to the British Museum in London and see the Parthenon frieze as a façade that explains the longing towards supreme power that the Athenians harboured in the Classical era. Jung would just marvel at the sheer beauty of the frieze and the artisanship needed to create this work of art. He would not see in the stones of the Parthenon their hidden ambitions, but simply see the Parthenon (Jung 1959, p. 203 n.63). Jung treasures the 'naivety', that 'priceless possession, or rather gift, which no creative person can do without' (Jung 1961b, p. 336). Jung tries to keep the self-criticism within bounds that, in too large a dose, may kill the creative offspring of the dreaming soul.

Dream 2 revisited: What was left and the open future

I promised earlier that we would take a closer look at the half-blind woman in the second dream. I suggested to the dreamer that this woman was also an image of herself. She had no vision of what her future would be. It was unclear what life had in store for her, even after reaching 80 years of age. In that sense she might consider herself very much as a blind person, or half blind. She could see only through 'a glass darkly' (1 Cor. 13). Or in the words of St Paul: 'Being therefore always of good courage, and knowing that, while we are at home in the body, we are absent from the Lord, for we walk by faith, not by sight' (2 Cor. 5.6, World English Bible 2002). But in her dream the Lord was far from absent. He was walking with both ladies. The Lord was in her dream thankfully within 'sight', although in spite of that she had to reckon with her partial blindness.

We were both satisfied with this interpretation of the half-blind woman. Life just went on and she became 80. She threw a great birthday party and showed me all the photos taken. She was clearly relieved to have passed that point.

Then, a few months later, she developed some minor physical problems. She consulted her local practitioner, who referred her on to specialists. In hospital they found out that she had cancer. The diagnosis was lung cancer with metastasis, which meant that the lungs were not the only organs affected. The news, as one can imagine, came as a blow. For weeks she was utterly devastated. Then, she began to adjust to the new situation. The symptoms were not too bad to start with. But soon they became more serious. She gradually lost all feeling in one side of her face. Her forehead, tongue, cheek, chin and the whole right side of her face became numb. A tumour was blocking one of the nerves in the facial area. And it got worse: the seeing faculty of her right eye was hampered as the nerve in the eyelid muscle lost its function to straighten and keep the eye uncovered. She could not even blink. Because of that she lost half of her eyesight.

Remember that months before, as she was still struggling with old age, she dreamt of this half-blind lady whom she took by the hand. All of a sudden I saw it happening. I saw that her dream was also literally becoming true.

Sometimes, dreams do seem to reveal the future. Jung said that this might be a way in which the unconscious works out the possibilities of the future. Dreams perhaps convey options from which one can choose. But they can also show that in the unconscious there is already knowledge for our consciousness in the offing.

Humility

This outcome was not expected by either one of us, at least not consciously, and certainly not by me. It is an example of how modest one should be about thinking in terms of a definitive interpretation. We should always be cautious in thinking that we have exhausted all possibilities. The second dream in particular shows that one probably never can be sure that one has run through all the significances of a dream. There may still be more layers waiting to be revealed.

I use the term 'modesty', but one can also speak of feelings of awe and humility that are often the response to something that outsmarts our wit. It resembles the outcome of the dreams of the biblical Joseph, who, still living at home with his family, related his dreams in public (Gen. 37). In the first dream sheaves of wheat bow before his own sheaf. Similarly in the second dream, the sun, the moon and eleven stars bow to his star. Joseph's family immediately guessed the significance of the dreams. And Joseph perhaps did too. Only years later did he find out that his dreams had contained indications of what would later become manifest. For he conjectured that his star was metaphorically rising and would eclipse the power of his parents and all his brothers. But he could not have guessed, then and there, that they would, in the end, be literally bowing to him in Egypt (Gen. 46.29ff).

Perhaps one should always be aware that dreams in general have a surplus of meanings that can hardly be grasped, and at best perhaps surmised. It is a reminder that we should be patient and always willing to review previous interpretations, and allow room for new ones.

Starting with dreams in pastoral care

A pastor does not need to be a certified expert in dream interpretation. Indeed, the true meaning of dreams can be decided upon only by the dreamer. The more I think about it, the more I see that just being attentive and willing to listen to dreams is appreciated more than what you say about their possible interpretations. People often know what dreams mean, even if they say they don't. Telling their dreams to you frequently carries in its wake an insight that opens up a path that in time leads to deeper knowledge. I have seen this happen too often to dismiss this as an exception. Speaking of dreams gives us a chance to be receptive and hospitable, and is as such precious in itself. Pastors should keep that in their minds and hearts; it is what people expect and ask for from their pastors.

I would like to finish with a few rules of thumb. These may, I hope, encourage everyone who serves a Christian community as a pastor as I do.

1 Be attentive if people, even in passing, hint at their dream life. Invite them gently to reveal more, but do not be too eager. It may look as if you are prying into affairs that are of no concern to you.

2 Do not be overbearing or too anxious to interpret what you hear. Let people always tell you what they think. Keep your thoughts to yourself. Remember that revealing a dream is an act of intimacy, and cherish the very fact that people share their dreams with you.

3 Stress the preciousness of every dream, even the most disturbing ones.

4 Encourage people to write down their dreams. This underlines their value and helps to see if they fit in with other dreams. Every dream contains a meaning even if it is not revealed yet. Explore whether it helps to distinguish between types of dreams. Is a dream a warning, a correction, or an encouragement? Remember that whatever you suggest, it is not your dream but theirs.

5 Try to connect dreams with a longing for healing, trust and love. Use their dream symbols in the prayers you share with the members of your community.

6 Give space to the silence in which Christ's presence can be felt. This space will inevitably give room for experiences that transcend our reasoning minds, insights that words cannot easily convey, things that eyes normally do not see.

7 Look at and listen to the members of your community with the eyes and ears of your heart. The more you do so, the more they will appreciate their own inner life, the language of their dreams, the soul within.

References

Jung, C. G. (1959), 'Gnostic Symbols of the Self', in *The Collected Works of C. G. Jung*, Vol. 9/II, New York: Princeton University Press, pp. 184–221.

Jung, C. G. (1961a), 'On the Significance of Number Dreams', in *The Collected Works of C. G. Jung*, Vol. 4, New York: Princeton University Press, pp. 48–55.

Jung, C. G. (1961b), 'Freud and Jung: Contrasts', in *The Collected Works of C. G. Jung*, Vol. 4, New York: Princeton University Press, pp. 333–40.

Keating, T. (1994), *Open Mind, Open Heart: The Contemplative Dimension of the Gospel*, New York: Continuum.

Lindijer, C. H. (1986), *In onze diepste dromen. Pastoraal omgaan met dromen*, Den Haag: Voorhoeve (Dutch).

Benefits of a Parish Dream Group

GEOFF NELSON

Introduction

This chapter will focus on a dream group I ran for seven years in the church that I was pastor of for 27 years, Whittier Presbyterian Church, in Whittier, California, USA (hereinafter WPC). For my Doctor of Ministry project, entitled 'Dream Groups in the Church', I ran four different dream groups for one year and wrote my dissertation based on the results. The dream group I'm writing about began as one of those four groups. When I shared the prospect of doing a dream group for WPC as part of my research there was a positive response from six or eight people. The group began meeting monthly in the autumn of 2005. The dream group became a regular part of the adult education offerings of the church, and is still running, meeting monthly.

My interest in dreams began in seminary and I've kept a personal dream journal ever since. In 2003 I had a series of experiences with my dreams that convinced me that it was time to study further the use of dreams in one's spiritual life.

Throughout the chapter reference is made to the International Association for the Study of Dreams (hereinafter IASD). The IASD brings together researchers, dream workers, artists and a variety of other people interested in dreams. Their ethics statement in particular is one of their outstanding contributions to the growing dream work movement.[1]

Background

I believe dreams and dream work can add much to the growth in spiritual practice of Christians. In American Protestantism, the last years have seen an explosion of spiritual practices: some are new, while many are rediscovered

---

1 I would strongly suggest anyone wanting to begin a parish dream group become familiar with the IASD ethics material (see p. 252). It may also be found at the IASD website at www. asdreams.org/ethics-and-privacy.

practices of the historical Christian Church. Practices such as lectio divina, praying the psalms, using a labyrinth and spiritual direction have all grown in popularity among Protestants. I believe dream work belongs among these practices. I believe dreams give us a ready, continual access to the work of the Holy Spirit in our lives. Dreams evidence an inner wisdom that each of us has that helps us realize what external events affect us and often gives us hints about how to address these external events. In these ways dreams have much to add to our practice of faith and should be included among current spiritual practices.

I also believe that the Church provides a helpful environment for dream work. A church is a community and the parish dream group members will be connected in a variety of ways and relationships in the life of the church. The availability of Bible study, worship, pastoral counsel, etc., all help provide an environment of trust and relationship within which dream work can thrive. Dreams touch upon powerful elements and experiences of life and the church has always provided a place where those experiences can be shared and the individual can be helped in his/her own growth. Worship in particular can provide a place where one can offer up one's dreams and dream work and confirm one's place in the larger experience of human life lived in the presence of God.

Through my work with dreams in the Christian life and the life of the church, I've come to see the following four ways that dreams help us.

- First is emotional honesty. Humans don't often acknowledge emotions that are unpleasant. We are usually conditioned that way by the culture or society around us. In the USA, I grew up with the expression 'If you can't say something nice, don't say anything at all.' Dreams will not speak nicely, but they will speak honestly. Dreams often tell us about things that we need to address in our waking life, but since we do not always want to face particular issues, our dreams may continually call our attention to those issues. Dreams may speak in a blunt fashion, impolitely, to get our attention. For example, if we are angry with someone, and anger is considered a negative emotion for us, our dreams may exaggerate our anger to the extent that we may dream of murdering the person we are angry with. That should get our attention!
- The second is what I call prioritizing our life. We have a variety of tasks, duties and obligations in our life. How do we choose which to address first? Which second? I believe that dreams can help us make that choice. For example, in my first church, during the first annual fundraising programme I had a dream that helped me decide who to visit in my church. The day before the dream I'd been looking over the membership rolls

and that night I dreamt about a family I'd not met yet. Based on the dream, I decided to visit that family as soon as I could. My dream helped me prioritize my pastoral duty of home visitation. I've seen the same process take place with physicians, teachers, and others. They are helped to choose what particular actions to take among all the possibilities that are open to them in their particular professions.

- Third, dreams provide another level of experience which can be very similar to some of the prayer and visionary experiences talked about in the Bible and other Christian literature. Jacob's dream at Bethel (Gen. 28.10–22) or Peter's dream at Joppa (Acts 10) provide great examples of the kinds of experiences all of us can have if we pay attention to our dreams. To provide experiences of God's immediacy, of God present to us in our lives, is one of the most powerful benefits of dream work in the parish. One way that we Christians might become more comfortable with our dreams is to make this link with the life of prayer.

- Finally, dreams enable us to be more open to the images and symbols that the Bible uses to tell us the story of our faith. Dreams and religion speak the same language, the language of symbol and image. When we become more familiar with our dreams and the images and symbols they use, we broaden and deepen our reading and understanding of the Bible. Beyond the dream stories referred to above, the parables of Jesus, the metaphors and images of the prophetic books, the book of Revelation, all become more readily understandable when we are comfortable with images and symbols, and we find those kinds of images and symbols in our dreams.

In these four ways dreams help us, providing a source of information that both augments and deepens our waking perceptions and abilities. I do not believe that we should let dreams replace our rational minds and the ways we have developed to live and pass on our faith. But I believe dreams can provide a most valuable addition to all those ways of learning and practising our faith. Dreams give us another level of information, in addition to those we usually use in our waking lives. These four elements of dreaming also provide some of the cautions about using dreams in our spiritual life. More will be said about those cautions later.

One distinction that may be helpful for the pastor considering a dream group is to remember the difference between therapy and spiritual growth. Some pastors are trained to do therapy, but most of us are just good listeners, with some training in counselling and basic psychology. Here the distinction between a dream group and group therapy is helpful. Therapy is designed for healing. A dream group, like other spiritual practices, is designed for growth. Though there are often similarities between growth and therapy, the degree of training and sophistication needed for therapy makes dream groups a more readily accessible option for most pastors.

The parish dream group

The format of the parish dream group mostly consisted of the following components:

- *Check-in.* An informal time of conversation, catching up on each other's lives and events that had taken place since our last meeting.
- *Opening ritual/prayer.* In our church group this opening ritual was in the form of a prayer, asking the aid of the Holy Spirit in our dreams and in our work together on them.
- *Presentations, discussion or instruction.* This part was used in the first year to offer educational information about dreams and dreaming, such as the physiological evidence of dreaming, an introduction to the symbols and images in dreams, and working with colour in dreams. After the first year, this component became an occasional element in the group format, addressing issues or questions that came up in the process of working with dreams. It may be helpful at the beginning of the group sessions to take some time for discussion and instruction about the qualities of dreams and dreaming and about issues that may have arisen in the previous session.
- *Circle of title and feeling.* This was an opportunity for each person in the group to make the title of a dream known and the feelings associated with it. This was not deep work, but an opportunity for the participants to introduce a dream. Then the choice of which dream to work with would be made.
- *The group's dream work.* This was the real work on the dreams for the evening, where considerable time would be given to each dream.
- *Closing ritual/prayer.* In our case, this was simply a closing prayer, giving thanks for the work done and asking for further guidance in and through our dreams in the future.

Possible parish dream group goals

What might be some of the goals that a parish dream group might set? Based on my experience with the previous four dream groups, and my experience with the long-term group at WPC, here are some suggested goals which I believe will be fairly easy to achieve.

Goal 1 To be more comfortable with our own dream life

All people dream, but few remember or pay attention to their dreams to the extent needed for a dream group. Some of the following goals help in this process of comfort. Some aspects of dream work, like better recall, more recall, various methods of recording and reporting on the dreams, are all part of the process of becoming more comfortable with our dream lives.

Goal 2 To learn the 'language of dreams'

Dreams speak the language of image and symbol. This is not the place to discuss the specifics of dream images and symbols. There is a wealth of published material and internet locations discussing images and symbols in dreams.[2]

Goal 3 To be more open to the metaphors and images of the Bible

As an extension of goal 2, becoming familiar with dream images increases group members' familiarity and comfort with biblical images.

Goal 4 To see what greater sense of creativity, freedom, sensitivity, awareness, tolerance, compassion might come from tending our dreams

The development of these qualities is one of the benefits of paying attention to our dreams. These are qualities usually admired and cultivated in the life of a parish. They can be developed and enhanced in the process of working with dreams in a parish setting.

Goal 5 To see how our lives of faith, our spiritual lives, are affected by our having tended our dreams more deliberately and regularly

This is exemplified by comments from the group participants, below.

Dream group member responses

The members of the dream group of Whittier Presbyterian Church kindly responded to some evaluative questions that were put together by me for

---

2 I would add a word of caution about such materials, as well as books that claim to be dream dictionaries. One of the basic principles of dream work as I practise it, and as is promoted by the IASD, is that only the dreamer knows for certain what the image or symbol may mean in their dream. Many dream images and symbols can have multiple meanings and associations.

the purpose of writing this chapter. The questions and their responses are as follows. I've also provided commentary from a pastoral perspective.

Question 1   What benefits did you find in the dream group?
Answers: Group closeness; learning experience; spiritual depth; opportunities to support each other more specifically than before the dream group began to meet; more effort thinking about my dreams; the dream group, being deeply personal, made me think about things on a deeper level – trying to get to the bottom of thoughts rather than accept them at face value.
Pastoral summary: The intimacy of a dream group takes place at a deeper level than may be achieved by other groups. What is it about dreams and dream work that gives it this special quality of intimacy, or allows such intimacy to develop? A colleague once said, 'Dreams are deep but not direct,' and I thought that was an excellent way to express this quality of dream work. Dreams reveal our inner selves in ways that we can cope with. When we recall a dream it means that we are able to work with the images, symbols and whatever message it makes.[3] This develops a closeness that can be provided in few other situations.

Question 2   What help did the dream group provide for you in your other work for WPC?
Answers: More aware of things with a much deeper feeling; it has been a help to clarify some issues we were having at the church and a chance to share and support the emotional upheaval that some of us were experiencing. It has also been of great support through good times and work at the church.
Pastoral summary: The closeness and intimacy engendered by dream work spills over into other parish activities where the members of the dream group are involved.

Question 3   What help did the dream group provide for you in your larger life beyond the church? (Like in your family, at work, etc.)
Answers: Becoming much more intuitive and learning to listen to my feelings and being more aware of those feelings; dream group shines the light on those areas in my life that are holding me back or interfering with having a clear vision of what needs to be done; sharing a dream with others gives clarity.

---

3 I've heard Jeremy Taylor, one of the founding presidents of the IASD, make this point repeatedly: the fact that we've recalled a dream means that we are ready to work with what it is trying to tell us.

Pastoral summary: In the area of personal devotion or spirituality, intuition and insight are touchstones by which we may measure growth and maturity in the Christian faith.

Question 4   What long-range benefits did the dream group provide?
Answers: (Dream group) has deepened my faith, as a few of my dreams were very spiritual – I have learned to listen to those dreams; deeper friendships, knowing that they are people I can always count on; problem-solving and insight into others' thoughts, realizing that it sometimes takes a village to come up with a plausible answer.
Pastoral summary: Dreams are considered meaningful as an aspect of one's faith and practice. Deeper and long-range friendships can be developed in a dream group. Such friendships help strengthen the life of a parish. Dream work can aid in problem-solving, and since problem-solving is part of what happens in the life of a parish, the benefit is clear. Hence there is deeper ministry taking place within the church or the dream group itself.

Question 5   In what ways did your dreams and the work done on them help you with being a faithful Christian, as well as a faithful member of WPC? (This may also apply to personal insights you may have had working with your own dreams which were NOT shared with the group.)
Answers: Being more intuitive and really listening to feelings has made me so much more spiritual and my faith has grown as a result; communication about the church and ways to serve it better; the ministry is mostly within our own dream group; our own introspection reflects our own Christianity.
Pastoral summary: Better and more open communication about church life matters. As in question 1, the closeness and intimacy engendered by dream work spills over into other parish activities where the members of the dream group are involved. As in question 3, the growth in personal spirituality can be seen in these responses.

Question 6   Did your participation in the dream group provide you with new or different opportunities for ministry? Does it still?
Answers: People who know that you belong to a dream group will come and want to share a dream, which of course you have to remind them that only they can truly interpret, but you can give an opinion or insight; it did give another area to share.
Pastoral summary: The fact that our church had an ongoing dream group made a difference in comparison with other churches. It made for interesting conversations in the cashier line at the grocery store!

Benefits to the pastor

Perhaps the greatest benefit of the dream group to me as the pastor of WPC was that the members of the dream group became my strongest supports in the ministry of the parish. They were able to consider new and different options for parish ministry, I believe as a consequence of doing dream work. They were also freer to speak truth to me as their pastor. They were the church members who were able to caution me or comfort me or in some other way expand our relationship beyond pastor and parishioner. This was a great benefit to me.

Cautions relevant to dream work

For a pastor or church leader considering a dream group in their parish, there are some precautions that I believe must be considered. Here are three that I believe are the most important.

'It is not for everyone . . .' Dream work is not something that has a universal appeal. Dreams arouse curiosity in many people, but to do the personal inner work that dreams require may not appeal to everyone. Because of the bizarre nature or deep power of some dreams, people's curiosity may be aroused when the topic of dreams comes up. But when dream work points in the direction of deeper personal issues, not everyone is willing to engage in deeper personal reflection. I've had very few examples of this kind of reaction, but they were dramatic examples. Any church leader considering dream work needs to be ready to shepherd people gently into the process, then be willing to shepherd some of them out of the process if it is not for them.

Second, there needs to be a willingness to address images or dream actions that violate our personal or Christian moral code. As mentioned above when speaking about the emotional honesty of dreams, dreams may picture death, suicide, murder, nudity, adultery, rape, and any number of other moral violations. It is most important to realize that these are images and symbols of our feelings, exaggerated as they often are in dreams. Taking dream images literally is often a mistake, just as taking biblical images or stories literally may miss the entire point of the image or story. Look to the Sermon on the Mount (Matthew 5–7) for some examples. Though this is a precaution, it can also serve as an opportunity for deeper education about the Bible, as mentioned above.

The third precaution has to do with the 'psi' elements of dreams and dream work. Psi elements are things like precognition, synchronicity or déjà vu. As common as many of these experiences are, they run against the rationalistic mainstream of our culture and therefore any preoccupation with them may not fit within the life of a local parish. But dreams will include elements of precognition, synchronicity or déjà vu, and when one begins to work with dreams, these psi experiences will happen more and more often. Anyone desiring to work with dreams needs to be, or become, comfortable with such experiences. This may provide some opportunities for pastoral care too, as long as the pastor him/herself is comfortable with psi experiences!

How does one start a group in a local parish?

How does one start a dream group in a local parish? First of all, the pastor or prospective group leader should be personally familiar with dream groups and dreams. Keeping a personal dream journal would be a first step. Sharing dreams and talking about them, and feeling comfortable doing so, would be another preliminary step. Training, sensitivity and group leadership are important for the one who will be in charge of the dream group.

Next, find out how much interest there is in a dream group in the parish. Are there enough people for a group? Even two people plus the pastor or leader is enough to begin. It may be wise to take a few months in preparation and advertising for the group. Perhaps a sermon may be preached on the topic, or sermon illustrations may include dream references. There are enough dreams in the Bible to provide material for a series of sermons.

Once there is a group ready to try it, the leader may want to do some kind of informal interview process with those interested, to be sure they are approaching dream work with as full an understanding as possible. Here is where the precautions mentioned above may be initially addressed.

After that work is done and the group is ready to begin, the leader needs to remember that the first meeting will set the tone for the future of the group. Small details in the process can always be adjusted, but the initial few sessions will establish the basic parameters of the group. It is wise to prepare group goals and group guidelines, ready to present at the opening meeting and gain agreement from group members before proceeding.

Once going, the group may need to help members with dream issues like dream recall or dream recording. Varieties of dream work such as art or drama can be introduced after the group has been going for a while and the participants are familiar with both the nature of dreams and dream work, and other group members, so that trust can be built.

Testimonial

I believe that dream work belongs in the Christian Church and that any parish can benefit from a dream group. This chapter is a mere sketch of the elements involved in dreams and dream work in a parish setting. I consider my experience as a pastor leading a dream group to have been one of the highlights of my career in ministry. I have now given my retirement energy in part to continuing to promote dream work in parish settings. That is how valuable I believe parish dream work to be.

12

Working with Dreams in Spiritual Direction
A Catholic Perspective

GERARD CONDON

The road to Emmaus

In the modern art section of the Vatican Museum, in a part rarely visited by tourists, a small woodcut by the German artist Karl Schmidt-Rottluff depicts the road to Emmaus (Luke 24.13–35), illustrating a story about the resurrection of Jesus. The artist, who had been a soldier on the Russian front, created the work in 1918, the year of his country's defeat. The landscape has a bizarre, dreamlike quality. The two disciples of the gospel story look like vanquished soldiers. In between them is Christ, his hand raised in blessing. The disciples fail to recognize the risen Jesus (v.16) even though they had been told that he was alive (v.24). His resurrection was also a transformation and they could not see him because of their lack of faith (v.25). Jesus makes sense of their defeat and leads them to a new interpretation of Calvary (v.26). As they break the bread, their hearts burn within them (v.32). They return to Jerusalem as liberated men who are capable of sharing the Good News (v.33).

The story of the two disciples on the road to Emmaus is a model for spiritual direction. Jesus accompanies the disciples on their way, just as the spiritual director walks with the directee in their faith journey. The spiritual director, like Jesus, invites the disciples to recount their stories (vv.17, 19) and actively listens. This attentiveness itself powerfully contributes to their sense of being accepted and understood. Having listened, and only then, does Jesus offer guidance. He goes beyond basic empathy, an accurate understanding of their situation, to demonstrate advanced empathy, an insight that the disciples themselves did not consciously possess (Egan 1990, pp. 122–36). Spiritual directors today, like Jesus, use the scriptures to broaden the disciple's comprehension of God's salvific will.

Approaches to spiritual direction

Spiritual direction is a regular (usually every three or four weeks) and confidential conversation hosted by the director for the benefit of the directee. It is underpinned by the belief that the risen Jesus continues to walk with his disciples. As Aelred of Rievaulx (1110–67) wrote in the opening lines of *On Spiritual Friendship*, 'Here we are, you and I, and I hope that a third, Christ, is with us.' Some commentators have wished to rename the ministry as 'spiritual accompaniment' or 'soul-friendship'. Others, however, have resisted this trend (Barry and Connolly 1982, pp. 9–12; Nemeck and Coombs 1993, pp. 83–94). The title 'spiritual' does not imply that the encounter is confined to the discussion of holy things. Nor does the word 'direction' intend a submission to the will of the director.

The ministry's title really refers to the presence of the personally communicating Lord in the life of the directee. The word 'spiritual' is the Pauline *pneumatikos*, the activity of the Spirit of God, as distinct from our own spiritual instinct (1 Cor. 2.12–13). The Holy Spirit is the real director and spiritual direction is a forum for listening to God's Spirit in the life of the directee. Much of the conversation may well be taken up with what is happening in the everyday life of the directee. However, the essential focus is on the implications this has for the directee's faith in God. Spiritual direction helps the person pay attention to the discreet movements of God's Spirit and to live out the consequences of that relationship.

The Christian ministry of spiritual direction has an ancient history that can be traced back to the Desert Fathers of fourth-century Egypt. They understood *diakrisis* (discernment) as the prerogative of the *abba* (father), who quickly told the person looking for guidance what they had to do. By the ninth century, the *anamchara* (soul-friend) of the Celtic monasteries was taking the directee's tendency to repeated failure into account. We do not acquire perfection overnight, but are accompanied on the journey by our soul-friend. Spiritual direction became a confidential internal forum where the directee was free to air their doubts and frustrations as well as their causes for joy. St Ignatius of Loyola (1491–1556), the patron saint of spiritual directors, was a central figure in the development of the ministry. He recognized that God addresses a personal vocation in each disciple. God's Spirit is to be found in the circumstances of my everyday life which, therefore, merit prayerful reflection and consideration within spiritual direction.

The best practices of psychotherapy and pastoral counselling have contributed much to the ministry of spiritual direction in the past 50 years. It was the psychology of Carl Jung (1875–1961) that first bridged the gap between psychotherapy and spiritual direction. Jung saw himself as the natural successor to the great spiritual directors of eighteenth-century France such as St John Vianney, the Curé d'Ars (1786–1859) (Kelsey 1968, pp. 13–14). Spiritual direction shares with all therapeutic relationships the goal of liberating the client. 'The glory of God', wrote Irenaeus of Lyons (d. 202), 'is the human being fully alive' (*Adversus Haereses*, 4.20). However, spiritual direction puts the psychotherapeutic aims of personal freedom and self-realization into the context of faith. The assumption is that it is God who can tell me who I really am and who I am called to be.

Dream work in spiritual direction

Jungian psychology is sympathetic to the ancient belief that, in some instances, '*somnia a Deo missa*' ('dreams are sent by God') (Jung 1961, para. 437). However, there are surprisingly few references to the use of dreams in spiritual direction over its historical course. Jerónimo Gracián, the confessor of Teresa of Avila (1515–82), listed dreaming as the tenth item in his twelve ways of the Spirit (Gracián 1933, pp. 238–9). But he discriminates between the majority of dreams, which have a purely physiological basis, and those with a spiritual origin. The latter can be of diabolical as well as angelic inspiration. The dubious origin of some dreams make all dream work an unreliable source for spirituality. In *The Ascent of Mount Carmel* (2.22.3), St John of the Cross (1542–91) would argue that God-sent dreams were only common in Old Testament times because direct revelation through Jesus Christ had not yet been established.

These assertions characterize the Catholic Church's suspicion around the use of dreams. It views the encounter with Christ as occurring through the official sources of revelation (especially scripture, tradition and the Magisterium) rather than personal experience. Taking a cue from the Bible (Deut. 13.2–6; Zech. 10.2), the Church associated dream work with oneiromancy: the divination of God's will through the use of dreams. This was condemned because knowing the mind of God was regarded as a divine gift, not a human endeavour. Visions from God, called private revelations, were regarded as extremely rare and would only be considered as valid when they conformed to the deposit of faith and were accompanied by a miracle. The everyday dreams of the ordinary faithful were not considered relevant to spirituality.

The distrust of personal experience in the Catholic Church reached its zenith with the anti-Modernist declarations of the early twentieth century.

However, in *Dei Verbum* (1965) the Second Vatican Council retrieved the biblical notion of revelation as a personal encounter with God that is accessible through a wide variety of means. Significant experiences of the divine are no longer confined to the mystical phenomena of the saints. All are called to holiness, according to their individual means (*Lumen Gentium* 1964, Chapter 5; Szentmártoni 2013, p. 60).

There had always been a latent stratum of Christian tradition which valued the role of personal experience in appropriating God's self-revelation. It is founded on the Pauline notion of the indwelling Spirit, who vivifies what has already been established in Christ (Rom. 8.9–11). The *Spiritual Exercises* of St Ignatius do not refer to the use of dreams in spiritual direction. However, his assertion that God's will is found through the discernment of spiritual movements in the interior life is sympathetic to the use of dream work in the ministry.

It was with a view to redressing the neglect of dream work in spiritual direction that I undertook my doctoral research in the 1990s (Condon 2008). My work was part of the general movement of recent decades to analyse dreams in places outside the psychotherapist's studio and the sleep laboratory (Shamdasani 2003, pp. 159–62). An appreciation of the dream work conducted in traditional cultures, coupled with the emergence of dream groups in the USA, has promoted the use of dreams in a wider variety of settings, including spiritual direction.

The argument for dream work

Dream work contributes to spirituality by creating a more wholesome sense of personal identity. Spiritual theology traditionally links self-knowledge with the ability to experience God. As St Augustine (354–430) wrote, 'Ever constant God, let me know myself that I may know you' (*Soliloquies* 2:1). Faith in God, like every relationship, demands a level of self-awareness to be authentic. The insight into the interior life provided by dreams uncovers some deeper truths about ourselves, thereby drawing us closer to God, whose Spirit dwells in the depths of human nature.

Dream work can also make us aware of God's movements in our lives. The relaxed state of the ego during sleep enables God's voice to be heard (Job 33.15–18) and hidden mysteries to be understood (Dan. 2.28–30). Thomas Merton (1915–68) likened the many images and ideas that flash before our minds each day to 'seeds of contemplation' (Merton 1961, p. 14). Dream images too can be counted among the 'germs of spiritual vitality' which are available to us if only we have the spontaneity to listen and respond.

The spiritual dimensions of dream work suggest the circumstances where it can be most useful in spiritual direction. Spiritual direction reflects more on the personal experience of God than ideas about God (Barry and Connolly 1982, pp. 13–27). Where the conversation is predominantly a commentary on public events and there is a detachment from the interior life, it may be helpful for the director to interject, 'Have you had any interesting dreams recently?' Dreams and the discussion of dreams help to engage the true man or woman and puts them in touch with their own experience.

Self-disclosure, or the 'manifestation of conscience' as it was traditionally called, is central to spiritual direction, but it is not easy. 'Lay bare your wound to your spiritual physician,' wrote St John Climacus (d. 605). 'Without being ashamed say: "Here is my fault. Here is my illness"' (*The Ladder of Divine Ascent*, 4). It normally takes several meetings with the directee for the director to win that trust. Even then the directee is always torn between the need to reveal oneself and hiding from that responsibility.

Dreams rise to the challenge of self-revelation through their circumspect language. They are, as Freud observed, 'the GUARDIANS of sleep and not its disturbers' (Freud 1953, p. 233). They disguise unacceptable wishes with a benign veneer. Jung, however, saw the dream as a relatively accessible, if poetic, psychic language. Being obtuse makes the dream's message, often a bitter truth, more palatable. As Emily Dickinson put it:

> Tell all the truth, but tell it slant –
> Success in Circuit lies
> Too bright for our infirm delight
> The Truth's superb surprise.

> (Franklin 1998, poem 1129)

The directee may already be aware of an embarrassing topic that they would like to share in spiritual direction. A dream narrative might be a circuitous way of hinting at the subject. The dialogue is made more comfortable because both director and directee can begin by talking about the dream as a curiosity. The narration of the dream can be a useful staging post towards a more direct treatment of the topic concerned. The discussion may draw on the dream's wisdom and lead to a new interpretation of that aspect of the directee's life.

Principles for dream work

Spiritual direction is an aptitude that combines the spiritual director's holiness with their pastoral counselling skills and knowledge of the Bible and Christian tradition. This personal and professional expertise instils confidence in the directee and helps self-disclosure. The director's knowledge about the basic principles of dream analysis can likewise encourage the directee to share their dreams. The following principles are offered as foundational best practice for the use of dreams in spiritual direction:

1 The dream belongs to the dreamer

Jung showed disdain for dream dictionaries, at least in theory, because the interpretation of each dream image depends on the personal associations of the dreamer (Jung 1945–48, para. 543). While the director may recognize the standard meaning of a certain image, this should only be offered by way of opinion. The dreamer is the final interpreter of the dream and so the director's question, 'What does this dream mean for you?' is essential.

2 Notice the emotional tone of the dream

In dream sleep the emotional centres of the brain are particularly active. Dreams are sometimes described as emotions in picture form. This may be in compensation for our skill at hiding our feelings in waking life. I usually begin a conversation about a dream with this question: 'What were the feelings you associated with that dream?' Those emotions are in themselves a self-disclosure.

3 What does the imagery represent?

Dreams have their own 'picture language' (*Traumbildsprache*) that conveys a message through images rather than words. The images generally signify aspects of the dreamer's own personality. Even in dreams of significant others (such as a best friend) the dream image is altered to express something of your relationship with that person rather than the person themselves. The surplus of meaning in the dream image can be interpreted using linguistic categories such as the pun, hyperbole, metaphor, sign, or symbol.

Freud confined the meaning of dream images to the semiotic: that is, signs for other material in the person's life, especially forgotten or neglected wishes from childhood. Jung argued that dreams can also connect us to fundamental propensities (*archetypes*), including that for God. Dream symbols use intelligible imagery that connects us to invisible realities.

Jungian dream analysis typically associates God's presence with circular images, which epitomize the underlying unity of creation. Another indicator is the presence of a 'supraordinate personality', such as a king or divine child (Jung, 1949, n.314). God's presence can also be expressed as the voice of conscience, independently asserting what is right. As we observe our lives through dreams, there is often a sense of being *sub specie aeternitatis* ('under the gaze of eternity') (Jung 1963, p. 3).

4 Dreams respond to the conscious situation

It is well documented that 'sleeping on' a problem can contribute to finding a solution the following day. Carl Jung held that the conscious and unconscious are in a constant state of confrontational dialogue (*Auseinandersetzung*), with mental balance being the desired outcome. He categorized three ways by which dreams function to respond to the conscious situation of the dreamer (Condon 2008, pp. 57–65).

Complementary dreams correspond with our awareness of an issue and generally reinforce its emotional impact. *Compensatory* dreams redress imbalances in the conscious mind. Such dreams typically 'tear down the proud and raise the lowly' (Luke 1.52). *Prospective* dreams are not so much predictions of future events as best guesses. They might address issues that we prefer not to plan for, such as a potential loss. While these three dream types are not explicitly religious, they neatly sum up a personal situation. That is itself a useful tool in contributing to the person's congruity before the Lord and in spiritual direction.

5 What are the implications for faith?

The dreamer's own associations are the primary method for working towards an interpretation. There may well be a straightforward message for the person's social, moral and spiritual life. The spiritual director may amplify the dream images with references to the Bible and other Christian sources. These would assist the directee in undertaking further work on the dream.

The spiritual director will want to put the dream's message into the context of the gospel. Often the dream's rationale operates in an instinctual and ego-centred way that runs contrary to gospel principles. Dreams that represent our sinfulness, whether potential or real, are not sinful, because they lie outside our free will. 'I thank you, Lord,' Augustine wrote, 'for not making me responsible for my dreams' (*Confessions* 10.30). Indeed, such dreams may serve a moral purpose by pointing out the damaging consequences of immoral actions. They serve to highlight our internal struggle with darkness and our need for salvation (Rom. 7.7–25).

The Christian critique of Jung is that his psychology bases its divine image on human experience. We may well dream of God as an awe-inspiring and amoral Olympian. The image of God in Christianity, however, is proposed by revelation and far exceeds that generated by perception alone. For this reason, when unacceptable wishes are vented in dreams they remain just that: unacceptable wishes.

The narrative structure of dreams

In spiritual direction I encourage the directee to tell their dreams in their own words. Prior to the meeting, they will have written out the full story of the dream based on the bedside notes they made on awakening. Jung observed that dreams generally follow the structure of classical Greek drama. There is an exposition of the setting and cast; this is followed by a *peripeteia*, a 'turning around' of the theme; then a crisis or impasse and finally a lysis or denouement (Whitmont and Perera 1989, p. 69). Dreams, though merely straws in the winds of consciousness, can ingeniously summarize the directee's situation. As stories they are far more memorable than dry facts. Their religious dimension is never too far away, as religion, like the dream, addresses the core issues of human existence.

Biblical criticism teaches us that even when a narrative is fanciful it can still deliver a powerful truth. We love stories because they stimulate the intellect and allow the imagination to flourish. They allow us to experience the full panoply of emotions and ideas all at once. In the five or so dreams we have each night we are by turns scared and enthralled.

The dangers we experience in dreams are allayed by the knowledge that it is 'only a dream'. Sleep comes all the more easily for the person who has faith in the presence of a loving God who delivers us from evil. Before going to sleep, children love to hear a thrilling bedtime story, with plenty of danger, because they know they are resting in the security of their parent's lap. In our adult dreams, divine love provides the place of safety from which we can continue to watch, hear, feel and learn (Condon 2012, pp. 52–3).

In conclusion, here are three abbreviated dream narratives, used with the permission of volunteers who have included dreams in their spiritual direction with me. The first two were narrated by final-year trainee teacher students. The third is from a long-term directee who has made extensive use of dreams in her personal work. You will see how the dreams neatly encapsulate a personal situation, while also raising questions for reflection and the discernment of God's will.

Patricia

I am in the kitchen of my new house with my mother. The atmosphere is cool and dark, and I step outside into the hallway. It is bright and airy and has a circular staircase that is much grander than my real house. However, it agitates me that the light switches are not all facing in the same direction. There is a doorway under the staircase which opens into a cave-like chamber. It leads through a series of rooms to a warm sauna and a cosy fireplace. I return to the hallway to find that it has been converted into a coffee shop. I become annoyed that there are strangers in my house. More people arrive and I ask a lady at the door: 'Are you charging people to use my sauna?'

The directee linked this dream to her preparation for an essay on Thomas Aquinas' interpretation of the commandment to 'love thy neighbour'. Patricia is naturally introverted (comfortable in her own company) and neat (annoyed over the up scuttled light switches), though her social skills have advanced considerably thanks to her teacher-training degree. She realizes that she has been spending too much time alone. The dream compensated her introversion with a call to be more hospitable. But she is left wondering if this openness will be costly.

Peter

We were running late for graduation day. I ask Rachel, my wife, to drive. She could drop me off at the door of the college and then find parking. I feel stressed in the car, but our daughter, Shelly, speaks words of encouragement. On arrival, I rush into the Great Hall. The ceremony, charged with a silent dignity, has already begun. I am embarrassed to be the last one in, but then honoured to be ushered to an empty seat in the front podium. I realize I am not wearing my graduation gown and wonder if I could receive the parchment without it. My thoughts turn to Rachel and Shelly. I look around but cannot find them.

Peter has 'parked' his family life over the course of his four years in teacher training and has relinquished the driving seat of his life to his wife, who has become the family breadwinner. The dream complements Peter's guilt at neglecting his family. It also delivers a positive compensation in his being called to the place of honour. In this case too 'the last will be first' (Matt. 20.16). Now that he is about to graduate, it is time to reprioritize family life.

Jessica

An elderly aunt has died and my husband, Connor, reluctantly agrees to attend the funeral. I join my family in the church which has a bright pink carpet. I cannot find Connor and am concerned that he has gone to the pub. The coffin is brought in with lots of white flowers and is followed by many people in liturgical dance mode. They take off their shoes on reaching the altar and insist that my family move to another part of the church, as we are in the space reserved for them. I leave and drive along a country road. I suddenly see Bran, our dog, playing in a garden with a light brown cocker spaniel. Bran is delighted to see me and I take him away, despite the protestations of a gardener. I still haven't found Connor and am afraid I'll never see him again.

The dream has obvious religious imagery: a sense of the sacred, in the removal of shoes on holy ground; liturgical joy, pink being the colour of Gaudete Sunday; and white flowers, representing the resurrection. But the dreamer perceives herself to be on the margins of the church (being moved to one side) and her husband does not want to join Jessica in prayer. She is anxious that she will lose him and in his stead finds their mutually beloved pet. I wonder how well the two halves of the dream are connected. The first part expresses her Christian hope in God, despite being pushed to one side by the Church. That same hope has yet to relieve her anxiety concerning Connor.

References

Barry, W. and Connolly, W. (1982), *The Practice of Spiritual Direction*, San Francisco: Harper and Row.

Condon, G. (2008), *The Power of Dreams: A Christian Guide*, Dublin: Columba Press.

Condon, G. (2012), 'Learning that is not Taught: Spirituality and the Dreams of Children', in *The Way* 51 (1), pp. 41–54.

Egan, G. (1990), *The Skilled Helper: A Systematic Approach to Effective Helping*, 4th edn, Pacific Grove CA: Brooks/Cole.

Franklin, R. W., ed., (1998), *The Poems of Emily Dickinson*, Cambridge MA: Belknap Press of Harvard University.

Freud, S. (1953), *The Interpretation of Dreams*, ed. J. Strachey, London: Hogarth Press.

Gracián, J. (1933), 'Peregrinación de Anastasio', in Idem, *Obras* 3, Burgos: Tipografia de 'El Monte Carmelo'.

Jung, C. G. (1945–48), 'On the Nature of Dreams', in W. McGuire, ed., *The Collected Works of C. G. Jung*, Vol. 8, New Jersey: Princeton University Press, paras 530–69.

Jung, C. G. (1949), 'The Psychological Aspects of the Kore', in W. McGuire, ed., *The Collected Works of C. G. Jung*, Vol. 9, Part 1, New Jersey: Princeton University Press, paras 306–83.

Jung, C. G. (1961), 'Symbols and the Interpretation of Dreams', in W. McGuire, ed., *The Collected Works of C. G. Jung*, Vol. 18, New Jersey: Princeton University Press, paras 416–607.

Jung, C. G. (1963), *Memories, Dreams, Reflections*, New York: Random House.

Kelsey, M. (1968), *Dreams: The Dark Speech of the Spirit: A Christian Interpretation*, Garden City NY: Doubleday.

Merton, T. (1961), *New Seeds of Contemplation*, New York: New Directions.

Nemeck, F. K. and Coombs, M. T. (1993), *The Way of Spiritual Direction*, Collegeville MN: Liturgical Press.

Shamdasani, S. (2003), *Jung and the Making of Modern Psychology: The Dream of a Science*, Cambridge: Cambridge University Press.

Szentmártoni, M. (2013), 'Mystical Experience – A Search for the Love of God', in I. Platovnjak, ed., *Karel Vladimir Truhlar: Pesnik, duhovnik in teolog*, Ljubljani: Univerze v Ljubljani, pp. 59–70.

Whitmont, E. C. and Perera, S. B. (1989), *Dreams: A Portal to the Source*, London: Routledge.

13

Out of the Mouths of Babes . . .
Hearing the Dreams of Children and Adolescents

PETER GREEN AND KATE ADAMS

Children and adolescents are prolific dreamers. Indeed, research shows that we dream more in childhood than we do in adulthood. For some children dreams can be particularly meaningful, and avenues outside the home such as church and school can offer them valuable opportunities to share their dreams. However, neither Christian pastors nor teachers are trained to respond to children's dream narratives. What follows is a response to this state of affairs. It is the product of a collaboration between two colleagues working in England. Peter Green is an Anglican priest of a theologically conservative tendency who has worked as a chaplain in schools: a role with responsibility for providing spiritual and emotional support for all members of the school community. Kate Adams is an academic and former primary school teacher with no religious affiliation specializing in the field of children's spirituality. This chapter focuses on the relationship between theory and practice, first drawing on Peter's experience as a school chaplain. Kate then illuminates key points from Peter's practice and demonstrates the links with research into children's dreams, before the chapter draws out implications for those working with children in school settings. Throughout we use the phrase 'spiritual dreams' to denote those dreams that contain divine imagery (such as God or angels) or to which children ascribe a divine source.

The spirituality of children and their dreams: a pastor's perspective

I've been an ordained minister in the Church of England for 25 years, and in the course of that time I've acquired (at a rough guess) about 600 books deemed useful for an Anglican priest – books on biblical studies, pastoral theology, church doctrine, church history and, believe it or not, spirituality. I reckon I've got about as many books on these topics to hand as most of my closest colleagues and clergy friends. In preparation for writing this I scoured the contents and the indices of those books looking for anything they might have to say on the question of dreams, let alone the dreams of children, and – outside biblical commentaries – the almost total silence was deafening.

On reflection, this is rather worrying given that I am more and more convinced that the logic of spiritual experience, out of which I believe the dogmatic core of Christianity arises, most likely has a huge overlap with dream logic. This view is suggested for a variety of reasons too lengthy to enumerate here but stems from the fact that, on those occasions when children and young people describe their experiences of the spiritual or the uncanny as part of our pastoral conversations, it is my residual impression that dream experiences constitute a significant minority of their accounts.

The reasons for pastoral reticence in my tradition to do anything beyond listening attentively and with respect to what children say on this matter can be guessed at easily enough. In my role as chaplain, whereby I talk with and listen to many children who share their cares and worries, I realize that (as with adults) there will be aspects of children's dreams that will probably only begin to make sense if one has a comprehensive knowledge of their life in general – at home, at school, and in their peer/friendship group. And inevitably, where I have had some separate knowledge of the child's circumstances, extreme tact was involved in dealing with dreams that seem to refer to traumatic experiences. In my own case, I have wondered whether I'm not haunted by the implication of Genesis 40–41, or Daniel 2, that the interpretation of dreams requires a special spiritual gift – or something akin to the discernment of spirits alluded to in 1 Corinthians 12.10. Yet, for all this, I have rather unreflectively evolved a fairly fixed pastoral strategy that governs my response to those occasions when a child chooses to share a dream experience. Aside of the fact that animals tend to feature more in the dreams of children than adults (Siegel and Bulkeley 1998), there seems to be a huge overlap between adult and child dream experiences – the anxiety dreams about an impending challenge, recurring dreams, occasional experiences of vivid dreaming, dreams that are generically realistic and dreams that are (to the child) either amusingly or worryingly 'weird'. Some relate dreams that have a directly spiritual character – and others attribute a spiritual meaning to a dream only in retrospect. Furthermore, I have a sense that the children who have spoken to me about this remember (or maybe even experience) a higher proportion of nightmares than adults generally tend to recount.

However, aside from the fact that children can be more unselfconscious in attributing spiritual significance to dreams than many adults, there are two things that strike me as demanding special pastoral attention:

- I have encountered children who with less inhibition than might be expected of an adult continue to fantasize during the day about the dream they can remember from the previous night's sleep and ascribe to the foundational dream a spiritual dimension. Sometimes this practice includes dream experiences that are aspirational, escapist, or generically realistic; but crucially – from an epistemological perspective – it also includes experiences that, in Andrew Brown's (2014) phrase, show a childlike 'preference for remembering and transmitting stories that defy scientific rationality'. Such a tendency seems to include the wish not just to remember and transmit stories characterized by dream logic but also to live in them. If nothing else, this should alert pastors to the fact that it's probable that a minority of the children who are part of their worshipping community are spontaneously framing their whole experience of religion or spirituality in a manner almost impossible to guess at.
- When children recount dream experiences to an adult who is predisposed to look for a spiritual dimension, they are inevitably more vulnerable to the tendency of such adults to measure the dream experience against an established inventory of religious images – adults with a Jungian outlook are, of course, particularly prone to this. A child may say (as recounted to me by a colleague): 'The Holy Spirit appeared in my dream – he was a bishopy kind of alien.' And the adult may spontaneously accept or reject that interpretation according to their dogmatic predilections.

Given that hitherto this analysis has stayed within fairly safe bounds, this last point simply reinforces an important pastoral consideration: that of dream interpretation. It seems to be wholly licit that one can ask whether the child him/herself attributes meaning to a dream. I have asked older children if they have had a dream that they thought had spiritual or religious meaning, and left any interpretation to them – though, of course, I have to bear in mind that children can sometimes be predisposed to offer answers to adults that they think will please.

As a pastor, when such conversations arise I generally do my best to reassure the child (should they require it) that spiritual experience in dreams is not strange or unusual – I will even say that I myself can remember having dreams that I think had a specific spiritual meaning. It has been my experience that children often only share an account of spiritual experience with adults (and peers) whom they trust: it seems that all too often such accounts are met with what appears to the child to be a patronizing or dismissive response. It has also been my experience that, when a child shares an account like this with me in the contemporary UK context, I should take this as an indicator of a certain level of trust that should be respected.

The spirituality of children and their dreams: an educator's perspective

Reading Peter's section was like holding up a mirror in places to my own experiences, even though we come from different backgrounds. And yet that is the beauty of spiritual dreams: for while imagery is often aligned to cultural background, dreams transcend boundaries. Carl Jung adopted the phrase 'big dreams' to describe those that 'stand out for years like spiritual landmarks, even though they may never be quite understood' (Jung 1946, p. 117). But what relevance might these big dreams, including those perceived to be connected to the divine, have for children?

A trip to the library to find out more resonated with Peter's remarks on how little his vast book collection tells him about dreams in general and the dreams of children in particular. Certainly, outside of the books directed at clergy, there are many books about dreams on the market, usually oriented towards the general public who wish to understand what their dreams might mean, alongside more academic tomes hailing from a range of disciplines. Yet the number of texts on children's dreams is minimal and those on children's spiritual dreams even fewer . . . yet what does exist affirms Peter's experience of working with children in different ways.

First, children often raise dreams as an integral part of their spiritual experience even when dreams have not been mentioned by the adults. Most certainly, dreams form a strand of the wider spiritual dimension of their lives (Adams, Hyde and Woolley 2008). They are often meaningful for young people; indeed, Jung himself observed that many big dreams occur in childhood. It is as if children are naturally predisposed to paying attention to them and reflecting on them even when their immediate environment may disregard dreams as fanciful notions or the simple processing of the day's events. Certainly, many dreams are characterized in this way, but some dreams are distinctly spiritual in nature. In a delightful and well-informed exposition of children's dreams, now regrettably out of print, Siegel and Bulkeley (1998, p. 162) describe the latter as distinguishable by their 'felt power, and experiential intensity and vividness'.

For some children, these dreams may contain explicit religious content. In my research, a Christian boy called David told me how he had argued with his best friend and subsequently dreamt:

> I was floating up through the clouds and I saw a concrete path. There was a large shining man and my friend stood there. The shining man floated away and I and my friend were left on our own together and I and my friend shook hands.

For David, the shining figure was God who, by floating away, gave the boys time 'to think' and the opportunity to resolve their differences 'in quiet instead of making up in crowds, or crowds of children'. Shortly after the dream, the two friends were reunited. David described the dream as 'a special' dream that showed him what God was able to do (Adams 2003, p. 109).

On other occasions there may be no explicit religious imagery at all (Siegel and Bulkeley 1998), and in such cases it is essential to hear the child's view – their understanding of the dream – in order to capture a sense of its richness and depth and to see how it can be part of the child's meaning-making. This point is superbly illustrated by ten-year-old Sarah, who described to me what at first glance appears to be a relatively mundane dream related to a daily concern. Her dream took place amidst nervousness about an upcoming cross-country running race that her school was hosting. The night before the race she dreamt:

> I was running in the race and I did it easily. Other children were in it and it wasn't hard for me, I just kept running and I finished the course. I wasn't the last one to finish either!

The temptation for adults to impose an interpretation on a child's dream is strong but must be resisted, especially in an educational setting, where listening should be the key. Here, Sarah revealed that she believed the dream had been sent by God to show her that she had the ability to run the race successfully (Adams 2003, p. 110). Without talking to Sarah, there would have been no sense of any perceived divine connection to what would otherwise have likely been set aside as a straightforward, almost mechanical, psychological response to a waking anxiety.

A second key resonance with Peter's experience lies in the matter of trust. In the cases I cite, I was taking the role of researcher, entering schools where I did not know any of the teachers or children. With the exception of a small number of children who had experienced a dream with a divine connection, but did not wish to share it (a right always to be respected, of course), those who consented to interviews (94 in my doctoral study) were very open to discussing their dream. Despite this, one third commented that they had never told anyone their dream before for fear of ridicule or dismissal (Adams 2014). For me, entering the schools as a stranger with a genuine interest in spiritual dreams, perhaps it was relatively easy for the children to be so open about such a personal experience. They could be confident that I would take them seriously, and hence not disbelieve them. This type of trust is of a different nature from that which builds up over many weeks, months or years with a teacher or other professional, but it is nonetheless a privilege that is afforded to researchers who work with children.

To end this reflection, it is important to highlight another key point evidenced by research: that it is not only children from various religious backgrounds who experience such dreams, but also those with no religious upbringing, which can easily be missed. The most poignant comment made to me in the course of my research, which encapsulates different points raised here, was from Paul, a nine-year-old boy from a secular background who dreamt of explicit religious imagery.

> I was on a cloud and God was there. I was crying and God told me not be upset. When I woke up I felt better.

I asked Paul if he had mentioned this dream to anyone else. 'Only my cat,' he replied. 'My cat always listens and never talks back to me.'

Concluding reflections

Four points of practical significance emerge from our dialogue, which may help others who work with children in schools and other pastoral settings.

- *Understanding the languages of dreams.* As David, Sarah and Paul's accounts illustrate, their dreams reflect their waking thoughts, which is to be expected given the relationship between the waking and dreaming states. But while neuroscience gives us insight into the brain's activity during dreaming – of firing neurons – the language(s) of spirituality adds a further, rich dimension.
- *Interpretation.* The only place for interpreting children's dreams is through dialogue in a therapeutic context. Clearly, a school is not such a place. Avoiding the temptation to impose an interpretation is sometimes difficult, but always necessary.

- *Trust and open minds.* Children's willingness to share their spiritual dreams requires more than trust in an adult confidant. They need to know that the adult also has an open mind with regard to the spiritual, something they often know instinctively.
- *Nightmares.* Any discussion of dreams with children is likely to initiate discussion of nightmares, even if unintended. Most are a common and normal part of childhood but a smaller number are the result of trauma. Where concerns about a child's welfare arise, the school's safeguarding policies should be adhered to.

Research suggests that when children elect to share their spiritual dreams with adults, this may happen only once or twice during their youth. Often children find this adult outside of their family home, making way for teachers, chaplains and other professionals who work with them to potentially undertake the role of confidant, a role that can only be described as a privilege.

References

Adams, K. (2003), 'Children's Dreams: An Exploration of Jung's Concept of Big Dreams', *International Journal of Children's Spirituality* 8(2), pp. 105–14.

Adams, K. (2014), 'Children's Dreams in the Classroom', in C. Hoffman and J. Lewis, eds, *Weaving Dreams into the Classroom*, Boca Raton FL: Brown Walker Press, pp. 17–30.

Adams, K., Hyde, B. and Woolley, R. (2008), *The Spiritual Dimension of Childhood*, London: Jessica Kingsley.

Brown, A. (2014), 'There's No Such Thing as an Atheist Baby', in *The Guardian*, 12 June 2014.

Jung, C. (1946/1954), *The Collected Works of C. G. Jung*, Vol. 17, London: Routledge.

Siegel, A. and Bulkeley, K. (1998), *Dreamcatching: Every Parent's Guide to Exploring and Understanding Children's Dreams and Nightmares*, New York: Three Rivers Press.

14

'For He gives to his beloved even in his sleep' (Psalm 127.2)[1]

Pastoral Care and Dreams in Hospitals and Nursing Homes

HANS DORNSEIFFEN

Translated by H. A. M. Zwemmer

Introduction

From 1976 to 2011 I worked full time as a pastoral counsellor in a general hospital and in a nursing home in Holland. Over the course of time I discovered that raising the subject of dreams for discussion often added a new dimension to the conversation. This was surprising for me as a pastor, and also for the patient. Looking more closely at my own dream world proved helpful. Literature and study provided me with the necessary qualifications and a deepening of insight. I have now come to regard talking about one's dream(s) as one of various pastoral instruments that can be used in a healthcare organization. In this chapter I would like to illustrate, by means of some real-life cases, how valuable an instrument this can be.

The singing bone

Once upon a time there was a king who offered to give his daughter in marriage to the person who could defeat the wild boar that terrorized his kingdom. Two brothers go off to accomplish this mission. The elder one is arrogant while the younger is naive and good at heart. Because of his kindness the younger brother receives a magic spear from a little man in

---

1 Trans: New American Standard Bible.

the woods, and with this spear he is able to kill the boar. With the dead animal on his back he comes out of the woods and meets his older brother who is just leaving the local pub where he had been drinking to pluck up his courage. He murders his younger brother, and buries his dead body under a bridge. Then he takes the swine to the king and he marries the princess.

However, God wants this crime to come to light.

After some time a shepherd finds a small bone close to that very bridge. From this bone he cuts himself a mouthpiece for his horn. As soon as he blows on it, he hears a little song:

> Dear friend, listen to me,
> thou blowest upon a bone of me.
> Long have I lain beside the water;
> My brother slew me for the boar,
> And took for his wife the King's young daughter.

The shepherd takes the horn to the king and the king understands that a crime has been committed. He orders men to excavate the bones of the younger brother near the bridge. The older brother confesses to the murder and is sentenced to death for his criminal act. The bones of the younger brother are reburied in a beautiful tomb at the churchyard.

It may be unusual to start this chapter with a fairy tale, but it is for a reason. In this folk tale by the Grimm brothers, different themes can be found, but the main one is that no matter how deep an injustice lays buried under the bridge, the truth will out. The power of the truth will force itself like a tulip bulb through the solid ground into the light of the sun.

The truth wants to be seen

One of my patients had experienced the same nightmare for several nights. This is what she told me:

> I am lying face down on a springboard and I am looking at the bottom of the swimming pool. The muddy bottom is covered with round cobblestones. One of the stones attracts my attention and I keep looking at it. Suddenly the stone trembles and it startles me. The stone breaks away from the bottom and it floats to the surface, towards me. Slowly it comes closer and closer. The stone turns into the face of my father and I scream with fear. I wake up in a pool of sweat.

This lady's father had died of cancer when she was only eight years old, and telling me about this dream gave her the courage, for the first time in 30 years, to talk about her grief. She had not been allowed to attend the funeral. Sitting on a doorstep she heard the bells tolling and said to herself: 'It is my father they are burying over there.' For 30 years this sadness and anger had remained hidden in a corner of her soul, but apparently now was the time for it to come out and be dealt with and accepted. After she had expressed this hidden anger, the nightmare never came back. The dream, like a coded letter to herself, had been read and understood.

It may have been a coincidence that I first set eyes on a book about dreams a few days before the start of my three-month clinical pastoral training. A new world opened up to me! The power of expression that dreams can have appealed to me and I decided to take the subject seriously and study it further. It was during one of the first nights of this training that I dreamt the following dream, which I titled 'Frosted brook in Austria':

> I find myself in the cellar/kitchen of an old residence which resembles my former student hostel. The floor is a boggy swamp and the water cannot flow. With a bamboo rod I jab into the drain pipes and after much pushing finally the water runs off spectacularly clean and clear. The water rises and a part of the ground floods with it and I have to make a channel for the brook. I remove a last remaining ball of grass. A fellow pastor decides to take a picture of the whole but his equipment is almost washed away with the stream. At the end of the cellar the water runs away through a street paved with bricks, and a big red broom stands against the wall. The land can be cultivated again.

It took several weeks to get some idea of the meaning of this dream. Skipping the details, I understood that during this clinical pastoral training I found myself in a learning process (student hostel). The state of my subconscious is still in a soggy condition – land and water are not yet separated (see Gen. 1.9) and not much can grow there. By pushing the drain pipes open with a bamboo cane I let the water run off from the marshy land. It becomes a broad stream that washes away in the corner of the cellar. The land is ready to be cultivated.

The bamboo cane puzzled me for some time. It did not ring a bell, until I remembered that I had read, about six weeks before the training, a book on English public schools in which the bamboo cane was often used as a form of punishment. It became clear to me that seven years of boarding school and junior seminary had left deep marks on my inner life. The training would be an opportunity to reorganize and to balance my emotional life.

How to deal with dreams

This personal experience with a dream (and the hundreds more that would follow) led me to reading the literature on this subject. I trained with a psychologist for six months and she taught me how to deal with my own and someone else's dreams. What I learned, from her and from the literature, to be of most importance when dealing with dreams is included in the following basic principles:

1 There are no fixed symbols. The meaning of a dream cannot be found in a dream dictionary.
2 One must be very careful not to be too rash in explaining someone else's dream. After having listened to a dream one may offer a guess about the meaning, but no more than that.
3 Only the dreamer can feel precisely what the dream is expressing.
4 When one is trying to interpret dreams it is always useful to ask for help from someone else. A second listener can notice details that the dreamer may have overlooked.
5 Working with dreams does not always lead to a direct result. Sometimes the understanding of the meaning of a dream comes later.
6 When talking about a person's dream(s) it is the dreamer who decides how far she or he wants to go.
7 When a person talks about a dream it is advisable to first listen to the whole of the story. Observe intently what feeling the dream activates in both the dreamer and the listener and recognize what special elements we have noticed. Sometimes it is helpful to make notes when a person tells their dream (which must be told in the present tense).

Dream group sessions

Dream interpretation is not generally regarded by ministers as one of their 'tools' for pastoral work. When I inquired about this during one of the general meetings with my 30 Catholic colleagues, it turned out that I was the only one of the whole Diocese of Haarlem who was actually using this instrument. Twice I delivered a lecture for them on the subject and there was some interest but little affinity. I have always regretted this. During my lessons for student nurses I also spent time talking about dreams and what they could mean to a patient. They always listened attentively and apparently years later often still remembered my teaching.

Analysing dreams seems to be primarily confined to the domain of psychologists and psychiatrists but at the same time in Holland there are numerous dream groups, where people tell their dreams and try to interpret them together. Specific exercises and regular practice provide help for the dreamer to find the meaning of the dream. It has often surprised me how people are able to take up the thread of their life again after having focused on and dealt with an inner conflict.

My basic assumption, however, remains that a certain modesty must be observed by pastoral workers when they use dream interpretation in their talks. This is why I always have a regular psychologist to whom I can refer a patient for further assistance.

Leaf and shadow on water

A woman of about 30 told me about a dream that recurred several times. In this dream she always tried on a black swimsuit with a print of large orange flowers. But this swimsuit did not fit at all: she exposed herself in it. 'What does this swimsuit remind you of?' I asked. This simple question released a torrent of words and feelings. Instantly it reminded her of her mother and how she had always taken her mother's opinion too seriously. Because of her own lack of self-esteem she often imitated her during her marriage. Deep down she felt very unhappy about this and the dream made clear what the problem was and how it could be solved.

Sometimes, after having been counselling a patient for a long time, I would notice that a conversation would stop; at the same time I would feel a resistance, as well as a longing to bring something up.

This was the case with a terminal care patient who had come to the hospital to die. I had visited Mrs Pieterse daily and after a while it seemed as if everything had been said, but still I noticed an indefinable sadness in her eyes. Our conversation stopped after a few minutes and I spontaneously asked her: 'Did you have a dream last night?' She seemed surprised and said that yes, indeed she had. 'It was a very short dream. I saw my mother standing in the far distance. She did not speak but was just looking at me.'

I asked her to close her eyes and to recall this image of her mother. Then I asked her what her mother would say if she could be there. Tears gathered in her eyes and she replied: 'Oh my dear daughter, it would have been better if you had not been born.' Through her tears she revealed her own story. She was born during the bombardment of Rotterdam in 1940; her mother gave birth prematurely out of pure fright. The bomb explosions shook her mother's bed and pieces of shrapnel battered the roof of the house. Her birth was two months early. Her father died later in the war and often her mother had little or no food to give her and her elder sister. This was what Mrs Pieterse had heard her mother say from the beginning of her life: 'It would have been better if you had not been born.' This statement had cast a shadow on her whole life. Two long conversations were enough to express her sorrow and enable her to move on. Mrs Pieterse, who had come to the hospital to die, felt much better after a few days and she was able to go home, where she was lovingly cared for by her husband for two months before she died.

Feelings of guilt

Sometimes ignoring a dream can give rise to feelings of guilt. This was the case with Mrs Zwart. She told me her story. It had happened 28 years previously. During the night her little son had come to his parents' bed because he had had a bad dream. She told him that his father was not feeling well and he had to go back to his own room. At breakfast she complimented her son for having been so obedient and asked him what this dream had been about. He told her that in his dream he had been run over by a truck. She soothed him by saying, 'But you know that dreams are not true, don't you?' Her son went to school, but not until he had said goodbye three times before walking out of the door. On his way to school he was run over by a dustcart that was reversing, and died. This denial had been a heavy burden on her life since then. Talking about her grief and this feeling of guilt helped her to make a serious effort to finally forgive herself.

From old to new

Mrs Janssen was a terminally ill patient who had some special experiences in the last weeks before she died. Sometimes when she dozed off, she would be talking to her husband. He had passed away 35 years ago but Mrs Janssen would see him standing in her room, dressed the way he had been when she buried him. This was Mrs Janssen's dream:

I am standing on the Dam in Amsterdam, in front of the Royal Palace. I know that there is a royal succession about to happen. The old queen will abdicate and the new queen will take her place and reign. On the balcony of the palace the queen appears. She wears a brilliant white dress, so beautiful that I am seized with emotion. But when I take a closer look I discover that the new queen is fastened to the palace with a chain.

We talked about the dream extensively. Her feeling about this dream was that it tended to refer to a future life – life after her death, to which she was looking forward with great faith. After some discussion this was her interpretation. The abdication of the old queen symbolically referred to the death of her sick body. To her, death is forthcoming, and that is probably why she is not present in the dream. Now the new queen stands on the balcony in a beautiful white dress. The white dress moves Mrs Janssen because to her a white dress is a symbol of her new life after death; in the same way as 'the angels in the beyond' are dressed in brilliant white.

Mrs Janssen felt that she was still between the old life and the new. The fact that the new queen was chained to the palace meant that she had not yet reached her new life. Mrs Janssen felt encouraged by the dream.

Mrs Janssen was a special person and at her deathbed I witnessed something extraordinary. She had a book of poetry that her husband had written long ago, and illustrated by hand. Mrs Janssen's wish was that I would read one of his religious poems at her funeral. She had chosen a poem titled 'From Old to New', and it started with the old year that would end on 31 December, moving on to 'passing away at our dying from the old life to the new life'. The poem was illustrated with a clock and the hands pointed to one minute before twelve.

I was sitting by her bed when she was dying and I picked up the book of poetry to reread this poem. I was absorbed in the text and it was very quiet. Suddenly the municipal alarm went off (all municipal sirens are tested monthly in Holland on the first Monday at 12.00). I looked at Mrs Janssen: she had passed away. Exactly at one minute to twelve she had breathed her last. She had gone from 'old' to 'new'.

15

Some Lessons from Prison Dreams:
A Personal Account

BART J. KOET

Introduction

In the Talmud, the immense collection of Jewish wisdom, a certain Rav Hisda says: 'A dream which is not interpreted is like a letter which is not read' (b.Ber 55a) (see Chapter 8, this volume). Later in the rabbinic dream book this adage is corrected and expanded: Has not Rav Hisda said: 'A dream which is not interpreted is like a letter which is not read? Say rather then, he should have a good turn given to it in the presence of three.' Thus, the rabbis urge to look for a positive interpretation!

However, the word 'dream' itself is ambiguous to interpret: is it referring to what's happening during sleep or is it the wishes for a life to be? An example of the latter is the nickname of a famous boulevard in Hollywood: 'The Boulevard of Broken Dreams'. Women who wanted to pursue a career in Hollywood would sometimes end up selling themselves on Sunset Boulevard in Los Angeles, and so this road earned its name as the place for broken dreams.

Prisons are places where one encounters people with their broken dreams too. Because I worked part-time from 1989 to 2004 as chaplain in one of the most complex prisons in the Netherlands, I heard about quite a few broken dreams during those years. But at the same time a lot of 'night dreams' were told to me, in private or in discussion groups. In the aforementioned Talmud text, it is said that it is always worthwhile to explain dreams in a positive way, and that is what I tried to do in the prison.

I have presented in the past both accounts of this use of the word 'dream'. Saskia Vredeveld, a documentary director, and I worked for two years in the prison trying to show how dreams could be healing (Koet and Vredeveld 2003). The aim of that endeavour was to illustrate that dreams could bring different cultures in prison together and how talking about dreams could bring an intimacy not only for those groups but also for some of the inmates. To a certain extent I consider the documentary as a failure, because it was quite difficult to create an atmosphere of intimacy and a sharing of feelings when the camera as a 'third eye' was present. However, it became a moving document of how a prison collects people who are living on the boulevard of broken dreams, and thus this documentary is still a revelation for many people.

In a later publication I described a discussion about dreaming with some interesting intercultural tensions, at the same time showing how such a discussion can immediately bring people from diverse cultures together. Just by talking about their visions or dreams the inmates could experience the extreme power of listening to dreams as food for thought, especially in the distressing situation of being in a prison. One could define those dreams as healing dreams (Koet 2009).

I started to work in the prison just after finishing my dissertation on the interpretation of the Old Testament in the New Testament. An inmate insisted on telling me his dream, and I realized that if I was able to explain in a methodical way the old wisdom of biblical literature, perhaps I would be able to try to interpret his dream with him (Koet 2009, pp. 226–7).

After this encounter I started to ask inmates about their dreams, and in religious services in the prison I used biblical dream stories. Even though religious services in a prison are often a little noisy, during the dream stories people remained silent. Further, I held dream groups with inmates. At that time in exegetical, academic circles there was a certain reluctance to study the dream texts of biblical times. Thus, I started to concentrate my research on texts that touched on the dream stories of biblical, classical, rabbinic traditions and the last years also in the literature of early Christianity (Koet 2006, 2012). In this chapter I offer – with some hesitation – some examples of prison dreams. Four dream lessons are presented: two of these lessons are derived from dreams of inmates and two from my own dreams.

Limitations and some methodological remarks

The confinement of dreaming to a psychological or physiological realm is relatively recent. For most of their long history, dreams have been treated not merely as an internally motivated phenomenon, but often linked to the realm of divinity, and thus I saw that it was in line with tradition to talk as a minister about the dreams of their 'flock'. However, it can also be worthwhile to pay attention – even in a superficial way – to the dreams of the pastor. First I sketch some limitations of such an approach.

A dream narrative is always only a reconstruction of a dream experience, and when we try to interpret a dream we are only interpreting this reconstruction of the dream. Even those people who keep a dream notebook on the bedside table, and who try to describe as precisely as possible their dreams, only write down a reconstruction of the dream. A verbatim account of a 'real' dream is beyond reach. In a prison context it is almost impossible for inmates to make a written report of such a dream narrative. Here I deal with the dream narrative in the form of a report I made after meeting with the inmate(s). Thus, we encounter the reconstruction of a reconstruction.

Although this chapter is experience based, it is certainly not written according to any standard of 'evidence based' research as is required in a social, psychological or scientific method. I present some case studies, but it is not possible to reproduce the material of our research. However, readers may be inspired to listen to their own dreams and learn from these dream narratives.

My specialism within theology is the interpretation of Scriptures and other sources, such as classical, rabbinic and early Christian texts. Methods for working with these classic sources are derived from or parallel to the scholarly interpretation of literature. The dream reports here are used as narratives and interpreted with a literary approach. However, with regard to the limited space of this chapter we will not detail the methodical steps.

My most important thesis is that considering a dream report as a narrative can inspire people working as pastoral counsellors to listen to the dreams told to them and maybe even to their own dreams. Ministers of all denominations are trained to listen in a careful way to the narratives of their traditions and thus it should be possible for them to listen to the dream reports of their flock and to their own dreams. These reflections could be considered as contributions to a special section of the theological discourse: practical theology.

In circles of dream workers several methodological steps are used when helping people to interpret their own dreams. Even in prison it is possible to create dream groups. However, in such a hectic and noisy context, it is often quite difficult to meet regularly or to give close attention to the dreams of an inmate. After all, a prison does not have the same facilities as the Carl Jung Institute! Thus, it was quite difficult to listen to their dreams in a systematic way. Sometimes I could follow some methodological steps, but more often I had to improvise.

In the context of this book, it is possible to show readers that one can see a dream report as a narrative and one can use literary methods to explain some of the elements of the dream. However, there is one rule that must be remembered. The most important insight of modern dream workers is that they try to guide the dreamer to find their own interpretation. For some dream workers it is almost dogmatic that one is not allowed to give an interpretation of someone's dream. This seems to be opposite to the way dream interpreters in the past saw their profession, and in other cultures today, convinced of their competence in explaining the dreams of everybody.[1] One of the most important tools is to ask questions. A more or less systematic interview concerning the details of the dream and the feelings of the dreamer can help the dreamer gain insight into their own dreams and hopefully also into their lives.

It is, in my view, not by accident that I, as a chaplain working in a prison context, was struck by the importance of dreaming for my pastoral clients. It is my experience that inmates have more time for listening to and becoming afraid of their dreaming than people who are free. This concurs with the observation that since biblical times there has been a relationship between dreaming and prisons. It is in a prison situation that Joseph, one of the most important dreamers in biblical (and Islamic) tradition, uses his skills of dream interpretation to explain the dreams of two other 'inmates'. One can find another example of dreams and imprisonment in a document from the beginning of the third century, the *Passio Perpetuae*, where Perpetua, the protagonist, receives dreams while imprisoned in a dungeon (Koet 2015). The great German evangelical martyr Dietrich Bonhoeffer writes in a letter to his parents that he is happy to receive dreams while in detention: 'It is remarkable that the days go quite fast here. It seems to me incredible that I am already three weeks here. I am happy to sleep at eight o clock. One gets the last meal at four o'clock and I did not know in the past,

---

1 See e.g. the introduction of Artemidorus (White 1975). In the rabbinic dream book one already finds a critique of dream interpreters. They seem to give positive interpretations of a dream for the rich and negative ones for those who cannot pay. The Talmud warns that it is dangerous to give negative interpretations, because the dream tends to follow the interpretation.

that that is a beautiful gift: I dream every night and it is always nice.'[2] In another letter to them he says that he is free in his dreams.[3]

When writing about the dreams of inmates there is a final problem that needs addressing here. As a minister I have confessional confidentiality. It is against the law of my country (and my church) to reveal important issues heard in personal encounters with my inmates. Thus, the dreams presented here are either presented with permission or reframed in such a way that the original elements are still there but the dreams are sufficiently anonymized to preserve confidentiality.

Dreams of inmates

The inspirational dream of a Mafia Capo

Imagine, your mother has two sons and you are not her favourite. You are doomed to become the black sheep in the family and you have fulfilled all the bad expectations of your mother. You seldom see her, or your brother, her favourite, who still lives with your mother who is widowed. You earned your money in all kinds of dark businesses and you became the owner of the biggest brothel in a nearby city. One day, you are sitting in the office of your business, overseeing the girls and their clients. You are a bit sleepy and then you see a customer entering. You look at the screen of the camera more closely though you do not know why. You look more closely still and suddenly, with a shock, you realize that the new customer is your brother.

This story is told by Adam Z, one of my clients in prison in Amsterdam. It is possible that it is a fantasy and thus may be not true, perhaps a lie: the prison is full of lies. Some people would use the word confabulation, more or less in a negative sense. As a scholar of literature I would not dare to use such a word. It is far too suggestive. We talk about a narrative and its variations: all are worthwhile.

---

2 Bonhoeffer 1998, pp. 51–2 (Urausgabe 36–37): 'Merkwürdigerweise gehen die Tage hier schnell vorüber. Daß ich hier 3 Wochen bin, scheint mir unglaublich. Ich gehe gern um 8 Uhr schlafen – Abendbrot gibt es um 4 Uhr! – und freue mich auf meine Träume. Ich habe früher gar nicht gewußt, was für eine glückliche Gabe das ist: ich träume täglich und eigentlich immer schön.'

3 Bonhoeffer 1998, p. 111. Like Bonhoeffer, quite a few Germans wrote about only being free in their dreams. The fact that sometimes one can be free only in dreams is beautifully documented by Charlotte Beradt (1968). It is a collection of dreams compiled by this journalist and smuggled out of Germany in code.

Thus, although the prison is full of lies, at the same time this story told me something about Adam and his feelings regarding his family. The story contains a truth for me to explore. A prison is a place where you can find truth in many forms, if you look for it and when you are prepared to read between the lines.

Adam was not a small criminal. He was a kind of *Capo*, a member of the 'nobility' of criminals, at least one of their baronets. I spoke quite often with him. He had quite a social side, and was caring – in his own way – for those inmates who had problems. Sometimes he referred them to me, sometimes he referred me to them.

One of the big themes of our pastoral discussions was his relations with women. He had enough money to impress them and he had several relationships at the same time. He was involved in bringing women from East Europe to the brothels of the Netherlands and he married Zonja, one of his own 'products'. However, he understood quite well that she married him for his money but he said that they had good times together when he was free. It was a calculated risk. She might leave him when he was in prison. Part of the calculation was that she needed his money to survive and he thought that she would stay with him as long as he could give her money via one of his underlings. So when she announced that she would like a divorce he suspected that she had a lover or had maybe found another unexpected source of money.

One day he asked me to come to his cell and he said to me: 'Listen, Bart, I know from the other inmates that you are always interested in dreams. Now I know why Zonja wants to divorce me. My dream told me. When I was still free, I realized that there could come a time when I could become a prisoner. In that case my business would stop and my friends would probably start to steal from me. As an insurance strategy I decided to hide three shoeboxes with a million dollars in them. I knew that I hid one box below the floorboards, and one in the garden of my holiday home, but I could not remember where I left the third box. This night I had a dream. I was in my house, in my bedroom. There was an enormous cupboard containing all my wife's shoes. In my dream I realized that the third box with one million dollars in was inside my cupboard, in the place where I keep my shoes. When I awoke, I knew for sure that Zonja has found the box and that thus she can afford to divorce me.'[4]

---

4 By telling this story I am not breaking my confessional privilege. Although I use a pseudonym for this inmate and his wife, after telling his dream he agreed that I could use his dream narrative for my publications.

Then he told me that he could not tell this to his friends or to her, because, according to the rules of his world, his friends had to punish her for 'the stealing' of this million dollar box. He preferred the loss of the million to hurting her. She had been a good companion and deserved her reward.

His story is one of the many dreams that were told to me during my chaplaincy in the prison. It is also an example of a problem-solving dream. We know that Nobel Prize winners have sometimes found a solution to their problem in dreams.[5] It is nice to add to this category a comparable narrative from one of the more 'important' inmates of a prison.

LESSON ONE: Speaking about dreams evokes interest in paying attention to dreams. Adam Z wanted to share his dream with me, because he knew that I was interested in dreams. It is my experience that sharing dreams (and here I use dreams in an ambiguous meaning) – often leads to more communication. Because the inmate and I had a good relationship, he – as an intelligent man – sensed that dreams are lessons and experienced in a dream that he could find some of his own 'wisdom' in his dreams.

Dreams about the father

This section presents a combination of different personages and dreams. In the years that I worked in the prison I heard many dreams encompassing various themes, but nightmares about severe fathers, in this combination, was one of the themes I encountered the most in the dream stories of my inmates.

'My father is sitting on a huge chair. He is silent and he looks angry.' This dream was told by a Spanish man in my prison discussion group. He was a proud man, well dressed and with the air of a gentleman. But you could feel the hate, or maybe even more the fear, for his dead father while he told the dream. I met this man only once before he was transferred to

---

5 A famous example is Niels Bohr, who was trying to work out the structure of the atom. He had sketched out many different designs, but none seemed to fit. Finally, one night in his dreams he saw the nucleus of the atom, with the electrons spinning around it, just like our solar system with the sun and planets. When he woke up, he knew the answer. Further testing and experiments proved it to be true. In 1922 he received the Nobel Prize for physics.

another prison. Thus, we didn't have the chance to discuss the relationship between his dream and his life.

However, with another man I was able to talk about his dreams for nearly a year. I met him for the first time during a group discussion. He was in his forties and came from somewhere in the region of the Mediterranean Sea and he started by talking quite fiercely. At the beginning of the discussion I had already noticed him but now he was making his presence felt with his story. He spoke with authority and it was obvious that he was used to an audience. In my thoughts I called him 'the prince'. He made a statement that dreams were bad. When I asked him about this it became clear that he often had nightmares. It was always more or less the same nightmare:

> Although he left the paternal home long ago, in his dream he is back at home. His father is there. He tries to leave his home, but then his father becomes angry and forbids him to leave. He has to stay in the paternal home. He is so scared of his father, he wants to escape, but he does not see a possibility for doing so.

This is his recurring dream. There are variations in details, but the result is always the same. He tells me about this dream and we talk about it. He tells me that he had a bad relationship with his father. And although his father passed away some years ago, the fear of his father returns in his dreams, just as it did when his father was alive. I say that a dream that is repetitive seems important. When you consider dreams as important, it is vital to give attention to repetitive dreams. The 'prince' asks me whether I can help him to interpret his dream. I tell him that he has to be the one to interpret it himself, but that I can help by asking some systematic questions.

Because I am a Roman Catholic chaplain and he is a Muslim, I propose that we ask the prison imam to assist our meetings. The imam, a gentle Moroccan, joins our sessions with pleasure. Once in a while we meet together in the cell of the inmate and we discuss his dreams. On one occasion he asks us to come to his cell. He has had a dream which was partly the same, partly different from his recurring dream. This time there are more different details than usual. He tells us his dream.

> He is travelling with his father and one of his younger brothers. They are travelling by tram. He has with him a holy book. That book was a legacy to him from his grandfather. At one of the tram stops his father seems to take that book from him or wants to take it from him. The father uses the younger brother as his messenger to take that book.

The man is upset and flees to his home. He is living in the house with his father. Thus, although it is totally different from the house of his parents, it feels like 'home'. Home is for him not really the same as 'at home'. In his dream he is looking for his book, or something like that. His father is still away. He knows that when his father returns, he will be sent away. The house feels like an insecure place. At the same time he sees that the house is untidy and he starts cleaning the house. His wife is in the house. Her presence feels like a support for him. They start to clean the living room. They move to a room that seems to be his. There is a bit of a mess in that room. The bed is not made. His wife helps him to make the bed, to clean the room. He is waiting for his father to return, with fear, but he is feeling the support of his wife.

He awakes with feelings of stress and fear and . . . relief. Although some of the interpretations seem to be obvious, it is his working on the dream that slowly reveals something of his changing feelings. He realizes that his wife, with whom he quarrels a lot, is a stable factor in his life. In a certain sense it is the antidote to the poisonous feelings around his father. The fact that in the dream his father left the home is to a certain extent also a relief. There is some freedom to talk about the diverse aspects of his father.

This is not the place to give a verbatim report of this meeting. I just want to relate one of the last dreams, from a few weeks before the 'prince' leaves the prison. He tells his dream:

The colours in the dream are dark, mostly brown. There is a lot of movement around his father, who is alive and in the middle of a bunch of people. Although there is no specific sign, the man realizes that it is the funeral of his father. He feels sorry that his father died.

We speak about this dream. It is again full of mixed feelings: regret, mourning, remorse, but also some fear and anger, and it is about death and life. There is even a reference to love, because he feels sorry that his father died.

The imam and I say goodbye to our 'prince'. He is full of new ideas, resolved to make it up with his wife, and take care of his child. After his release I heard that he got a job, and the fact that – as far as I know – he never returned to prison is a good sign. It suggests that his life really could have changed. It could indicate that talking about his dreams about his dead father was a new start for his life. He seemed to have left behind, to

some extent, the fear of his father and had started looking for new relationships with his wife and child.

LESSON TWO: In western society a Christian minister encounters a
Muslim man who has lost contact with his roots. Although in Muslim
tradition dreams are important, the man rejects dreams, because they
are frightening. When the Christian minister proposes to listen to his
dreams, he opens up; when the imam joins the sessions, the man can face
his past. Listening to dreams seems for him a possible way to reconcile
with his dead father. The cooperation of a Christian minister with an
imam is for him also an indication that it is possible to reconcile his
different spheres of life. Listening to his dreams about the past opened
a future for him.

Working in the prison: my own dreams

Walking with an inmate

One of my teachers at the university where I read theology was Yehuda
Aschkenasy. He was a survivor of several concentration camps including
Auschwitz and Buchenwald. He decided that if he survived the war he
wanted to teach Christians about Judaism with the aim that they could
live peacefully together. After the war he began doing what he promised
himself. He became, I believe, the first Jewish rabbi to teach Judaism at a
Catholic academic institution for the study of theology. He was an inspiring
teacher and one of the most important things he taught his pupils, Jews
and Christians alike, was the joy of learning. He showed me from the
beginning the reciprocity between learning and doing, and that became
the basis for my scholarly work *and* for my practical work, first in a parish
and later as chaplain in the prison, and even for my scholarly work as a
teacher at the university.

His motto was that you could always learn from a situation and that
when a situation was very nasty the only positive element of such a situation was that you could learn from it.[6] Because Aschkenasy as a teacher
believed that his students were *his* teachers, learning with him could
become a lifelong relationship and there was always reciprocity involved.

---

6 His attitude is comparable to an HIV-positive man who took part in Gay Pride in San
Francisco with a text on his T-shirt: 'Positive is an attitude not an illness'.

He managed to stay in touch with many of his students and the learning process never stopped.

As a New Testament scholar who at the same time was working in prison, I was one of his pupils with an unusual combination of experience and that may have been the reason why his disciples invited me to speak at an honouring party on the occasion of his eightieth birthday. One student called me and asked: 'Could you tell us in ten minutes how you use what you learned from Yehuda in your practice?' I thought that that would be quite difficult, and because it was for the birthday of such a special teacher, I hesitated. But that night I had a dream:

> I am walking in a street in Amsterdam, not far from Central Station, side by side with Adam Z (whose narrative is detailed above). He is talking about his problems with his girlfriends. He has three girlfriends and now one of them wants to leave him. He does not want to lose her. He talks on and on. I am a little bit embarrassed about the situation. What can I add to such a story? Thus, I start talking to him. 'Okay, Adam, that is difficult but the only thing you can do now is to learn from it.'
>
> Adam stops abruptly in the middle of the road and says, becoming angry, 'Oh, you, always with your learning, always learning.'

And that was the dream. It was so funny that in the dream Adam typified me in such a concise way, and I was able to use this dream in my speech honouring the rabbi. In my dream Adam typifies my work, but at the same time mocks it.

This dream became the introduction of the *laudatio* of Yehuda Aschkenasy, because the dream contained the kernel of my work. I learned from him how important learning is, but at the same time it concurred with his experience that the learning process is not easy and thus I could use my dream in my speech.

The rabbi taught me that working with inmates is a learning process, for the inmates and even more for me. My experience as prison chaplain can be defined by this lesson. As a chaplain I am often considered to be a helper. However, some people, and especially inmates, are often not inclined to be helped.

I am not a helper, but consider myself as a pupil; thanks to my inmates I learn to know myself and the world. I do not only give, I receive at the same time, and probably I get more than I give (see Matt. 25.9). Yet, I am not the only one who learns. At the moment that an inmate notices that you take him seriously, that you can learn from him, his confidence grows.

Shame and guilt can slowly disappear and the whole process can be a real boost for his injured self-esteem. If an interaction is good, one can see how detainees and minister learn together.

When reflecting on my work as chaplain, a dream came that helped me to explain my work in a playful and clear way. For ministers, storytelling is an important tool to share wisdom and to give models for reflection. While I worked with inmates with dreams, my own dreams became – from time to time – important too, and gave me images to express the kernel and the dilemmas of my work.

LESSON THREE: Literature helps us to understand the *condition humaine*: the human condition. Dreams are a special form of literature. The dream narrative was for me a key text in explaining my work to the audience of the eightieth birthday party of Yehuda Aschkenasy. Telling stories was his trademark. Thus, I began the speech with my own dream narrative attuned to the teaching style of my rabbi.

My nightmare: I have to stay a night in the prison

After five or six years working in the prison I had a dream:

> In that dream I have to stay the night in the prison where I work. It is not because I am being punished. There is, for one reason or another, no possibility that I can go home. They bring me to the cell. The cell is twice as big as a normal one, or maybe even bigger. Instead of a wall, there are windows to the corridor. Because I am 'the father', as inmates in the Netherlands call their pastoral counsellors, I get the privilege of a roommate with whom I can play cards. Playing cards is a popular pastime in the prison. Also because of my special position I get a big bottle of Dutch gin! Still I feel *horrified* by the idea that I have to stay the night in a cell and I am enclosed for a whole night in the prison.

LESSON FOUR: Life in prison is harder than you think.

This is a fascinating dream and I do not need to reflect too long on it. American prison movies – even such a romantic one as *The Shawshank Redemption* – teach us how hard life in a prison is. However, life in prison in the Netherlands is quite different and there is a tendency for many to argue that these prisons are like luxurious hotels. This dream shows how horrifying it is to be in prison, how awful it is to not be free; this can sometimes be forgotten, but my subconscious does not forget it and thus lets me experience it in a dream. It is funny that a dream tells me, the prison chaplain, what it is like to be imprisoned and thus be not free, because many inmates have told me that in prison it is only in their dreams that they can feel freedom.

Conclusion

Evidence-based research is the basis of social and psychological scholarship. At the same time researchers use in their hermeneutics definitions that find their origin in literature. In my scholarly research of ancient wisdom literature I see dreams as narratives and thus as literature. Dreams are a special form of narrative literature.

In this chapter I have presented some dream narratives with a specific context: the prison. All these dream narratives have one thing in common. They help the dreamer to listen to their own lives. Interpreting your own life can never be just the result of evidence-based research. Of course there are biological facts, but the evaluation of these facts is always the result of thinking, and for thinking we can use the methods of literature. Dreaming is one particular way of such thinking. Like literature there is always more than one interpretation of a dream. Dreams and literature are an invitation to think.

References

Beradt, C. (1968), *The Third Reich of Dreams: The Nightmares of a Nation, 1933–1939*, Chicago: Quadrangle Books.

Bonhoeffer, D. (1998), 'Widerstand und Ergebung: Briefe und Aufzeichnungen aus der Haft', in C. Gremmels, E. Bethge and R. Bethge, eds, *Dietrich Bonhoeffer Werke Bd 8*. München: Gutersloher Verlaghaus.

Koet, B. J. (2006), *Dreams and Scripture in Luke-Acts: Collected Essays*, Leuven: Peeters.

Koet, B. J. (2009), 'Discussing Dreams in a Prison in Amsterdam', in K. Bulkeley, K. Adams and P. M. Davis, eds, *Dreaming in Christianity and Islam: Culture, Conflict and Creativity*, New Brunswick NJ: Rutgers University, pp. 226–35.

Koet, B. J., ed. (2012), *Dreams as Divine Communication in Christianity: From Hermas to Aquinas*, Leuven: Peeters.

Koet, B. J. (2015), 'The Prophetic Identity of the Martyr Perpetua: A Narrative Mystagogy', in P. van Geest, ed., *Seeing Through the Eyes of Faith: The Mystagogy of the Church Fathers*, Leuven: Peeters.

Koet, B. J. and Vredeveld, S. (2003), *Bijlmer Blues*, idea and content by Bart J. Koet, directed by Saskia Vredeveld. Broadcast among others by Humanistische Omroep, for example 25 and 28 June 2003, and also in other countries.

White, R. J. (1975), *Artemidorus Daldianus, The Interpretation of Dreams. Translation and Commentary*, Park Ridge NJ: Noyes Press.

16

A Dream Friendly Attitude in Ministry and Chaplaincy
Dreams in Pastoral Supervision[1]

SJAAK KÖRVER

Introduction

In this chapter I argue that dreams should have a natural and legitimate place in pastoral supervision by looking for connections with the characteristics of the supervisory learning process. Within the framework of supervision, the supervisor as well as supervisee may dream about their own work and life and about the supervision process and the relationship with one another. In this chapter I limit myself to one scenario: the supervisee's dreams regarding their work and life brought up within the supervision framework. Using three vignettes from a supervision process, I discuss, successively:

- What (pastoral) supervision aims at and which processes play a role in it.
- The place that dreams can have in this process, and in particular the surprises that dreams can present – beyond the routinely and hence seemingly logical frames within which work and life are often restricted, and which can interfere with learning.

Dreams can draw attention to new possibilities and anticipate decisions to be made. Dreams are rarely topics of reflection in theology, ministry and pastoral supervision, which is in contrast with certain forms of new spirituality. Between 1960 and 1991, papers about dreams in the context of ministry appeared regularly, in particular in American journals: *Journal of Pastoral Care*, *Journal of Pastoral Counseling* and *Pastoral Psychology* (e.g. Kildahl 1968; Howe 1986; Lindijer 1990; Doehring 1991). In the

---

1 This contribution is a revision of a presentation given at the annual congress of the International Association for the Study of Dreams, Kerkrade, the Netherlands, 24–28 June 2011.

same period, very few Dutch contributions about ministry and dreams were published (Roscam Abbing 1984; Lindijer 1986; Lindijer and Speet 1990). In Roscam Abbing's paper, the dream is discussed in the context of the use of imagination and symbolism in ministry. Scarcely any reference to the theme of dreams can be found in practical theology handbooks, except as an expression of the unconscious (Clinebell 1966) or as a reference to Freud's and Jung's views on humankind (Heitink 1999). The use of dreams in supervision is – and this is no surprise – to be found predominantly in the literature about psychoanalytic supervision (e.g. Kildahl 1968; Olsson 1991; Ogden 2005) or supervision in the setting of drama therapy (Pendzik 2008). In the Dutch language I could find only one paper about working with dreams in supervision (Hanekamp 1986). Reflection on pastors' dreams also gets a very raw deal (Kildahl 1968; Lindijer 1986, pp. 152–9). In recent years, however, a revival can be observed in regard to research into the relationships between religion, theology and dreams (see Chapter 1, this volume) and the place of dreams in ministry (e.g. Bulkeley 2000; 2009; Davis and Hill 2005; Stranahan 2011).

Which view on dreams?

As a starting point I consider it for (pastoral) supervision productive to approach dreams as images and narratives that can gradually acquire meaning in the reflection on developing as a better professional.[2] Freud saw dream interpretation as the *via regia* to the unconscious, and somewhat provocatively asserted that reflection on one's own dreams is the leading way of becoming a psychoanalyst (Freud 1955/1943). Pastors and pastoral supervisors don't have to become psychoanalysts, but by paying attention to and reflecting upon their symbolic reality – including their dreams – they can become sensitive professionals who never cease to let themselves be surprised. Of course, dream images are rarely clear and comprehensible at first sight, but on closer consideration they often provide an alternative view on the issues with which clients are struggling – in particular when the dreams are connected with the story that a client tells or is trying to tell.

---

2 Pastoral supervision is usually described as supervision to pastors (ministers, chaplains, clergy) in which the specific themes, methods and dilemmas inherent in the pastoral profession are the key features. However, pastoral supervision is also described as supervision carried out in a pastoral way, i.e. in which pastoral methods co-determine the supervision process (Andriessen and Miethner 1993; Haan 1999), or as a supervision format in which the spiritual aspects of professions working with people are taken into account (Klessmann 2004). Here I keep to the first description.

Let us elaborate on this view first by taking a closer look at some practical examples and what these convey to us about the specific type of learning that is taking place within the process of supervision.

Vignette 1 An identity without a habit?

In a supervision session, a chaplain reports the following dream.[3]

> Everything is red. Things are mostly red, it's not about the shape. It's a funeral. Someone is lying – alive – in a coffin. The coffin is open. The person lying in it wants out, and sits up. I push him back, together with the other pallbearers. The coffin has to be put on the catafalque. I'm not only one of the pallbearers, I'm also presiding at the funeral. I'm wearing a habit. Everything is red. The person lying in the coffin wants to stand up again. The pallbearers push him back. At a certain moment, I have to go out briefly. When I return, my habit has gone. The coffin has to get on the catafalque. The pallbearers again push back the person lying in the coffin. I've lost my habit.

The supervisee works in a prison, having previously worked in a parish. He seems to be stuck in a rut. Some elements from his narrative are as follows: no pleasure in his work any more; a looming conflict with management; a paralysing feeling caused by the increasingly stringent instructions from the bishops; physical complaints and sleeping problems. In the supervision sessions, it becomes clear to him step by step that he is in a state of crisis. He says that he has never properly grown up, that he never had a father figure to usher him through life, that actually he should try to find other work (maybe even another profession), but that he is too afraid to take steps in that direction. Then he reports the dream in red. He adds that when he woke up he was not feeling anxious at all. He had immediately thought of Barnett Newmann's 1966/67 painting 'Who's afraid of red, yellow and blue?', which he had recently seen a picture of. The following questions occur to him: 'Am I blocking myself? Is it me lying in the coffin? Is the coffin a symbol of my present position? Am I pushing myself back? Does red mean enthusiasm, life, blood, guts?' He is surprised that the images are red rather than black; he would have expected black, in view of his dejection and apathy. And

---

3 The chaplain involved has given permission to make use of the dreams mentioned in this chapter.

a second surprise is that, at a certain moment, his habit is missing. Is he already internally taking steps to abandon his position, searching for more freedom and for a new identity? An identity without a habit?

Supervision is about learning: learning how to (better) carry out a profession working with people. This learning has a number of layers: learning to increasingly integrate thinking, feeling, volition and acting, learning to integrate person, profession and the concrete work situation, and learning to learn. This threefold objective of the 'Dutch supervision concept' can be compared to a three-lane motorway; supervisees can switch lanes if necessary, but in their learning process they need all three lanes in order to be able to move forward (Van Kessel and Haan 1993; Siegers 2002). In the dream, and in particular in reflecting upon it, integrating it into his own professional self-awareness, it becomes clear that this chaplain switches lanes regularly. His first duty is to find renewed inspiration in his professional functioning, beyond the routine of constantly conforming to a job that has become a straitjacket. This implies reflecting on his ideals, on his strengths and weaknesses, and on his knowledge and methodical skills (should they be lacking). He has to think about his theological views regarding his ministry, about his organizational sensitivity and his career plans, and about the gaps in them. After this, he has to switch to the lane of a better integration. His thinking ('it's a well-paid position in which surely I can make it to my retirement') does not harmonize with his feeling of 'I feel exhausted and dissatisfied, I'm dying here' . . . nor with what he wants: 'I want to escape from this trap'. This challenges his behaviour: 'I have to start applying for a new job or to try to find a new challenge in my present job.' Subsequently, he occasionally changes gear and takes the third lane, asking himself how he can stay 'sharp' in his daily practice and go on working 'with enthusiasm and passion'. The task here is to learn how he can go on to learn permanently and, as it were, develop an 'internal supervisor' (Casement 2013).

Vignette 2 Spreading one's wings

In the next session, the supervisee reports a dream that he has had in the meantime.

I am in some kind of fairytale park, a kind of Disneyland. A plank is sticking out of an open window, and is hanging over a fairytale landscape. A fantasy animal walks across the plank and flies away. I ask someone:

'Can I do that too?' 'Yes', is the answer. 'But I don't dare, can I sit behind you on your bike?' That's okay, and together we ride across the narrow plank and fly away.

With wonder and joy the chaplain reports this dream in which he can fly, or, to be more precise, fly away, and dares to spread his wings. We discuss a couple of questions. Is the fairytale park the childhood that he has been unable to leave behind? Or is it the spurious world of the Church in which he has lived? Or is it about both possibilities? The supervisee also asks himself: 'Is the cyclist a side of me that I have within myself, but that needs developing? Or does it indicate that as yet I still need the help and guts of someone else?' The dream has surprised him, because it speaks of strength and daring, of the courage to spread his wings, to be who he is. That is a side of himself that he hardly knows. In fact, he always aims for compliance, safety and caution (Körver 2006). This surprise may be the most important function of dreams in the framework of supervision.

This is also what the chaplain tries to master. The dreams surprise him, and subsequently he lets himself be surprised. He accepts stirrings in himself other than only rational considerations and arguments, and hence brings up his dreams in supervision. Initially, he has no idea what, for him, the meaning of the dreams is. He just surmises that they have something to tell him. Through an open 'dream friendly attitude' he establishes, in his reflections, connections between the images and symbols in his dreams on the one hand, and on the other his person, his profession and his practice. He learns something about his professional functioning and his ways of learning, but he also learns something about himself in particular. In this process, his dreams play an essential role precisely because they draw his attention to aspects of himself that he did not know very well and to the possibility of new professional perspectives. In addition, his dreams help him to avoid wanting to immediately solve the uncertainties in his everyday professional functioning. He becomes aware of the potential creativity of his doubts; precisely these doubts keep him 'sharp' so that he continues his search for new inspiration and passion.

Vignette 3 'Words of life everlasting'

Our chaplain goes on dreaming. A third dream is as follows:

I'm in a group and I'm chosen jointly with some other, younger men. We're standing together in a group. The conversation is led by X, the then cantor in the monastery. A fellow monk and classmate, Y, takes over the conversation and explicitly involves me. It is about the acclamation, 'Thou hast words of life everlasting, to whom else would we go?'

In the 14 dreams explored in the course of this chaplain's supervision process, elements from liturgy appear on a regular basis. The dreams in this way indicate an important framework of the supervisee. He returns to the time of his training and formation. It is obviously important to take these spiritual/religious roots into account when searching for new perspectives.

Dreams announcing new forms and contents of awareness

We will deepen psychologically the approach of dreams as a narrative tool.

Dreams have a particular integrative power

In the complex interplay of person, profession and concrete work situation, it is not only reflection and cognitive abilities that play an important role. Other dimensions of human existence are shown to be essential too: corporality and the senses, being connected to others and to previous and next generations, different states of awareness, spirituality and religiosity, the world of spirits, angels and apparitions. And the world of dreams. Just like other images and symbols, dreams have a particular integrative power. They are able to bring together the various dimensions within the person, and subsequently the person's position in their environment, which fits in with supervision's objective of integration.

Simultaneous presentation of continuous and discontinuous elements

Research evidence shows that dreams reflect a person's emotionally most important issues, activities and experiences in their waking existence. There is, in particular, continuity between dreaming and the waking existence, which also implies that there is a connection between a dream's religious/spiritual contents and the dreamer's religious life. But next to that, there is also discontinuity, which, as a contrast, can refer to new ideas, possibilities and energy with a view to decisions that have to be taken in waking life (Bulkeley 2009). In their images and moods, dreams not only organize and interpret reality but, in their symbolizing function, they provide new perspectives on that reality.

Dreams as intermediate play areas of the imagination

In the context of the efficacy of rituals, the American sociologist and anthropologist Thomas Scheff (2001) talks about the importance of aesthetic distance. This term indicates that, in order to be able to deal with a major life event in a ritual, the person concerned has to be a participant as well as an observer. They have to be able to simultaneously occupy an inner and an outer perspective. The distance to the event should not be too close, as that would mean mere reliving. At the same time, the distance should not be too great, as that would only lead to a detached rational consideration. All this applies also to the interpretation of dreams – dreams that, just like rituals, can be understood as intermediate play areas of the imagination between on the one hand the internal world of the individual and on the other the realistic external world of objective facts (Winnicott 1971; Jongsma-Tieleman 1996). Imagination, including dreams, can be seen as a higher order function of human cognition (Koning 1998). In dream imagery a different kind of awareness announces itself.

Taking dreams seriously in pastoral supervision

These insights are particularly valuable to work with, given the complexity of the learning process that is intended in the supervision process. A quote from the American philosopher Donald Schön (1987, p. 93) shows:

> The paradox of learning a really new competence is this: that a student cannot at first understand what he needs to learn, can learn it only by educating himself, and can educate himself only by beginning to do what he does not yet understand.

Schön proposes to designate a professional's competent actions as artistry, as being artistically minded, as creativity. A central feature of creativity is that a question or problem can be put in a different framework, i.e. that reframing takes place (Capps 1990). This means that a professional is able to improvise, and to apply scientific and professional knowledge in new ways. In this framework, explicit attention to surprises, to situations running differently from what is expected, to results that were not planned, to outcomes deviating from the model or the theory, has centrality of place (Körver 2009). A professional who is receptive to surprises becomes aware of the knowledge and experience steering his actions at an unconscious and intuitive level, of his tacit knowledge (Polanyi 1967). This person will also be disposed towards negative capability (an expression coined by the English poet Keats), being willing to let uncertainties and doubts exist and not constantly on an impatient quest for answers and solutions (Van Praag 2005). And finally, this professional is able to be receptive to serendipity, to the principle that fortunate and unexpected discoveries often occur by chance (Van Praag 2005).

A dream friendly attitude simultaneously takes into account these various dimensions and layers in awareness – which is also already important to professional pastoral functioning as such. But next to that, taken together the above means that a supervisor should be especially alert when a supervisee brings up a dream – indicating that a supervisee senses intuitively that the dream might be significant in the learning process.

Several types of actions can be helpful for a supervisor to take the dream seriously.

- Invite the supervisee to describe the dream in as much detail as possible – in the present tense, including seemingly trivial and inconsequential elements – and explore together with the supervisee precisely why these specific elements feature in the dream.
- Attention should be paid to the most vivid moments, the abrupt and unexpected transitions, the most bizarre aspects and the patterns that are most strikingly symmetrical or, on the contrary, dissimilar in relation to waking life.
- The reflection moves simultaneously across the events in the 24 hours preceding the dream, discussing the crises and fears possibly playing a role in the present stage of the supervisee's life, and the way in which the supervisee views their (spiritual) development.

This approach can be summarized by referring to American psychologists Davis and Hill's *Cognitive-Experimental Dream Interpretation Model*, which describes three stages of interpreting a dream:

1 Exploring, in as much detail as possible, the images from and the feelings during the dream, while the dreamer/supervisee talks freely about what comes to mind in relation to the dream.

2 Deciphering the meaning of the dream, in which there is constant attention to the values and principles playing a role in the dreamer's/ supervisee's life.

3 Designing a plan for applying the gained insights in the supervisee's life and work.

(Davis and Hill 2005)

Alongside this, be aware that a supervisor may be able to utilize the dream as an opportunity for exploring the supervisee's professional and personal development; but only the dreamer, the supervisee, can provide a valid interpretation of the dream (Howe 1986; Bulkeley 2000; Stranahan 2011).

Concluding remarks

More states of awareness than just the rational are found in spirituality and religion. Many people, including those in modern western societies, are coping with the difficulties and struggles in their lives with the help of convictions, actions and experiences that reach into that 'other world' (Orsi 2007; Subbotsky 2010; 2011). In psychoanalysis, dream interpretation is seen as the *via regia*, the royal road, to the unconscious. In analogous ways, reflecting on dreams in pastoral care can be understood as a doorway to other layers of awareness, to the world of imagination and belief, to the world of archetypes and symbols, maybe to the world of the divine. As Drewermann (1984) boldly states: 'Dreaming imagination, rather than conceptual thinking, determines religious elementary experiences, and thought comes always later and is more superficial than images. Hence, we have to start from dream images, if we want to understand from within the biblical images of redemption in their lasting validity.'

It certainly behoves theologians and chaplains to learn to be open to these other dimensions of human existence, in themselves as well as in their clients. Supervision can be useful in this. Supervision can help them to pluck up the courage to abandon the restraint of rational thinking and be open to the surprises put forward by awareness of symbols, by dreaming imagination. Dreams merit a place in pastoral supervision precisely because they often outline in special ways the dilemmas and perspectives with which chaplains are confronted in their (personal and professional) development. In this context, it is important that pastors learn to approach their clients' experiences not only at the substantive level, but also functionally. Dreams and spiritual experiences can express a specific (theological) content, but can also have a significance or function in coping with more or less powerful events and situations (Berger 1974; Pargament, Desai and McConnell 2006). Paying attention to dreams in supervision will develop a 'dream friendly attitude' (Ogden 2005) in pastors, which will help them to be receptive and attentive to the diverse layers of awareness within themselves, and in particular, based on this sensitivity, enable them to consider clients' special dream experiences.

References

Andriessen, H. C. I. and Miethner, R. (1993), *Praxis der Supervision, Beispiel: Pastorale Supervision*, Heidelberg: Asanger Roland Verlag.

Berger, P. L. (1974), 'Some Second Thoughts on Substantive versus Functional Definitions of Religion', in *Journal for the Scientific Study of Religion* 13(2), pp. 125–33.

Bulkeley, K. (2000), 'Dream Interpretation: Practical Methods for Pastoral Care and Counseling', in *Pastoral Psychology* 49(2), pp. 95–104.

Bulkeley, K. (2009), 'The Religious Content of Dreams: A New Scientific Foundation', in *Pastoral Psychology* 58(2), pp. 93–106.

Capps, D. (1990), *Reframing: A New Method in Pastoral Care*, Minneapolis: Fortress Press.

Casement, P. (2013), *On Learning From the Patient*, Hoboken: Taylor and Francis.

Clinebell Jr, H. J. (1966), *Basic Types of Pastoral Counseling*, Nashville, New York: Abingdon Press.

Davis, T. L. and Hill, C. E. (2005), 'Spiritual and Nonspiritual Approaches to Dream Work: Effects on Client's Well-Being', in *Journal of Counseling and Development* 83(4), pp. 492–503.

Doehring, C. (1991), 'Approaching Dream Narratives and Interpretations with a Hermeneutic of Suspicion', in *Journal of Pastoral Counseling* 26, pp. 6–17.

Drewermann, E. (1984), *Tiefenpsychologie und Exegese: Band I: Die Wahrheit der Formen: Traum, Mythos, Märchen, Sage und Legende*, Olten, Freiburg im Breisgau: Walter-Verlag.

Freud, S. (1955/1943), 'Über Psychoanalyse: Fünf Vorlesungen' (Five Lectures on Psycho-Analysis), in S. Freud (ed.), *Gesammelte Werke: Chronologisch geordnet*, Vol. VIII: Werke aus den Jahren 1909–1913, London: Imago Publishing, 1957, pp. 1–60). *The Complete Psychological Works of Sigmund Freud* (The Standard Edition), Vol. 11, London: Hogarth Press, p. 3ff.

Haan, D. (1999), 'Pastorale supervisie in Nederland: Een verkenning' (Pastoral Supervision in the Netherlands. An Exploration), in *Supervisie in Opleiding en Beroep* 16(4), pp. 3–20.

Hanekamp, H. (1986), 'Droombewerking als leermiddel' (Processing Dreams as a Training Tool), *Supervisie in Opleiding en Beroep* 3(2), pp. 5–12.

Heitink, G. (1999), *Practical Theology: History, Theory, Action Domains*, manual for practical theology, Grand Rapids MI: Eerdmans.

Howe, L. T. (1986), 'Dream Interpretation in Spiritual Guidance', in *Journal of Pastoral Care* 40(3), pp. 262–72.

Jongsma-Tieleman, P. E. (1996), *Godsdienst als speelruimte voor verbeelding: Een godsdienst-psychologische studie* (Religion as a Play Area for Imagination: A Study in the Psychology of Religion), Kampen: Kok.

Kildahl, J. P. (1968), 'Six Dreams of a Clergyman in Psychoanalysis', in *Pastoral Psychology* 19(4), pp. 8–10.

Klessmann, M. (2004), 'Pastorale Supervision? Die Bedeutung theologischer Feldkompetenz für Supervision im Raum der Kirche' (Pastoral Supervision? The Significance of Theological Field Competence within the Church), in *Wege zum Menschen* 56, pp. 377–90.

Koning, B. (1998), 'Levenswijsheid verbeeld en geleefd' Wisdom Pictured and Lived), in *Praktische Theologie* 25(1), pp. 45–61.

Körver, J. (2003), 'The Pastor on the Boundary of Biography and Profession: The Courage to Continue', in B. Roebben and L. van der Tuin, eds, *Practical Theology and the Interpretation of Crossing Boundaries: Essays in Honour of Professor M. P. J. van Knippenberg*, Münster/ Hamburg/London: LIT, pp. 247–61.

Körver, J. (2006), 'Voorbij aan voegen, voorzichtigheid en veiligheid: Klinische Pastorale Vorming en de professionalizering van de geestelijk verzorger' (Beyond Compliance, Caution and Safety: Clinical Pastoral Education and the Chaplain's Professionalization), in J. Doolaard ed., *Nieuw Handboek Geestelijke Verzorging: Geheel herziene editie* (New Handbook of Chaplaincy, revised edn), Kampen: Kok, pp. 759–72.

Körver, J. (2009), 'Jezus Sirach als pastor en supervisor avant la lettre: de onmisbaarheid van ervaringsleren en pastorale supervisie in de opleiding van pastores en geestelijk verzorgers' (Jesus Sirach as a Pastor and Supervisor before the Terms Existed: the Indispensability of Experiential Learning and Pastoral Supervision in the Training of Pastors and Chaplains), in H. W. M. van Grol and P. J. van Midden, eds, *Een roos in de lente: Theologisch palet van de FKT: Opstellen aangeboden aan Panc Beentjes bij zijn afscheid als hoogleraar Oude Testament en Hebreeuws aan de Faculteit Katholieke Theologie van de Universiteit van Tilburg* (A Rose in Spring: Theological Palette from FKT: Essays in Honour of Panc Beentjes at his Retirement as Professor of Old Testament and Hebrew at the Faculty of Catholic Theology of Tilburg University), 5 Utrecht: Faculteit Katholieke Theologie, pp. 127–35.

Lindijer, C. H. (1986), *In Onze Diepste Dromen: Pastoraal Omgaan met Dromen* (In our Most Profound Dreams: Dealing with Dreams Pastorally), Den Haag: Voorhoeve.

Lindijer, C. H. (1990), 'Working with a Pastoral Dream Group', in *Journal of Pastoral Care* 44(4), pp. 373–7.

Lindijer, C. H. and Speet, E. (1990), *Werken met Dromen: Mogelijkheden van Omgaan met Dromen in het Pastoraat* (Working with Dreams: Possibilities of Dealing with Dreams in Ministry), 's-Gravenhage: Meinema.

Ogden, T. H. (2005), 'On Psychoanalytical Supervision', in *International Journal of Psychoanalysis* 86(5), pp. 1265–80.

Olsson, G. (1991), 'The Supervisory Process Reflected in Dreams of Supervisees', *American Journal of Psychotherapy* 45(4), pp. 511–26.

Orsi, R. A. (2007), *Between Heaven and Earth: The Religious Worlds People Make and the Scholars Who Study Them*, 2nd edn, Princeton/Oxford: Princeton University Press.

Pargament, K. I., Desai, K. M. and McConnell, K. M. (2006), 'Spirituality: A Pathway to Posttraumatic Growth or Decline?', in L. G. Calhoun and R. G. Tedeschi, eds, *Handbook of Posttraumatic Growth: Research and Practice*, Mahwah NJ/London: Lawrence Erlbaum Associates, pp. 121–37.

Pendzik, S. (2008), 'Dramatic Resonances. A Technique of Intervention in Drama Therapy, Supervision, and Training', in *The Arts in Psychotherapy* 35(3), pp. 217–23.

Polanyi, M. (1967), *The Tacit Dimension*, New York: Doubleday.

Roscam Abbing, A. D. H. (1984), 'Fantasie in het pastoraat' (Fantasy in ministry), in H. Faber (ed.), *Handboek Pastoraat: Pastorale Perspectieven in een Veranderende Samenleving* (Handbook of Ministry: Pastoral Perspectives in a Changing Society), Deventer Amersfoort: Van Loghum Slaterus, De Horstink, pp. 7, 1–16.

Scheff, T. J. (2001), *Catharsis in Healing, Ritual, and Drama*, Lincoln: Authors Guild Backinprint.com.

Schön, D. A. (1987), *Educating the Reflective Practitioner: Toward a New Design for Teaching and Learning in the Professions*, San Francisco: Jossey-Bass.

Siegers, F. (2002), *Handboek Supervisiekunde* (Handbook of Supervision), Houten: Bohn Stafleu van Loghum.

Stranahan, S. (2011), 'The Use of Dreams in Spiritual Care', in *Journal of Health Care Chaplaincy* 17(1), pp. 87–94.

Subbotsky, E. (2010), *Magic and the Mind: Mechanisms, Functions, and Development of Magical Thinking and Behaviour*, Oxford: Oxford University Press.

Subbotsky, E. (2011), 'The Ghost in the Machine: Why and How the Belief in Magic Survives in the Rational Mind', in *Human Development* 54(3), pp. 126–43.

Van Kessel, L. and Haan, D. (1993), 'The Dutch Concept of Supervision. Its Essential Characteristics as a Conceptual Framework', in *The Clinical Supervisor* 11(1), pp. 5–27.

Van Praag, P. (2005), 'Over serendipiteit en reflectie tijdens het handelen: Elementen van de grondhouding van supervisoren' (On serendipity and reflection in action: Elements of the supervisors' basic attitude), in W. Regouin and F. Siegers, eds, *Supervisie in Opleiding en Beroep: Verzameling Tijdschriftartikelen uit de Periode 1982–2002* (Supervision in Training and Profession: Collected Journal Articles from the Period 1982–2002), Houten: Bohn Stafleu van Loghum, pp. 169–82.

Winnicott, D. W. (1971), *Playing and Reality*, London: Tavistock.

Zijlstra, W. (1971), *Seelsorge-Training: Clinical Pastoral Training*, München: Kaiser.

Dream Narrative 5

Finding Deep Emotional Healing and Reconciliation through a Dream

RUSS PARKER

My own interest and growth in understanding of dreams was brought about by a dream that dramatically changed my life.

One morning in 1975, when I was a lay Baptist minister, I was sitting in my upstairs study preparing notes for a sermon. My eyes were open and I was awake, but from time to time my mind would drift into a sort of waking-dream or daydream. The picture that began to form in my mind was of an old toy fort that resembled one I had been given when I was five years old. Now the fort was of life-sized dimensions and I was standing right in the middle of it. For some reason I knew that I was a very young child, and as I looked up at the battlements I could see Arthurian knights patrolling. I could feel the hot sun on my head and I felt so safe and warm. Suddenly all this peace and security was shattered. Out from a square hole in the floor of this old fort came what looked like a long tongue of huge, sticky fly-paper; it seemed alive and immediately it grabbed hold of my head. I struggled hard to get free and stay in the fort but it was a losing battle. Relentlessly I was pulled down through the hole and driven along a dark tunnel; all the while my face was being smashed into the walls at either side.

As I sat there in my study that morning I was acutely aware of feelings of rage and anger rising up from deep within me.

What was really startling about this dream was that, as the feelings of anger began to come to the surface, there came a string of memories, all of which contained the same expression of angry rage. The most immediate was from a few days earlier. It had been my turn to babysit with our son Joel, and I had been at it from about midnight until the early hours of the following day before he drifted off into sleep. However, an hour or so later he woke up and started crying again; my wife was fast asleep in another room, and after all it was still my shift. I can remember feeling really angry at him for being awake; this time when I lifted him out of his cot it was not to give him comfort but to take my anger out on him.

I completely lost control and began to shout at him and strangle him. It was only the intervention of my wife that prevented any physical damage being done. I felt so ashamed of myself; here I was, a Christian minister strangling the life out of my son like an angry vandal.

I had had a number of these outbursts in my life and I had prayed about them, but nothing seemed changed in my behaviour. I wanted to be free but felt really trapped in my feelings. It is interesting to note, by the way, that the dream was triggered by a recent experience and that this is often the reason why we have certain dreams.

The rest of the memories were all directly connected with my mother. When I was about ten years old my mum asked me to run down to Parson's corner shop to buy some cigarettes for her. I was enjoying a game of football in the street with all my friends and my two brothers and sisters. I felt picked on and, I remembered, I ran off to do the errand in sheer rage at this and called my mother all the swear words I could think of as I went.

The other memory was of a later time, when one of the boys from our street was told to move away from our house; apparently he was sitting on our fence and my mum told him to go up to his own house and play. Sydney was his name and he climbed back on that fence just as soon as my mum had disappeared into the house and he began to call out loudly, 'Mrs Parker is a dirty old cow.' Mum was having none of this and so she sent out my younger brother to hit him and send him packing. The job was duly done, but Sydney was not to be dismissed that easily. I was in the house that day and I knew in my heart that my mum would ask me to go out next and I just hated the thought of it. Well, the command for me to go and do likewise came. I went out and I could feel the cold anger beginning to well up inside me against my mother, and when I reached Sydney I put my hands around his throat and began to squeeze hard. He began to choke and I had to be dragged off him. The anger was directed at my mum but Sydney had become the focus for it. I suddenly grew afraid of how I felt towards my mum but there was no reason I could think of for feeling like this.

These and other memories linked up to the dream picture, and I could feel them all with the same intensity as if they were actually happening again. I have already mentioned the times I had prayed for help over my feelings, but now it seemed that I was beginning to get somewhere. I believe that this waking-dream was a gift from God and that he gave me the presence of mind to write it down straightaway before I forgot it. And so I hurried downstairs to share it with my wife Carole who was working in the kitchen. I made her stop everything and sit down to listen.

Her immediate reply was to say that the dream seemed to be a symbol of being born (having been both a nurse and a mum probably helped to give her this immediate insight). The sticky flypaper was the umbilical cord and the dark tunnel was the birth passage. Instinctively I felt this was right, and as I began to acknowledge that my feelings of anger could in fact be related to how I was born, I knew that I was on the trail towards being healed. But couldn't all this be just a bit too far-fetched? After all, what is in a dream? I began to be a little concerned that I might be running away with myself and getting out of my depth. And on top of all this, there were the real difficulties in our relationships with my mother that stood in the way.

She had had a very hard life and had been divorced from my father for about seven years by this time. Her health had suffered and in her own eyes she had lost everything that had meant so much to her; her home had gone and the man she still loved was married now to someone else. Consequently she had retreated into a world of make-believe. Her switched-on television was her constant companion; she seldom went out or visited anyone. She would tell me stories of having been approached by handsome men on the bus who asked her for a date. We all knew that she was fantasizing and compensating for the break-up of her marriage. Needless to say, I felt more than reluctant to go to see my mother and ask her, 'How was I born?' But go I did.

I asked her if she could remember anything or was she drugged up at the time. Very calmly she told me that I had been born at home and that she was fully aware of the events. 'Your birth was as normal as all the rest,' she said, 'except for one thing. You were born with an enlarged head and they had difficulty in getting your head to come out, or so the doctor said, and you didn't need a slap to make you take your first breath. You came out kicking and shouting with the most brilliant red hair I had ever seen on a baby. You looked like a carrot.' Apparently I got the nickname Rusty which, with the passage of time, became Russell.

I can remember being profoundly moved as I listened to my mother and I felt very tearful. Some hurt deep inside me was being touched and I welcomed it. I also felt a new regard for my mother and so, very deliberately, I asked for her forgiveness for all the anger and hate I had felt in the years gone by. 'It's a bit late in the day I know,' I said, 'but I mean it, Mum, please forgive me.' I wasn't really prepared for what happened next. My mother told me that I was the first person in her whole life who had asked forgiveness of her. She then told me all about her life and childhood. Her mother had died when she was three, and she was raised by her half-sister who had an affair with her father. She had been beaten as a child and had felt lonely all her life. She married my father during the early years of the war, and among the various difficulties that followed was the announcement that my father wanted a divorce. The shock and anger she felt gave rise to a period of depression and drunkenness, the effect of which was a brief affair and the birth of a daughter. At the end of the war, my father came home, his hopes of marrying another woman dashed. When he discovered what had happened he gave my mother the choice of saving the marriage by giving up her daughter or keeping her daughter but ending the marriage and losing her son. She gave away her baby girl, but had felt guilty all these years and, 35 years later, still longed to see her daughter again. 'Can God ever forgive me?' she asked. I told her that if God could forgive me my sins he could surely forgive hers too. So she asked me to pray with her and I had the joy of leading my mother to a true faith in Jesus and the knowledge that she had been forgiven. I found this to be one of the most meaningful encounters of my life.

The most notable results of this experience have been the inner healing of my emotions. I have the usual ups and downs like anybody else, but no longer do I have the rage and anger. Jesus has healed me. I became aware of feeling more whole and together than ever before. Second, my mother started living in the real world and we found that we could relate normally for the first time as adults. She found a new freedom with the rest of her children, and so was able to share with them her secret and, perhaps for the first time in her life, feel really accepted by those she loved. And second, I began to respect and take notice of my dreams. All this healing and restoration had come about as a result of following through a dream. I believe that this was under the guidance of God. I started to share my experience with others and so began a journey that would teach me the value of dreams for use in healing and deliverance ministry. But I needed a proper foundation and framework to work with dreams, and I found my starting point in the Bible. Here there were further discoveries that would deepen my respect for dreams.

Dream Narrative 6

Christ's Message to a Diplomat

EDY KORTHALS ALTES

I consider it a great privilege to share with you the exceptional dream which changed my life. It is a privilege, as dreams are being dreamt again in this time of transition. The title above may surprise some readers because diplomats are not supposed to be dreamers, but professionals, with both feet firmly on the ground, confronting hard reality. But they have to combine realism with vision, otherwise our world would be a much bigger jungle than it is today!

In this chapter I will focus on three elements of working with a dream:

1 The context of the dream.
2 The dream itself.
3 Its consequences.

The context

For a correct understanding of the dream we should look at its context. In my case it was a conflict of conscience during the Cold War. For some years I had felt a growing concern about the arms race. Well over 70,000 nuclear weapons exist, many ready to be triggered, in an extremely vulnerable world. I had my doubts about the wisdom of the deterrence doctrine. Was the prevailing security concept not lagging behind the grim reality created by the spectacular achievements in science and technology? Did the destructive power now in feeble human hands not *force* us to adopt a new security concept? Soothing declarations that these arms were not for use did not reassure me. The risks of managing an apocalyptic potential seemed to me too great.

A decisive moment was reached with US President Reagan's Star Wars Program. By stressing its defensive nature, the dangerous consequences were deliberately played down. In essence, however, we were dealing with the development of a fourth theatre of warfare: in space. From this moment on I felt a strong urge to take a public stand on the issue.

This led me into a serious conflict of conscience. I was working as a Netherlands Ambassador in Spain, representing a NATO country, so I had to, of course, stand fully behind its policies. This conflicted with my personal assessment of the urgency to change course.

The question 'What can I do?' became an existential one for me. It could no longer be shrugged off with a simple reference to the obligatory loyalty to government policy. We are, after all, not puppets, but human beings, fully responsible for our actions and omissions, towards God and our fellow men. This internal struggle lasted nearly five months; it ended all of a sudden with an unusually intense and coherent dream during the night of 29/30 September 1984.

The dream that changed my life

I saw many people on a square, in front of a church. The church was full. At first I didn't want to go in until an elderly woman took me by the hand and showed me an empty seat in one of the left front rows. A large wooden cross was hanging over the altar. To my surprise sawdust was falling down from the wooden cross. (Perhaps this was a symbol of an inner crisis of a self-centred church?)

While looking at the cross, I experienced an intense compassion for the suffering Christ (an unusual experience for me as a Protestant). At the very same moment, I saw in the living eyes of Christ the pertinent question: 'And you, what have you been doing with your possibilities, with what you know, in this crucial period?'

This direct confrontation with the suffering and living Christ was an overwhelming experience, impossible to describe. Suddenly, a different situation: a conversation with a leading figure with a vague face. I spoke, with some emphasis, about faith and life. He hardly listened and suddenly handed me two volumes saying: 'Here, read these, it is about peace. Very important now!'

My immediate reaction was: 'But this is exactly the field in which I am deeply interested. Peace and social justice, now. I am looking for relevant action in this field.' Suddenly he looked at me, saying: 'See to it that you will be ready in 1982!' I was surprised and responded, 'But we are living in 1984!' This was directly followed by a brusque and decisive statement: 'End '85 you have to be ready, begin in '86!'

Waking up at 4.45 a.m., I felt an immense relief. My inner struggle had come to an end. I knew that I had to take a stand. This dream changed my life. A process began that would ultimately make me free to accept new responsibilities. But on the road towards freedom there were some serious obstacles. There could be no question of abandoning my duties at short notice. Moreover I had to overcome three prevailing contemplations:

1 Your concern may be right, but your analysis is wrong.
2 Why not wait another four years until your retirement? You can avoid a lot of trouble.
3 What an incredible pretence to think that you as an individual can have the slightest impact on this vast and complex problematic area.

The first one took me some time in checking and checking again. High-ranking colleagues in the Foreign Office tried to convince me that there was no arms race and the Star Wars Program was of a purely defensive nature. Serious study finally confirmed to me the accuracy of my own analysis.

The second rationalization looked particularly tempting. It opened the possibility of 'continuing life as usual' in Madrid, working in a most interesting and agreeable post. In this way, all sorts of difficulties would be avoided, such as a premature ending of a career that had given me much satisfaction; inevitable friction with colleagues; and the loss of substantial material privileges. All of these, however, could not do away with my conviction that a turning point in East–West relations had to be reached soon. The coming years would, in my opinion, be decisive for a real breakthrough.

However, the third argument presented the greatest difficulty. This had a paralysing effect. Indeed, what could one hope to do against the enormous forces controlling the arms race? Was Don Quixote not, for all of us, an eloquent warning against fighting windmills?

Obviously I was not alone. Millions of people were actively engaged in protests against the arms race, among them even several retired politicians and military commanders. Decisive for me was, however, the persistent force of the dream, kept alive by the daily practice of reading an outstanding Benedictine Prayer Book. Faith in the living Christ is not merely an intellectual understanding, it has to be lived in obedience to the call of the hour. There can be no split between a private part of our personality in which faith is cultivated and a functional part ruled by different values. Ultimate Truth addresses the whole person.

In the middle of 1985 the road was cleared.

The consequences

After several efforts I succeeded in drafting a full-page article against the madness of the arms race. I submitted this to the minister of Foreign Affairs telling him about my intention to publish it in a leading Dutch newspaper. The reaction could be predicted, as it was most inopportune at a time of the lively debate on cruise missiles. The refined practices of classical diplomacy were put into play, from gentle persuasion to the knife in the velvet glove: recall from Madrid. This did not have any effect, as I felt committed to take a stand. I offered my resignation, not only because I considered it the right thing to do in case of conflict with my minister, but also because I wanted to be free to work towards a more adequate security concept.

The years following my resignation I consider as the most important period in my life. I tried to serve the cause of peace and justice through a range of interrelated activities at national and international levels. Most of these were in the context of the Pugwash Movement, the Netherlands Council of Churches and the World Conference of Religions for Peace.

Quite a number of lectures, articles and conferences followed. These, together with five books, were enough for my wife to complain that the life of a retired diplomat can be much more hectic than life during active duty!

Let me end with three observations. First, it is with deep gratitude that I look back on the dream that changed my life. For the first time, I grasped the essence of the words of Jesus: 'I am the Way, the Truth and the Life.' Rather late in life, I discovered that this truth becomes real by *going* the way you have to go, living up to your vocation. In accepting the challenges, getting on our feet we receive Life! Second, I must admit that I would never have solved my conflict of loyalty relying solely on abstract norms and values. The final decision to go all out against the arms race was based on the direct confrontation in the dream, which galvanized my faith.

Finally, the pertinent question in my dream is not addressed to me alone, but to all human beings. In essence it is the question in Genesis which God posed to Adam: 'Where are you?' This is a highly relevant question at this time of crisis: not only for diplomats and politicians but also for others holding a position of responsibility. All of us are called upon to stand up in this critical epoch for the preservation of human values for a more peaceful and just world. This acceptance of personal responsibility seems to me the inevitable outcome of the obedience and respect we owe to Ultimate Reality.

Acknowledgements of Sources

The publisher and authors acknowledge with thanks permission to use material under copyright. Every effort has been made to contact copyright owners and we would be grateful to be informed of any omissions.

Bart Koet's chapter, 'Rabbinic Dream Work' is reproduced by permission from the original, slightly different version, 'Over droomuitleg bij de Rabbijnen', in *Collationes* 29, 1999, pp. 27–47.

Amira Mittermaier's chapter, 'Muslim and Freudian Dream Interpretation in Egypt' is from the book, *From After Pluralism*, edited by Courtney Bender and Pamela E. Klassen. Copyright © 2010 Columbia University Press. Reprinted with permission of the publisher.

Russ Parker's Dream Narrative, 'Finding Deep Emotional Healing and Reconciliation through a Dream', is from his book, *Healing Dreams: Their Power and Purpose in your Spiritual Life*, SPCK Classic, 2013.

IASD Dreamwork Ethics Statement

IASD celebrates the many benefits of dreamwork, yet recognizes that there are potential risks. IASD supports an approach to dreamwork and dream sharing that respects the dreamer's dignity and integrity, and which recognizes the dreamer as the decision-maker regarding the significance of the dream. Systems of dreamwork that assign authority or knowledge of the dream's meanings to someone other than the dreamer can be misleading, incorrect and harmful. Ethical dreamwork helps the dreamer work with his/her own dream images, feelings and associations, and guides the dreamer to more fully experience, appreciate and understand the dream. Every dream may have multiple meanings, and different techniques may be reasonably employed to touch these multiple layers of significance.

A dreamer's decision to share or discontinue sharing a dream should always be respected and honoured. The dreamer should be forewarned that unexpected issues or emotions may arise in the course of the dreamwork. Information and mutual agreement about the degree of privacy and confidentiality are essential ingredients in creating a safe atmosphere for dream sharing.

Dreamwork outside a clinical setting is not a substitute for psychotherapy, or other professional treatment, and should not be used as such.

IASD recognizes and respects that there are many valid and time-honoured dreamwork traditions. We invite and welcome the participation of dreamers from all cultures. There are social, cultural and transpersonal aspects to dream experience. In this statement we do not mean to imply that the only valid approach to dreamwork focuses on the dreamer's personal life. Our purpose is to honour and respect the person of the dreamer as well as the dream itself, regardless of how the relationship between the two may be understood.

www.asdreams.org/ethics.htm#dreamwork_ethics
Association for the Study of Dreams

Index of Biblical References

1 Corinthians		Ecclesiastes		Joel	
2.12–13	193	3.14	138	2.28	5–6
12.10	204	5.2	7, 142	2.28–32	6
13	178	5.3	142		
		5.6	7	Luke	8
1 Kings				1.52	198
3	9–12	Galatians		24.13–35	192
3.5	10	2.20	173		
3.5–15	11			Mark	112
3. 16–18	12	Genesis	110, 250		
3.16–28	13	1.9	212	Matthew	84
12.15	10	20.3	6	1.20–25	8
		28.10–16	6	1–2	7, 8
1 Samuel		28.10–22	184	2.12	8
8	10	28.12	92	2.13–15	8
8.11–18	10	28.16	9	2.19–20	8
		31.11–13	6	2.22	8
Acts	8, 9	37	180	5–7	189
2.17–21	7	37.40–41	6	20.16	200
10	184	40–41	204	25.9	227
16.9–10	8	41.15–25	140	27.19	8
		46.29ff	180		
Daniel				Numbers	
2	204	Jeremiah		12.1–8	6
2.28–30	195	23.28	140	12.6	7, 142
				12.6–7	140, 144
Deuteronomy		Job (Hiob)		12.6–8	6
13.1–5	140	7.14	7		
13.2–6	194	33.15–18	195	Proverbs	
24.1	8			5.2	xvi
				29.18	6

Psalm

127.2   210

Romans

7.7–25   198

8.9–11   195

Sirach

34.5   7

Zechariah

10.2   142, 194

Index of Names and Subjects

Aboriginal 27–8

adolescents (see children and adolescents)

Ahmad, Al-Hagg 147, 148, 149, 151, 159

Alexander the Great 9, 12

anthropology 6, 18, 20, 64 (see also culture)

anxiety 21, 22, 29, 46, 60, 71, 102, 126, 176, 177, 201, 204, 207

archetypes 22, 42, 197, 239

Aristotle 3, 5, 6

Aschkenasy, Yehuda 226–8

Augustine of Hippo, St 4, 195, 198

Babylonian Talmud (Berachot 55a–57b) 134–45, 217, 220n

Bonhoeffer, Dietrich 220, 221n

brain xvi, 16, 17, 37, 38, 39, 41, 43, 44, 45, 47, 48, 49, 50, 60, 62, 69, 72, 164, 197, 208

brain map 40

Carrique, Pierre 3–4

Catholicism (see Christianity)

children and adolescents xvii, 18, 27, 66, 69, 72, 74, 199, 203–9

Christianity 8, 15, 33, 95, 96, 104, 110–12, 119, 134, 165, 173, 180, 182–4, 188–9, 191, 193, 195, 197, 198–9, 201, 203–4, 207, 218, 219, 226

Catholicism 84, 95, 99, 102–3, 104, 106, 111, 192–201, 213, 224, 226

Protestantism 84, 111, 173, 182–3, 248

Colby, Kenneth 22

collective unconscious 42, 75

colour 17, 47, 55, 61, 120, 153, 185, 201, 225

conflict(s) 13, 29, 30, 31, 40, 44, 45, 46, 48, 49, 52, 54, 56, 111, 131, 214, 233, 247, 248, 250

consciousness xv, 4, 16–7, 18–9, 30, 33, 39, 60, 81, 83, 95, 98, 135, 167, 169, 179, 199

crisis 64, 105, 110, 113, 199, 233, 248, 250

culture xvi, 8, 12, 16–34, 38, 43, 64, 66, 95, 104, 109, 110, 111, 113, 117, 119, 124–5, 126, 127–8, 134, 136, 149, 155, 183, 190, 195, 206, 217, 218, 220

d'Andrade, Roy 21–2, 25, 26

David, King 10–12

death 8, 9, 10, 11, 13, 22, 24, 26, 29, 31, 33, 43, 69, 77, 80, 81, 84, 86, 103, 105, 109, 112, 144,

149, 156, 157n, 174, 176, 178, 189, 211, 216, 224, 225

desire(s) 24, 46, 112, 128, 148, 152, 154, 155

dream incubation 11, 18, 99, 139

dream as intersubjective phenomenon 68-9

dream interpretation xvi, 5, 14, 19, 20, 23, 24-5, 27, 28, 31, 32, 33, 42, 43, 62-8, 94, 96, 97, 98, 99, 100, 105, 106-8, 110-13, 116, 122-3, 125, 130, 131, 134-5, 137, 141, 142, 143-4, 145, 147-52, 153n, 155-9, 162, 167, 173, 179-81, 188, 192, 196, 197, 198, 200, 204, 205, 207, 208, 213-14, 216, 217, 218, 219-20, 224-5, 227, 229, 232, 237, 238, 239

dream narratives xvi, 4, 6, 9, 10, 11, 12, 37, 38, 42, 43, 56, 66, 72, 74-9, 80-7, 94, 100, 102, 104, 105, 106, 107, 109, 113, 135, 143, 144, 161-4, 166-9, 196, 199, 203, 219-20, 221, 223, 226, 227, 228, 229, 232, 233, 236, 243-6, 247-50

dreams recounted in pastoral counselling xv-xvi, 44, 67, 83, 85, 93, 94, 120, 121, 124, 126, 174, 176, 200, 201, 207, 210-11, 212, 214-15, 215-16, 221-3, 223-4, 224-6, 227, 228, 233, 234-5, 235-6, 248-9

dreams in published studies 23, 40, 41, 42, 44-5, 46-7, 48-9, 53-4, 54, 55-6, 97, 102-3, 156, 161-2, 166

dreams shared within a group xvii, 22, 23, 24, 29, 32, 46, 71, 91, 92, 93, 100, 107, 109, 110, 113,

129, 168, 181, 182-91, 213-14, 246

Drewermann, Eugen 111-12, 114, 239

Eleazar, Rav 143

emotion 38, 39, 41, 43-7, 50, 52, 54, 55, 56, 59-60, 61, 63, 68, 69, 70, 71, 91, 93, 96, 98, 99, 100, 114, 120, 130, 139, 175, 183, 187, 189, 197, 198, 203, 213, 216, 236, 243, 246

ethnography 18, 20, 21, 31, 32, 33, 64, 114, 147, 158 (see also culture)

forgiveness 83, 85-7, 92, 98, 245

Freud, Sigmund 10, 14, 38, 41, 47, 51, 62-3, 65-6, 134, 144, 147-8, 149, 150-2, 155, 156, 157, 158-9, 177-8, 196, 197, 232

George, Marianne 32-3

God 5, 6-7, 8, 9-11, 15, 19, 75, 76, 77, 79, 80n, 81, 95-6, 98, 107, 111, 117, 119, 122, 124, 125, 128, 129, 131, 132, 134, 135, 138, 140, 142-3, 144, 145, 155, 158, 162, 163, 165, 166, 167, 173, 175, 176, 177, 183, 184, 192, 193, 194-6, 197-8, 199, 201, 203, 207, 208, 211, 244, 246, 248, 250

Graham, Larry Kent 116, 117

Graham, Laura R. 25-6

Gestalt therapy 44-7, 56, 116

Grün, Anselm 95-6

Hallowell, Irving 22

Hartmann, Ernest 41, 44, 51, 53, 59

healing 5, 16, 22, 24, 25, 26, 28, 29, 30, 37, 38, 48, 75, 95, 98, 99–100, 108–9, 125, 149, 163, 181, 184, 217, 218, 243–6

Hisda, Rav 138–41, 217

Hobson, Alan 39, 59

Holy Spirit (see Spirit, Holy)

Ignatius, St 193, 195

imagery 37, 39, 41–4, 47, 56, 59, 91, 94, 175, 177, 197, 201, 203, 206, 207, 208, 237 (see also symbols and symbolism)

Islam xv, xvii, 106, 147, 147–59, 224, 226

Jacob 6, 9, 92, 110, 184

Jesus 7, 8, 75, 76, 84, 87, 112, 184, 192, 193, 194, 246, 250

Johanan, Rav 138, 140, 141

Joseph, St 6, 110, 198, 220

Judaism 5, 7, 8, 135, 139n, 142, 217, 226

Jung, Carl G. xvi, 22, 38, 39, 41, 42–3, 52, 55, 68, 74, 76, 79, 165, 177, 178, 179, 193–4, 196, 197–9, 206, 232

Kant, Emmanuel 3, 14

Kennedy, John F. 5–6

Kessels, A. H. M. 5

Kilborne, Benjamin 24–5

Kittel, Gerhard 8

Koet, Bart 65, 100

Kracke, Waud 23

Krakow, Barry 143

Kramer, Milton 44, 61, 62

Krippner, Stanley 143

Lacan, Jacques 155, 156, 159

Lindijer, Coert 173

Mary 8, 92, 163

Matrix, The 4

Matthews, Gareth 4–5

miracle(s) xvii, 102–9, 111–13, 124, 137, 194

Morgan, William 28, 30

Moses, Prophet 6, 7, 8, 11

Muhammad, Prophet 148, 149, 155n, 157–8

Muslim (see Islam)

myth(s) 23, 25–6, 31, 43, 55, 66, 81, 111

Nathan, Tobie 64–6

neuroscience xvi, 38, 48, 53, 62, 72, 208

neurobiology 52, 61

neuroimaging 37, 39, 48

neurology 17, 39, 43, 70, 144

neurophysiology 16, 17

neuropsychology 16

New Testament 7–8, 111, 135, 218, 227

Nietzsche, Friedrich 147, 159

nightmare(s) xv, 20, 26–7, 29, 30, 43, 61, 65, 69–70, 72, 99, 132, 204, 209, 211–12, 223–4, 228, 243

non-REM (NREM) 38–9, 61

Oepke, Albrecht 7

Old Testament 5, 7, 8, 13, 140, 194, 218

oneirocritic and oneiromancy 22, 23, 25, 27, 28, 30, 194

Oppenheim, A. L. 5

parish dream group 182–91

pastor(s) xvi, xvii, 4, 80–6, 91, 94, 98, 100–1, 123, 125, 145, 173, 175, 180, 182, 184, 189, 190,

191, 203, 205, 210, 212, 219, 232, 239-40

pastoral care xvi, xvii, 77, 116, 125, 173, 180, 190, 239

pastoral counsel(ling) xvii, 70, 91, 183, 193, 197

pastoral counsellor(s) xvi, 210, 219, 228

pastoral supervision 231, 232, 237, 239

Paul, St 8, 9, 99, 173, 178

Perls, Fritz 44

Perpetua, St 14, 220

Peter, St 84, 202

PET scan 39

Pindar 3-4

Plato 3, 5

premonition and prediction 19, 22, 29, 63, 77, 106, 108, 109, 198, 215

problem resolution 18, 39, 41, 44, 47, 48-56

prophecy 8, 26, 142, 144, 149-50, 152, 154, 157n

Protestantism (see Christianity)

psychoanalysis 24, 58-9, 61, 62, 64, 65, 66, 68, 150-1, 155, 239

psychologists 38-9, 101, 147-8, 151, 152-3, 155, 213, 214

psychology 16, 38, 39, 47, 53, 132, 148-50, 152, 154, 157, 173, 184, 193, 199
  Freudian 151, 158, 159
  Jungian 116, 194
  religion xvii, 91

psychosystems 116-32

psychosystems map 117-18

PTSD (post traumatic shock dreams) and imagery rehearsal treatment 43, 56

Qur'an/Koran 25, 148-9, 150, 155, 156, 157

recurring dreams and nightmares 28, 41, 69, 70, 72, 83, 97, 99, 102, 107, 139, 153, 204, 214, 224-5, 225-6

REM 38-9, 42, 43, 44, 47, 48, 50, 61, 62

Samuel, Judge and Prophet 10

Samuel, Rabbi 142-3

Sanford, John 97, 99

Scriptures 6, 7, 8, 9, 14-15, 81, 100, 192, 219

Shamanism 24, 27, 28, 29, 30-1

sharing dreams (see dreams shared within a group)

Shaykh Nabil 155-8, 159

society xvi, 16-34 (see also culture)

Solomon, King 9-14

Spirit(s) 5, 21, 22, 26, 27, 28, 30, 31, 32, 33, 149, 150, 157, 177, 194, 195, 204, 236
  Holy 8, 183, 185, 193, 205

spiritual direction 91, 183, 192-201

spirituality 74-5, 99, 104, 124, 188, 194, 195, 203, 205, 206, 208, 231, 236, 239

Stickgold, Robert 39, 53

subconscious 62, 83, 212, 229

Sullivan, Kathleen 99

symbols and symbolism 24, 25, 41, 42, 43, 75, 77, 84, 97, 99, 156, 166, 168, 181, 184, 185, 186, 187, 189, 197, 213, 216, 232, 233, 235, 236, 239, 245, 248 (see also imagery)

symbols: cave 75-6; clothing 214; death and rebirth 43; dying 77; female vs male 44-5; female and male integration 54; crib 78; cross 248–9; dark tunnel 243; death 24; dog xv; falling xvi; flying/ airplane 40, 78; fruit 24; God 198, 207, 208; house and home 67, 97, 99, 224; hunting 31; illness 42, 77; lost possession 103; marriage 24; Mary-icon 67; people – abstract: black woman 77; dark guiding characters 43; monks 76; people – associative: parent, sibling, partner 41, 67, 224–5; running race 207; shadow 76; snake 75–6; swimming suit 214; vestry 75–6; vehicle 78; village 40; white people 24;

Tedlock, Barbara 25
therapist 37, 41, 47, 56, 64, 68, 71, 125, 167
  psychotherapist 51, 66, 195
Tiberia, Vincenza 22

Tibetan dream yoga 18
Tonkinson, R. 27–8
Torah, Hebrew 7
transpersonal dreaming 31–2
Troy 8–9
Turner, Edith 33

unconscious 24, 39, 41, 42, 43, 45, 48, 95, 127, 147, 152, 155–9, 177, 179, 198, 232, 239

vision(s) 5–7, 9, 12, 14–15, 19, 23, 26, 31, 32, 65, 83, 86, 108, 121, 140, 142, 144, 150, 153–4, 156, 157, 187, 194, 218, 247

Wallace, Anthony F. C. 24
witchcraft 29

Ziwer, Mustafa 150, 152, 155, 156